HOW TO UNDERSTAND THE ENTIRE UNIVERSE

part 1

by

Ethan Renoe

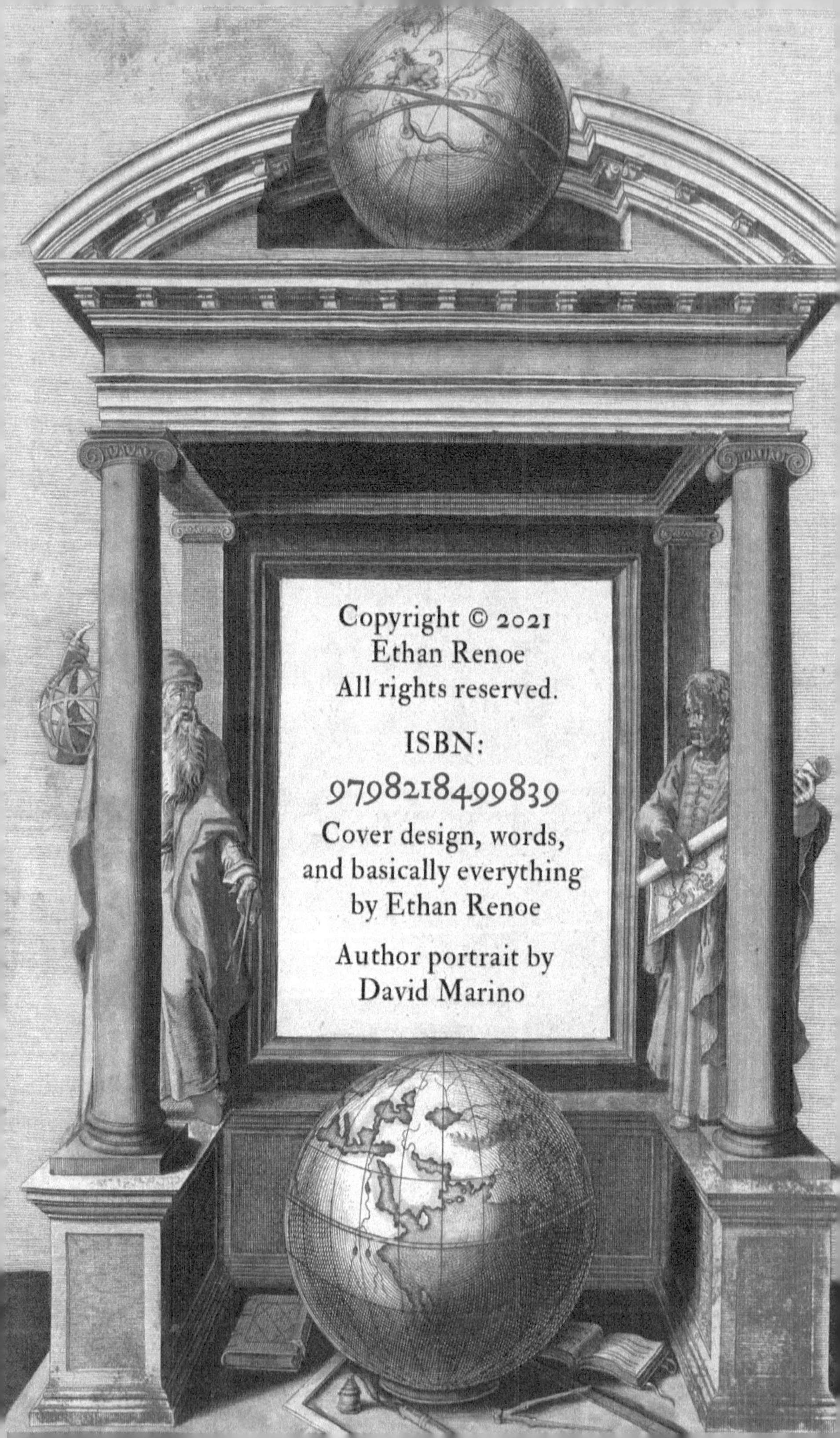

ISBN:

9798218499839

Cover design, words, and basically everything by Ethan Renoe

Author portrait by David Marino

Dedicated to Johnny

My boy, my **** *****, my little boop.

Thanks for becoming instant friends with me in Los Angeles and making that season less weird (or more, depending on how you look at it), less painful, more creative, and more adventurous.

I knew we'd click from the first time we talked, back when you had long hair and a Corolla and I also had a Corolla. Look how far we've come! You're getting married and I got a new car.

Not only did we click, but you've become a lifelong friend and a caring, wise mentor(ish). Despite the fact that you're way older than me, we always joke and hang like homies. I'm so grateful we randomly got connected in LA and that 5 years later, you still put up with me! Can't wait to be your best man!

(Plz make me your best man)(*Second edition update: he didn't.*)

CONTENTS

WHAT DID I MISS?

or,
Previously, on Earth

or,
"wtf just happened?"

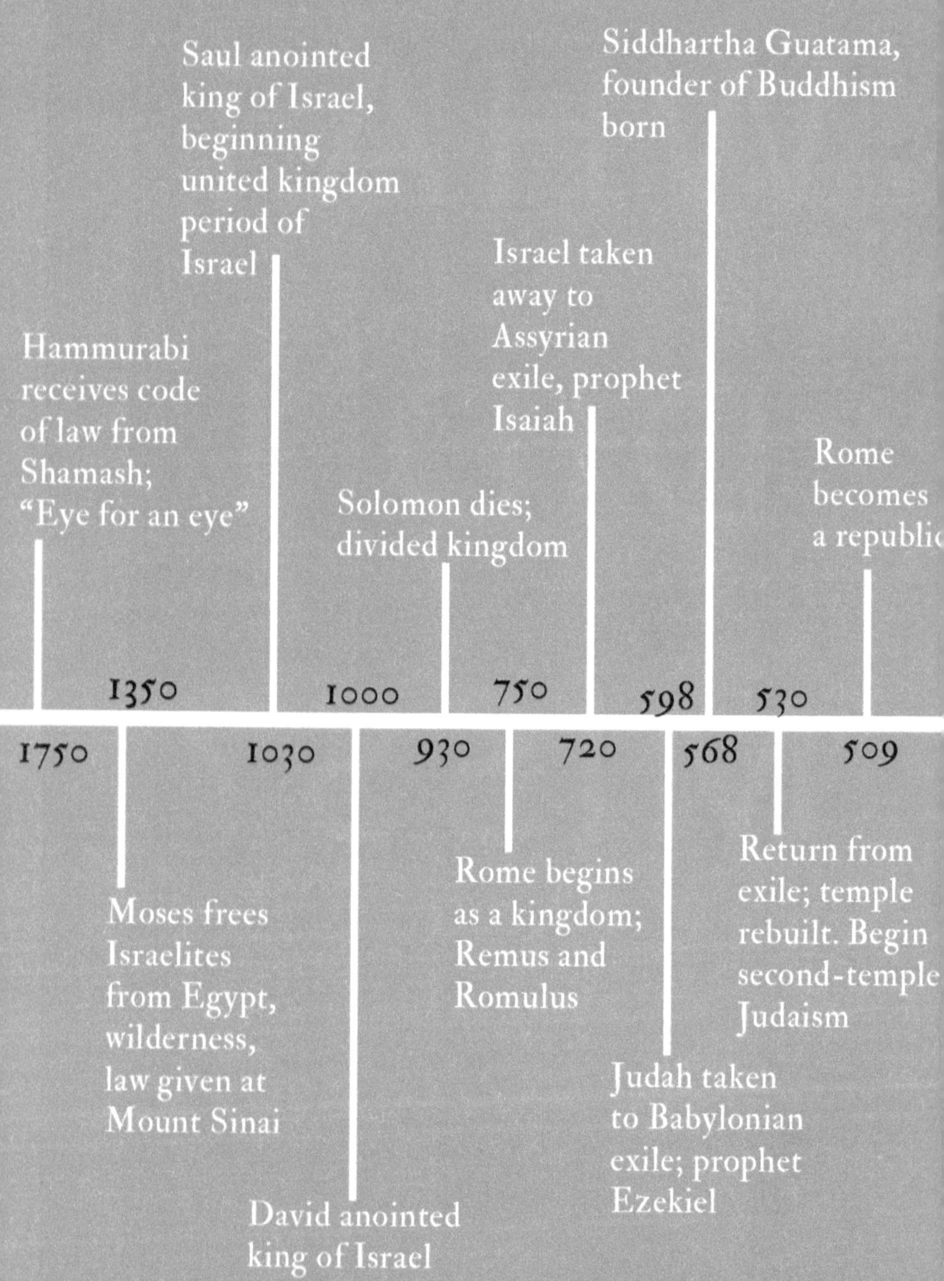

Most dates on this timeline are approximate estimates

Inter-Testamental Period
(time between Old & New Testament)

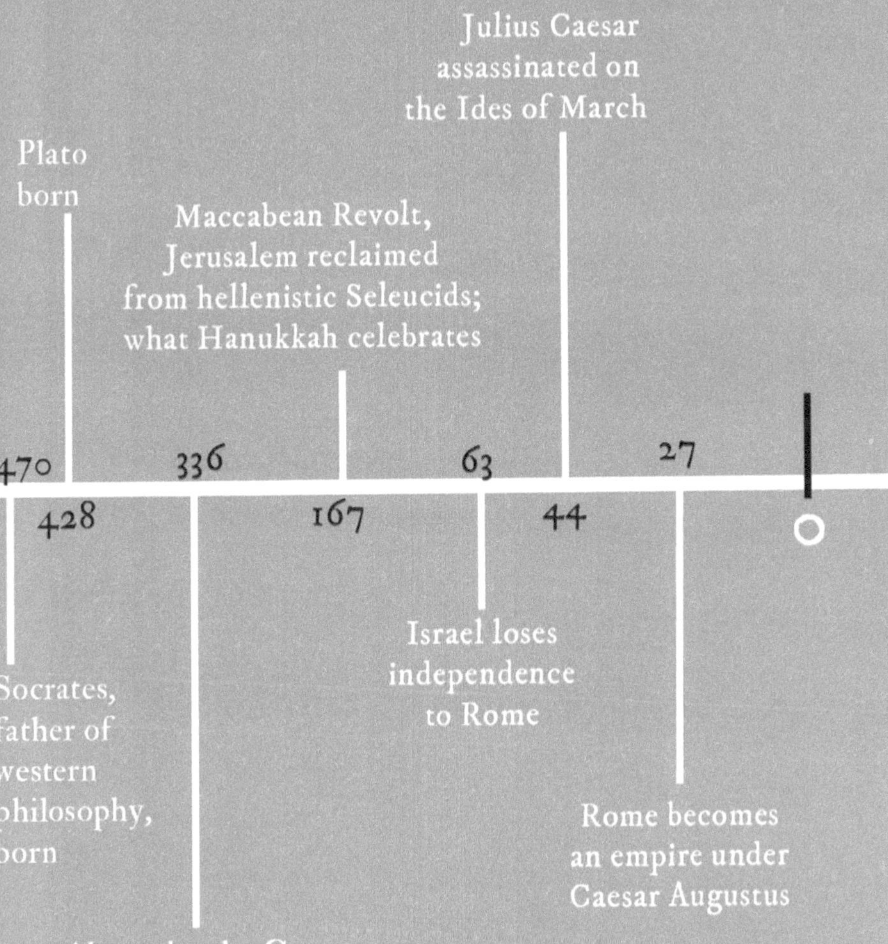

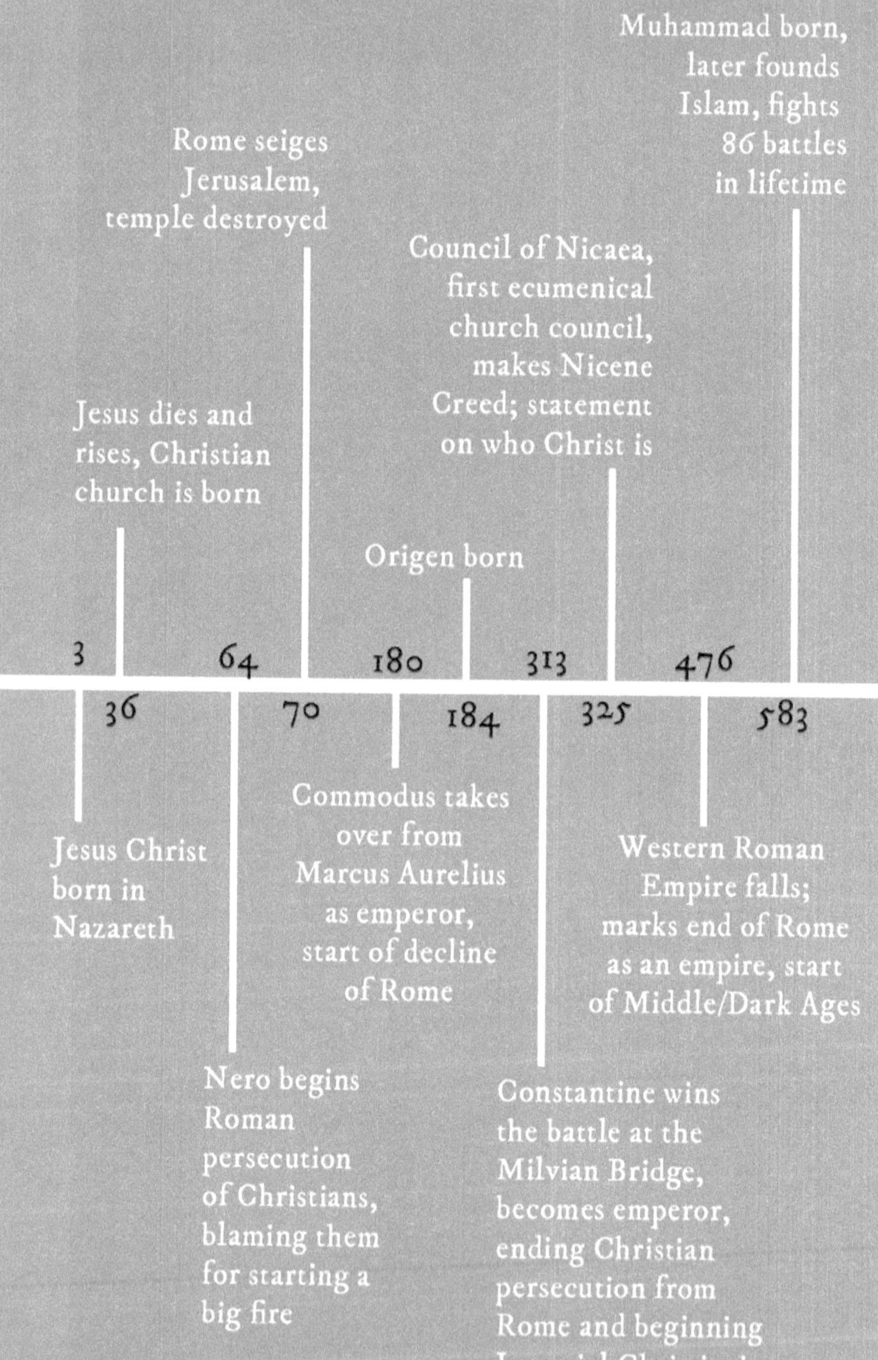

Muhammad born, later founds Islam, fights 86 battles in lifetime
Rome seiges Jerusalem, temple destroyed
Council of Nicaea, first ecumenical church council, makes Nicene Creed; statement on who Christ is
Jesus dies and rises, Christian church is born
Origen born
3
64
180
313
476
36
70
184
325
583
Jesus Christ born in Nazareth
Commodus takes over from Marcus Aurelius as emperor, start of decline of Rome
Western Roman Empire falls; marks end of Rome as an empire, start of Middle/Dark Ages
Nero begins Roman persecution of Christians, blaming them for starting a big fire
Constantine wins the battle at the Milvian Bridge, becomes emperor, ending Christian persecution from Rome and beginning Imperial Christianity

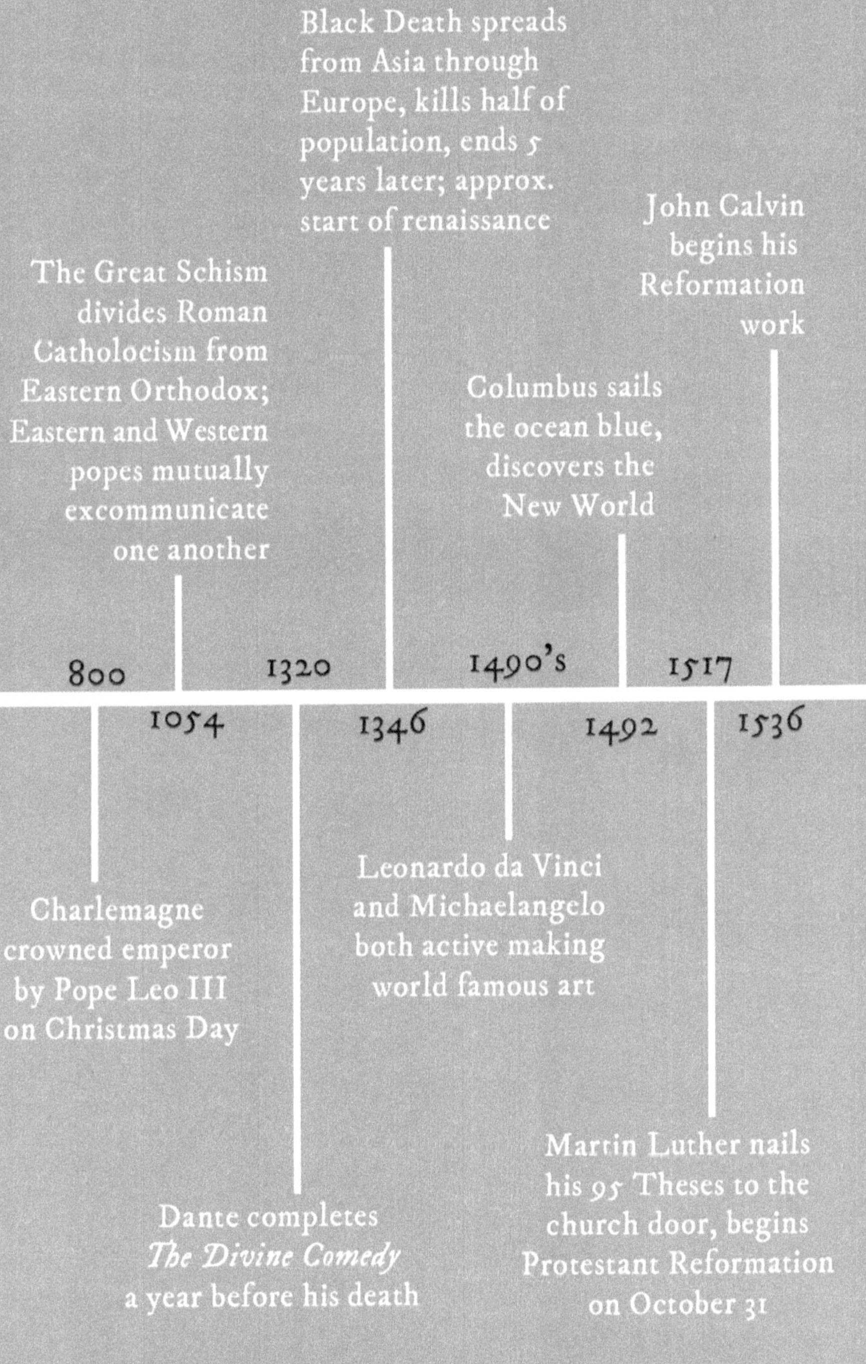

Black Death spreads from Asia through Europe, kills half of population, ends 5 years later; approx. start of renaissance

John Calvin begins his Reformation work

The Great Schism divides Roman Catholocism from Eastern Orthodox; Eastern and Western popes mutually excommunicate one another

Columbus sails the ocean blue, discovers the New World

800
1054
1320
1346
1490's
1492
1517
1536

Charlemagne crowned emperor by Pope Leo III on Christmas Day

Leonardo da Vinci and Michaelangelo both active making world famous art

Dante completes The Divine Comedy a year before his death

Martin Luther nails his 95 Theses to the church door, begins Protestant Reformation on October 31

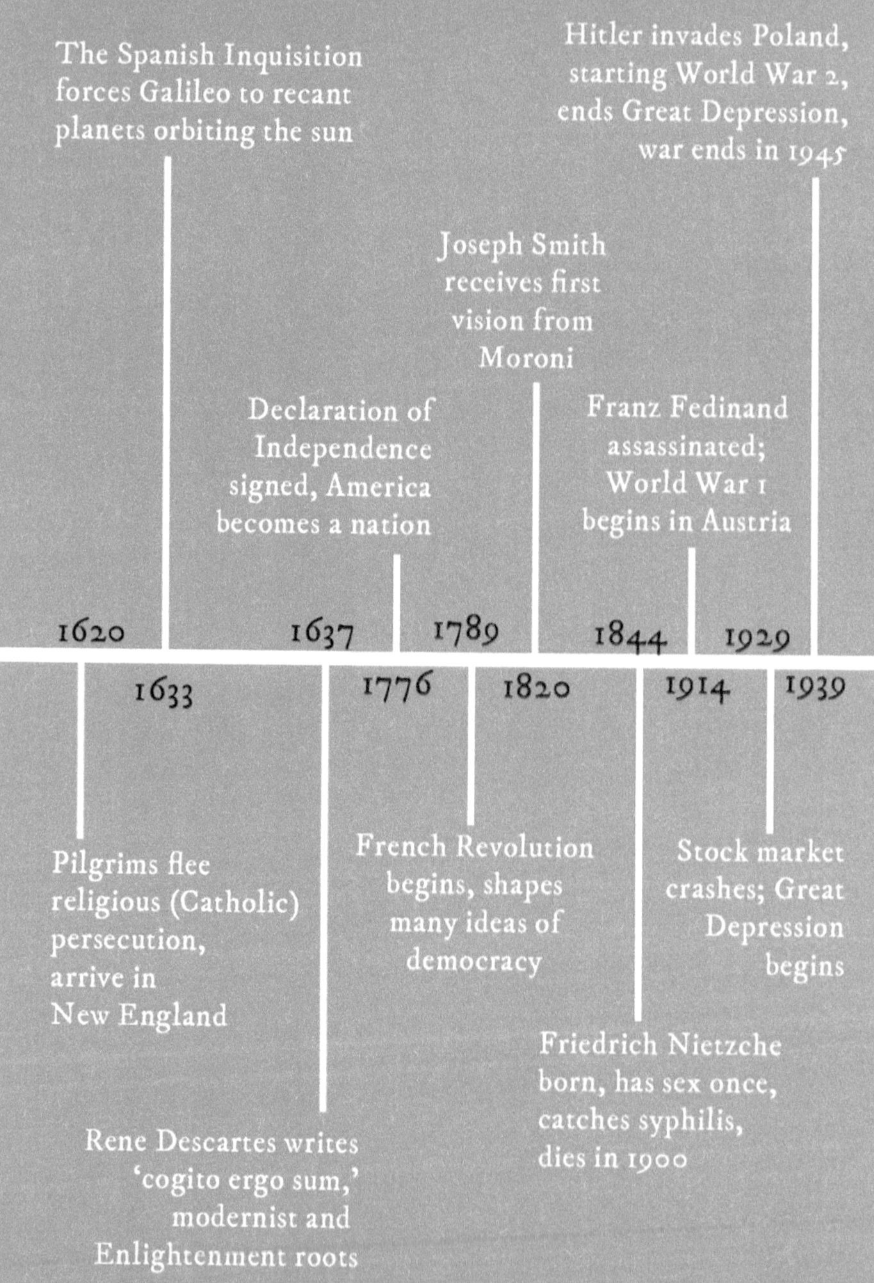

The Spanish Inquisition forces Galileo to recant planets orbiting the sun

Hitler invades Poland, starting World War 2, ends Great Depression, war ends in 1945

Joseph Smith receives first vision from Moroni

Declaration of Independence signed, America becomes a nation

Franz Fedinand assassinated; World War 1 begins in Austria

1620
1637
1789
1844
1929

1633
1776
1820
1914
1939

Pilgrims flee religious (Catholic) persecution, arrive in New England

French Revolution begins, shapes many ideas of democracy

Stock market crashes; Great Depression begins

Friedrich Nietzche born, has sex once, catches syphilis, dies in 1900

Rene Descartes writes 'cogito ergo sum,' modernist and Enlightenment roots

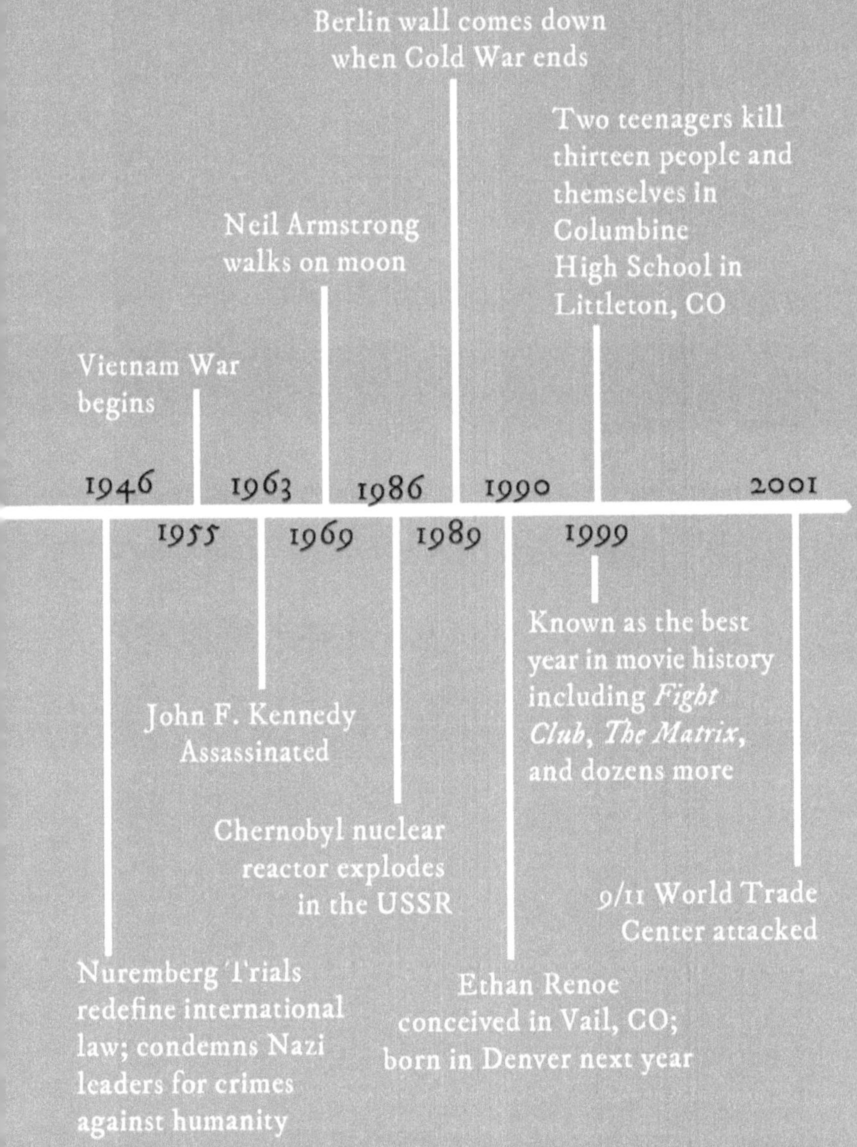

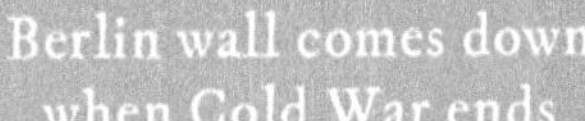

Berlin wall comes down when Cold War ends

Two teenagers kill thirteen people and themselves In Columbine High School in Littleton, CO

Neil Armstrong walks on moon

Vietnam War begins

1946
1955
1963
1969
1986
1989
1990
1999
2001

John F. Kennedy Assassinated

Known as the best year in movie history including *Fight Club*, *The Matrix*, and dozens more

Chernobyl nuclear reactor explodes in the USSR

9/11 World Trade Center attacked

Nuremberg Trials redefine international law; condemns Nazi leaders for crimes against humanity

Ethan Renoe conceived in Vail, CO; born in Denver next year

"There are these two young fish swimming along and they happen to meet an older fish swimming the other way, who nods at them and says "Morning, boys. How's the water?"

And the two young fish swim on for a bit, and then eventually one of them looks over at the other and goes "What the hell is water?"

—David Foster Wallace, *This Is Water*

Foreword
Jump

"HEY I'M ETHAN AND I LIVE ON YOUR FLOOR. WANNA JUMP OFF A BRIDGE?"

This is how I met the author of this book you're about to read, back in August of 2014. Before Ethan was 'The Shirtless Wonder,' everyone just wondered why he was always shirtless. In my case, there was a very valid reason that my first encounter with this fellow lacked a shirt; preemptive de-shirting is necessary to jump off a bridge into the Chicago River (just so long as the US Coast Guard had something better to do that day than busting conservative Christian college kids looking for unconventional thrills).

&

Something you may not know about Ethan is that his lighthearted, spontaneous spirit is just the preliminary layer in this jawbreaker of a human. Beneath the good vibes and hilarious demeanor is a man that pours his heart and soul into his creative endeavors. The amount of time, energy, and scrutiny he puts into his books would shock you more than his Thomas The Tank Engine towel and his fists-up impersonation of Charles Bronson.

Have you ever had to look an uncomfortable barista in her exhausted and bloodshot eyes as she asks you to leave, so she can lock the joint up for the night and go home? I know Ethan has. Did you know her name because this happened so frequently? Yes, Ethan does.

Have you then walked to another Starbucks open 24/7 to continue writing until the next (and now second consecutive) AM? Yes, I have been there to see Ethan do it myself, both to offer another set of eyes and ears in the creation of his earlier works, and mooch off his Starbucks Gold Card.

With all this being said, I would like to personally challenge you, as Ethan puts it so well, "to be gentle with people, and hard on ideas." As hard as he's worked on this book, he didn't toil over his words to receive something as cheap as an "amen" from the masses (he has the comment sections from shirtless videos for that).

Don't just plow through this book and shelve it. That's what the scroll function of Twitter is for. In a day and age where we are bombarded by cheap words, know that the words of this book were painstakingly written and rewritten, discussed and debated, until finally they became what they are now.

Push back on the ideas presented in this book that don't sit well with you, with all your might. Ask your friends, family, neighbors, or church members what they think. Heck, shoot Ethan a message! Harness the synergy of mind and emotion; for this book, you're going to need both of them. Get into heated conversations that bring both parties to a point of greater knowledge, understanding, and respect for one another. There's no greater honor you could give an author than letting his words live on in you after he's released his work to the world.

&

Quite like the fateful day of the plunge, you may not realize just who, or what might come knocking on the metaphorical door of your heart and mind, and what ramifications a simple "heck yes" might result in. For me, that fateful "heck yes" led me to forsake my benevolent grandmother's pleas to be safe, and set the stage for many more "heck yesses" to date. Sorry Grandma!

The 20-something foot jump brought me not only into the most thrilling and unsanitary water I have ever swam in, but also into an equally thrilling and "unsanitized" lifelong friendship. Much like my first interaction with Ethan, you are about to read a book that is thrilling, adventurous, and unsafe in all the right ways. Freefall into new ideas, even if that means braving unexpected belly flops of bewilderment in areas of thought that were once unprodded (or smacked at 50MPH).

Maybe you didn't realize in picking this book that an invitation to jump came standard, but it does. You know you're about to read a book, but have you ever read a mind? A soul? Tell your grandma sorry before you start if you must, but by all means, take the plunge.

-Noah Reynolds
Missionary in Asia
Ethan's favorite human on the planet

Trade your certainty for awe

—Silent Planet, "Dying in Circles"

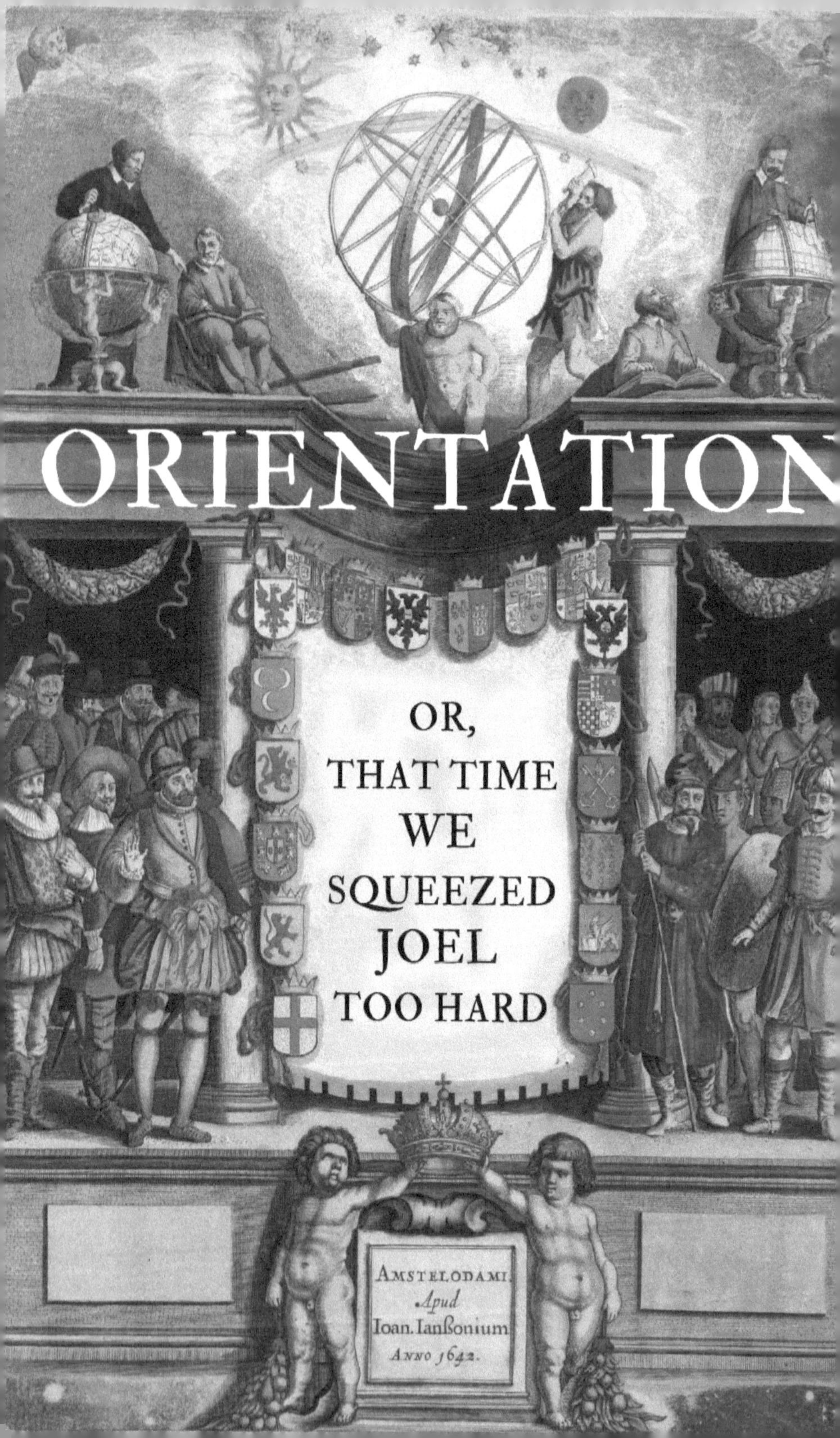

ORIENTATION
OR,
THAT TIME
WE
SQUEEZED
JOEL
TOO HARD
AMSTELODAMI.
Apud
Ioan. Ianßonium
ANNO 1642.

You ever hold your breath exhaled and have a friend hug you as hard as they can until you black out? It's kind of fun, kind of dangerous. You wake up on the floor and forget what day it was, where you are, who you're with, and how you got there.

It seems like an eternity of white oblivion, until it slowly fades away as the oxygen surges back to your brain and over the next minute, and you remember what was up.

One time in Brasil, a friend and I sandwiched our other friend Joel in between us and squeezed hard. He fell to the ground once we released him and we thought he was kidding. His glossy eyes stared into space until slowly he regained presence of mind and stood up.

We had squeezed all the air out of his body, and when he came to, his brain needed a minute to reorient itself to reality.

Where are you?
When are you?

Who are you? Who are all the people around you?
How did we get here and what is going on?

Each of us is born into this crawling planet and we're supposed to know what is going on? It's like God gave us a cosmic squeeze and dropped us onto the crust of the earth.

"They'll figure it out."

The problem is, we lie to one another.

We see thousands of advertisements a day telling us who we need to be, what we lack, and what we need to have. We hear the words of leaders who want money and assume they're being honest. We watch as our friends and also supermodels paint the primmest version of themselves across their social media platforms.

We lie to ourselves. We think we're too fat or too skinny or too weak. Our eyes are untrustworthy. Our memory sucks.

Seriously.

Some studies asked people where they were when they first heard about 9/11. Then they asked them the same question ten years later and half the people gave different answers. Your brain isn't nearly as reliable as you think.

&

Life is a slow way to die

I'm 30. Cells in my body now die faster than they reproduce and I'm always tired. I have a list of body parts that don't work anymore and I'll keep adding to it until none of them do. Maybe I felt it years before but denied it;

the best is yet to come! I'm only getting stronger!

You keep telling yourself this until you can't.

I was born and assumed I was oriented to the world and its workings, but now that I've begun to die, I'm reexamining who and what, exactly, oriented me. And toward what?

Like the demagogue in the highest seat of the world, we tell ourselves what we want to hear, regardless of whether it's true or not. In my head I'm young and spry but in my body I'm aging and tired.

We don't see things as they are; we see them as we are.
Don't trust every thought you have.
Or every feeling.

Trust nature because it doesn't lie. Try not watering a plant while you keep it in a dark room and see if it lied about photosynthesis. Throw a rock in a pond and tell it not to ripple.

Trust people's pasts, because that's what brought them to where they are. Don't trust what they say they will do (or heck, any of their words for that matter), but trust their life stories. In the end, your life story was the realest thing about you.

Our stories and our old baggy bodies eventually become so intertwined that life has squeezed all the pulp out of us and both rest together beneath a stone with a date on it. All that's left of you will be a name and a stretch of time, so the story you told with those two tools had better be pretty freaking good.

And despite what you heard growing up in America, your story is not about how much money you made, although money—and what you do with it—is important. As is work and friends and sex and technology and travel.

All of these things (as well as everything else) play a role in understanding you.
Your life.
Your story.
The world.
The universe.

Telling a good story with your life is much easier said than done, and the first step is figuring out where the h-e-c-k you are. And when you are. And what all has happened before you got here so you can get caught up.

So that's what this book, and the following ones in the series, aim to do. I want to examine those questions: Who are we, when are we, how did we get here, and as a result, to borrow from Francis Schaeffer, how then shall we live?

&

Imagine, if you can, nothing.

According to philosophers, it is impossible to think about nothing.

So, imagine space. Imagine that you're floating in space, but in this space there are no stars, planets, comets, or even space dust. It's just you, floating there with absolutely no reference points.

Now imagine that someone asked you where you are. How would you describe it? You'd have no way to describe where you are, because location is always a matter of referring to something else.

I'm near the McDonald's at the corner of State and Chicago.
I'm next to the front door of the Willis Tower.
I'm in a field at 39.935822, -102.406772, which of course is a reference from the equator and prime meridian, respectively.

If there is nothing to refer to, there is no location. How do you know where you are without reference points? And how do you know what to refer to without being taught them?

When we talk about geographical reference points, most people tend to agree. I doubt any of us, except maybe cartographers, have gotten into an argument about where something is in relation to something else.

But when it comes to more abstract ideas, like life, humanity, right and wrong, we are all oriented to slightly different objects.

If you're born into the Christian universe, you have oriented yourself to a certain set of ethics and thoughts, and much of this is shaped by culture and language (Christianese). Hindus are born and oriented into the same planet as us, but a different universe. Same with Buddhists, Muslims, and so on.

Many of the most cringe-worthy moments of my life have been watching culturally uneducated Christians attempt to have evangelistic conversations with non-believers. They barrage these cultural outsiders with in-language and think they're doing something profound. But we'll come back to this later.

Understanding the universe and how it works begins with acknowledging your own reference point. Where were you born, and into what type of culture? Even my best friend Dave —also born into a white, loving, evangelical, suburban Colorado family—has a much different view of the world than I do.

Everyone tends to assume that they are born with perfect orientation and an objective understanding of the universe, but that simply cannot be true. Acknowledging this in yourself takes humility, an open mind, and of course, this book to set you straight.

It also means diving into science, history, and philosophy to help us grapple with some big-picture, objective truths in order to discover capital-T-Truth.

Where are we in the universe?

We must orient ourselves to *something* or else we are nowhere.

&

"But Ethan, you're predominantly a pedantic douche so why should we listen to you and your understanding of God, history, philosophy, et al.? In the words of Michael Scott, *Who...do you think you are?*"

Good question. About a year ago, I conducted a survey among my email newsletter subscribers. I asked why they continue to read my blogs and books, what they would like to see more of, and are they on any prescription medication, since they still follow me?

Many of the answers reflected the same sentiment, summed up best by this response from one reader:

"I appreciate the lens with which you view the world."

There was a theme of people appreciating *how* I think, even if they disagreed with some of my conclusions. Learning how to think involves a heck of a lot of orientation and context. None of us are good at it, but we can improve.

This book, or series, is an attempt to explain *how* I see the world; how I think and arrive at the conclusions I do. It may not be objective—it is, after all, my way of explaining why I see the world the way I do, as best I understand it.

This book is the prescription of my lens.

&

And this book has gone through at least two iterations prior to the one you're holding, and both themes emerge repeatedly throughout the pages.

Initially I was going to title it *Zoom Out*. Because most issues are a compounded mosaic of a million other issues so that you end up thinking through the far end of a telescope, rather than examining a bigger picture. We humans have a tendency toward growing myopic and locked into place. We make up our mind on an issue before considering all the facts—especially those presented by 'opponents.'

Liberal media or conservative talk radio.
Pick your poison.

So Zoom Out. Look at more sources and open your mind.

The other idea was to call it *A Series of Precarious Balances*, as life is largely a matter of finding the proper balance between two extremes. Any time you polarize to one side or another, on nearly any issue, you'll get into trouble. You'll be imbalanced.

As I wrote the chapters, I realized that applying this filter to every issue 1) has already been done by folks like Ezra Klein as well as every Greek philosopher when discussing virtue and 2) I realized I wanted to do more than talk about finding the proper tension between two ideals. (You could say I zoomed out, LOL!)

So I landed on this title for the series: How to understand the entire universe. Because that's what we're after here. Not ethics or balance or politics or any *one* thing; but all of it. Everything. The whole universe and all that happens within her boundaries.

The "How" refers to how we think; how we got where we are. It's not an attempt to describe every single thing ever. As you know, a book like that would have trillions of pages. Instead, it's about forming thought and padding out trails toward truth.

I quickly realized I could not fit every thought, story, and epistemological root into one book, so I'm trying to group together similar ideas. This volume is heavy on philosophy, death, worldly systems, money, and balance. The next one could be more focused on sex, animals, the combustion engine, and whipped cream. Who knows!?

We will start with time, aliens, and the Garden of Eden and move swiftly to popcorn as a means of understanding God's holiness. I hope you brought a seatbelt and maybe a neck brace.

Hopefully the transitions don't give you too much whiplash. Then again, you're ripping around a star on a planet traveling 1,037 miles per hour (or, like, 40,000 km/h. I don't know, I didn't look up the conversion) and somehow manage not to break your neck, so you should be able to follow along.

I believe in you.

e

Ano Domini, September, 2021

The Deep
Future

here is everyone?" exclaimed Enrico at lunch one day.

His friends probably looked at the physicist and wondered just what was going on inside that balding head.

Enrico Fermi, credited with the thought experiment known as Fermi's Paradox, had just realized why logically, humans are most likely alone in the universe.

Imagine, for illustration, that the universe has existed for 100 hours.

Of these hundred hours, humans have existed, in all of our recorded history, for about the last two minutes. Everything we have learned in social studies class, from the hunter-gatherers to Jeff Bezos tooting himself up into space has occurred in the last two minutes.

universe
begins

humanity
begins

That means an alien civilization could have spawned in some other galaxy, say, 50 hours ago, and by this time they *definitely* would have concocted some form of interstellar travel. Think about it: On a timeline that long, why would they emerge at the same time as us humans? Or even a few 'minutes' before us? We got into space in 2 minutes and they've had 50 hours.

If there were sentient life out there, they would have found us by now.

Or perhaps they last about 5 'minutes' before going extinct, but that was 43 hours ago and we missed each other by hundreds of millennia. And they were on an earthlike planet on the other side of the universe, in a galaxy hundreds of lightyears away. The chances that we would overlap time-wise, much less geographically, are incredibly slim.

The probability of them being at the same developmental stage as us, spawning at the exact same time humanity happened to on earth (or within a few thousand years), and invading our planet like they do in the movies, is so slim that you'd have a better chance of jumping to the moon.

Of course, the 'minutes' in that metaphor were hundreds of thousands of years, most of which we weren't around for.

Or perhaps, continues Fermi's reasoning, they *have* found us and have chosen not to make themselves known to us. They have no interest in conquest or resources on earth, so have not made any attempt on our planet. Or perhaps they are watching, observing, and remaining hidden, possibly with something called a Dyson Sphere. This raises a lot more questions, but these are mere theories built upon theories.

Chances are, we are alone in the universe.

You can look up at the starry sky and know with relative certainty that cosmic gasses and solids and gravitational quirks are slamming into one another up there without observation or inhabitance. The vastness of space rips and roars and boggles our minds—and only *our* minds. Our lonely, colorful, humid planet is the only one making noise and spouting exploratory missions into the rest of the cosmos.

Minus, of course, whatever caused the "Wow! Signal," but you can Google that one for yourself…

&

There is a project called the ten thousand year clock. Thinkers, sociologists, and even science fiction writers wanted to make a clock that would run for ten thousand years.

Think about that for a moment.
You may have just glazed over the number.

All of our recorded history is roughly 4-5,000 years old, and they want to make something that will last twice that long. Think of how drastically humanity has changed in that amount of time, and think about how quickly our progress has increased just in the last ten years.

That's a *huge* amount of time.

The number of generations between Jesus and you, times five.

A different project wanted to create signs warning people to turn back to avoid stumbling into radioactive nuclear waste. They want these indicators to communicate clearly to humans 10,000 years in the future so they'll steer clear of this area.

Welcome to the world of nuclear semiotics, or the study of symbolism and communication with people in the distant future.

Well, you can't write the signs in English. Language changes faster than my roommates go through toilet paper. Beowulf, the earliest English story/poem was written about 1,000 years ago and we couldn't understand a word of it today. Look at the first sentence:

> Hwæt. We Gardena in geardagum,
> þeodcyninga, þrym gefrunon,
> hu ða æþelingas ellen fremedon.

(And no, "We" doesn't mean "we," nor is the following word "garden." That's how much our language has changed.)

Now multiply *that* time frame by ten.

Language shifts and evolves faster than sand blown over the face of the dunes. How many words have you used today that didn't exist 5 years ago? 10 years? 20?

"I'll shoot you a text."
Say that to someone in the 80's and they will think you're blasting them a book for school from a cannon.

"I'm streaming a movie."
Why would you throw your VHS tapes in a river?

See how quickly language changes? Granted, it has changed much faster in the past few decades than ever before, but the point remains: How do you communicate with people living 10,000 years in the future?

(Also, how do you expect to pick up an ancient document like the Bible, written 2-4,000 years ago and understand it without incredible effort, research, and context? But we will save that point for later.)

You can't rely on symbols either, as they change just as much as language. The color pink used to be seen as majestic and manly, while blue was perceived as gentle and feminine. Even the image of a skull hasn't always indicated death to some non-Western cultures, so we can't be sure that it will communicate danger to all humans in the far future. Symbols, like language, are highly embedded in the culture in which they are used.

Language, which shapes how you think and see and experience the world, comes and goes.

Symbols make connections, tell stories, create culture, and also...change.

Humans live and die.

The world is in flux.

The nuclear committee considered ideas like a priesthood which would keep alive legends of a dark and evil danger living in the caves where the nuclear waste was stored (they looked at how long present religious traditions have been passed down, and how humans keep these alive for centuries, either out of fear or love or both), or a vast forest of concrete thorns.

Ten thousand years is a long, long time.

And it's a fraction of a million years.

Which is a tiny slice of a trillion.

And a few trillion years from now, the universe will die.

Each second, the spinning particles of atoms slow by a nanoscopic amount. Think of atoms like a basketball being spun on a player's finger: it doesn't spin forever. Eventually it slows down, wobbles, and comes to a stop. This will happen to every atom in the universe, eventually. Energy is not an endlessly renewable resource at the atomic level. All the heat and energy and light and motion of the universe will ultimately fall still.

This is called the Heat Death of the Universe.

It's the moment at which, forecast nuclear physicists, the Big Bang will be undone. Every electron orbiting its nucleus will make a final lap around and putter out like a hula hoop after its user gives up, or a spinning top that lost its steam.

All will fall motionless and dark and quiet.

The universe has an expiration date.

Welcome to the deep future.

&

I'm a Christian, but don't espouse *all* the traditional views of the Young Earth crowd or a literal reading of all of the Old Testament. This change in my thinking is a recent one too, as I've learned to un-read the Bible through an American/scientific lens and re-read it closer to how the original audiences would. But that's also for a different chapter.

Now, taking historical, philosophical, and scientific factors into account, and considering the wild amount of time everything has, or could have, existed, let's look at two things:

First, the timing of Christ is uncannily eerie if he was not God and did not know exactly when to enter into human history. Rodney Stark, in *The Rise of Christianity*, outlines many of the factors in the pre-Constantinian era which led to Christianity's success. For example, Christ came when the infrastructure of the Roman empire was at its zenith, but the quality of the emperors would soon wane, causing the empire to fall within a few centuries.

Sociology has proven that major transitional periods are when the largest number of people convert to Christianity, and the Roman roads allowed the message of Christ to spread far faster than at any other time in history. That, as well as plagues in the empire and a handful of other historical factors (Jewish wars, destruction of the temple, Hellenization across Europe and Asia) reveal a timing that is not only uncanny but impossible.

No human gets to choose when they are born, much less what events will happen after their death. In the vastness of time, the precision of Christ's appearance must be more than mere coincidence...almost as if he *chose* when to enter into our world...

Second, I return to a verse from the Bible which has been a favorite for years, Ecclesiastes 3:11—

> God has made all things beautiful in their time, he has also set eternity on the hearts of men.

It may be easy for some of us, especially those of us raised in Christian homes, to glaze over the word 'eternity' without giving it a second thought. Yet when we take time to think about how long time really is, we realize that our minds begin to cave in at about 10,000 years.

That's not even a tenth of a million,
far less a billion,
and a billion doesn't even come close to eternity.

If we can remove our scientific caps for a moment and don our human hats, how true is that verse? Haven't we had longings and emotions which seem bottomless and far deeper than mere instinct?

A friend of mine recently became a Christian after years of being an atheist. She had a revelatory moment alone in her car and began crying. She said there simply *has* to be more than being born and dying and then that's the end. In a way, the overwhelming grandness of eternity proves to me that there is more to this world than what we can see and prove.

Perhaps this is not a scientific or rational argument, but an emotional one. Maybe the two work together hand in hand to point us to the source of this eternity. Compare the slow passing of time to the vastness of infinity and realize there must be *something* carrying these atoms along through time and space.

Think of how slowly an oak tree grows but how fast you get old.

Consider how badly you longed for that one lover to come along for *years*, or perhaps how deeply you were cut when you lost them in a second.

This eternity planted inside our hearts is more than just ancient wisdom literature—it is experienced fact. When I consider the Deep Future and Past, everything works out too perfectly to be chance. We did not find ourselves here by accident in light of everything. After all, the only thing I've ever witnessed which comes close to matching the immensity of the Deep Sciences is my own heart;

the beauty of new life and the black depths of grief;
the way liberated people dance;
the red rage in my vision when I lose my temper;
and the gentle yet explosive excitement of a first kiss.

If we believe Christ is the ground of our being; the source of our existence, it's not hard to imagine Him entering into our reality and demolishing our expectations. These arguments may not convince the more scientific-minded of you, but it's all overwhelming me enough to stay in the embrace of an invisible God a little longer. He's an invisible God who became visible for our sake, when the time was exactly right (Galatians 4:4).

Thinking big thoughts re-orients my mind to appropriately 'see' God in His proper context:

That Person who existed before eternity, and continues after it ends.

That thing which is bigger than all things.

The one able to place eternity on the hearts of humans.

You burn with hunger for a food that does not exist.

—David Foster Wallace, *The Pale King*

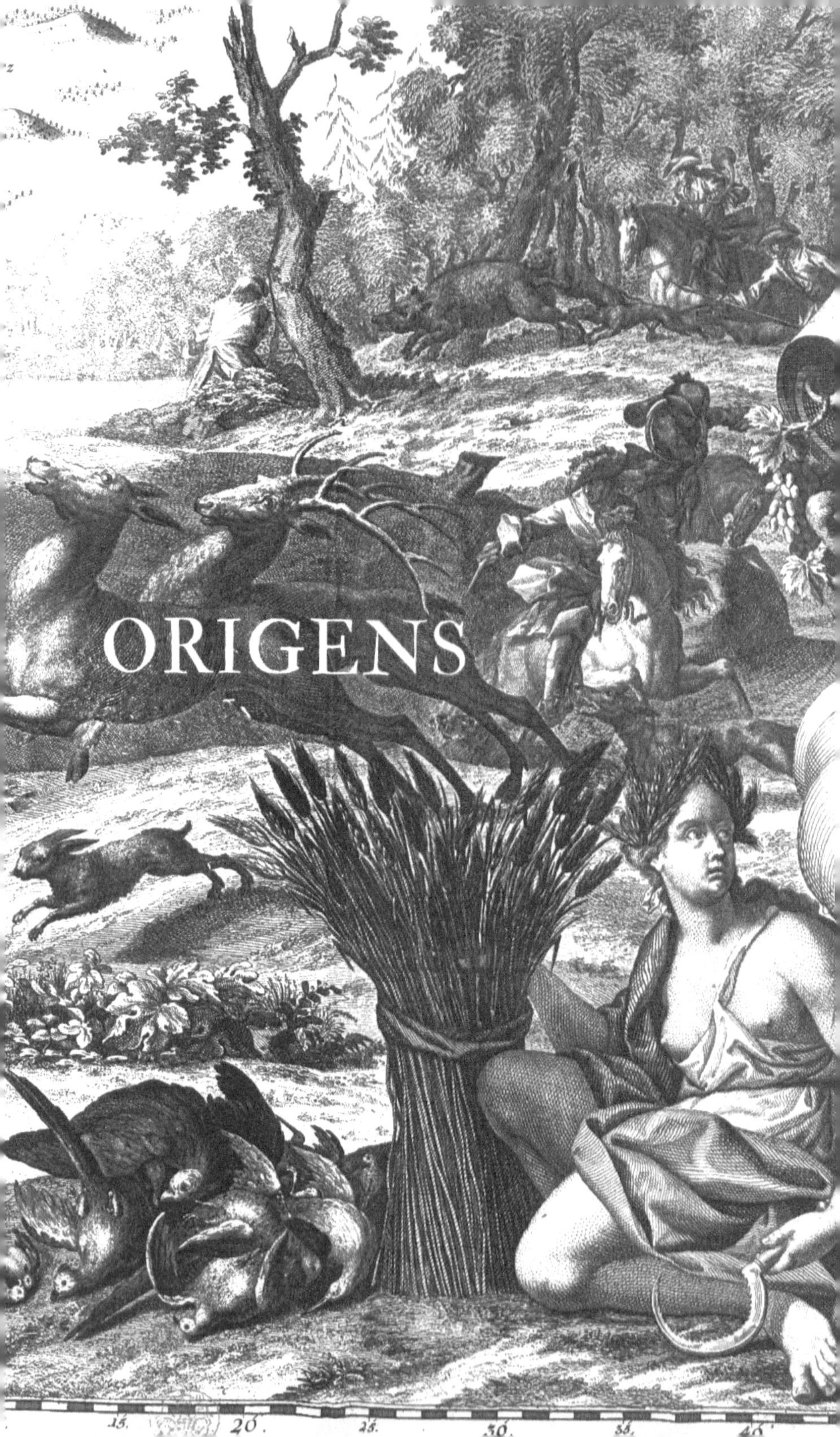
ORIGENS

hen I first began this book, I thought I'd have to reach all the way back into the origin of human history and rebuild everything about how the world works from infinity-BC until now. Thinking it through again though, we don't necessarily need to know the origin of something to understand how it works.

Take, for instance, a little houseplant. I don't need to know the complete genus history and micro-evolutionary ancestors of a plant to know how it functions in the world today. All I need to know is that if I water it and give it sufficient sunlight, it will live. If I deny it these things, chop all its branches off, or pull it out of the dirt, it will die.

Every time I fall too deep into a web of conspiracy theories, or read too much abstract philosophy, or just forget who and what to trust in the world, it's helpful for me to remember that nature is honest. You can always step back from the internet, or your conspiracy-crazed friend and remember that plants always tell the truth. So does the sun. And mountains. You can always return to the coast and find the ocean singing the same deafening song it has been for millennia.

Which is more real, anyway: the past or the present?

What are the things that can't lie? Where can we locate some sense of normalcy? If we begin our construction of the world, or at least our perception of it, with things that can't lie, or at least can't be disproven, we will be in somewhat of a better place than if we try to build our reasoning upon abstract theorem or philosophical conjecture.

&

I recently had a conversation with a man who holds two Masters degrees and a PhD, all in theological or biblical fields. He lands on the conservative side of most issues, and as we discussed biblical interpretation, particularly Genesis, he insisted that without a firm foundation of our origins, we can't know anything else. If we don't know exactly where humans came from, how can we know where we are now?

In other words, he meant, if Adam and Eve were not literal, how can we know that *anything else* in the Bible was?

This is a logical argument, or fallacy, known as the Slippery Slope. It's easy to poke holes in, as with most slippery slope arguments. The person isn't arguing for something crazy; they're just talking about what they mean. In this case, we are talking specifically about Adam and Eve—a piece of literature written in poetic form, in the structure of similar legends from the same time period.

It's a slippery slope, then, to jump to Jesus and suddenly say "If Adam and Eve aren't true, then how do you know about Jesus??"

Because it's a different type of literature.

Because there are at least two thousand years between the composition of the two records.

Because the stories of Jesus aren't written like metaphorical, deeply symbolic poems.

The Bible is a library of diverse genres, and to read them all as if they were the same genre does an injustice to the authors as well as the meaning of the text. Heck, in this book you're holding, I have poems as well as accurate historical accounts and scientific theorems. When you read these different genres, you don't assume the poems are 100% literal, or that the scientific measurements are allegorical. Yet this is exactly what we do with the Bible, particularly the Adam and Eve narrative.

Whenever I teach on Adam and Eve, I read Emily Dickinson's account of a sunrise to the students:

> I'll tell you how the Sun rose –
> A Ribbon at a time –
> The Steeples swam in Amethyst –
> The news, like Squirrels, ran –
> The Hills untied their Bonnets –
> The Bobolinks – begun –
> Then I said softly to myself –
> "That must have been the Sun"!

But how he set – I know not –
There seemed a purple stile
That little Yellow boys and girls
Were climbing all the while –
Till when they reached the other side –
A Dominie in Gray –
Put gently up the evening Bars –
And led the flock away –

Then I take some clip from a scientific textbook on a sunrise:

Sunrise: the rise or ascent of the sun above the horizon in the morning as a result of the rotation of the Earth. Sunlight refracts as it travels from the vacuum of space into Earth's atmosphere. As its wavefronts graze the upper atmosphere, light bends downward, meaning we see the sun higher in the sky than it actually is. The oranges and reds occurring at sunrise are due to the absence of higher-frequency blues and violets because higher-frequency sunlight has been scattered by tiny molecules in the atmosphere. When the Sun is close to the horizon, light that grazes Earth's surface is lower-frequency reds and oranges that survive scattering. Hence the reddish-orange colors of sunsets.

Then I ask my students, "Which is more true?"

They usually spout out the same answer: "They're both true, just different!"

And that's exactly it.

When we read Dickinson, we don't imagine that she *literally* saw ribbons falling from the sky, or church steeples going for a swim. We know that she is using poetic language—why? Because we go into it knowing that we're reading a poem. We also don't accuse her of being a liar, or for saying things that are untrue—they are true in their own poetic way. Perhaps *very* true in a personal, experiential way which can be just as real—though not literally or scientifically—to the writer.

When we read the scientific description of the sunrise, we also interpret it with a different pair of glasses on our minds. We know that the things happening have been scientifically observed, and can be witnessed exactly as described in nature.

It's also worth noting that this type of exact, literal writing would not be invented until the first couple centuries AD at the earliest, when people grew curious about how exactly the world works. Up until that point, it was all legends of dragons blended with seeds of reality. Karen Armstrong, British author and scholar, agrees that "preoccupation with literal truth is a product of the scientific revolution."

On top of all that, The tales in Genesis were passed down orally for hundreds upon hundreds of years. Some scholars believe that the Israelites didn't have a written language (Hebrew) until the time they established themselves as a nation under King David, several generations after they fled Egypt around 1350 BC.

Steve Falkenberg, professor of religious psychology at Eastern Kentucky University, observed:

I've never met anyone who actually believes the Bible is literally true. I know a bunch of people who say they believe the Bible is literally true but nobody is actually a literalist. Taken literally, the Bible says the earth is flat and setting on pillars and cannot move (1 Chr 16:30, Ps 93:1, Ps 96:10, 1 Sam 2:8, Job 9:6). It says that great sea monsters are set to guard the edge of the sea (Job 41, Ps 104:26).

So why, exactly, people think that a literal, scientific reading of the first several chapters of Genesis is the most accurate has come to baffle me. We aren't reading it accurately when we do that; we are reading it like 21st century westerners, not ancient near-easterners. And we still spout the phrase, "Read it as the original author meant it for the original audience!"

Do not mishear me: the story is still packed with *truth*, the same way Emily's poem is. We learn truths about humans, about God, and creation. And what we learn about these three categories are *drastically* different from the creation stories of the surrounding people groups.

The Babylonian creation story is called the *Enuma Elish* and it paints a much different picture of how God, humans, and creation interact, and how they began. The gods are chaotic, violent, unpredictable. Humans are their slaves and are always inches away from pissing off the gods. And all of creation was an accident that got kicked out of heaven.

Can you see how, if you grew up hearing this version of creation it would inform a much different way of thinking and life? You would primarily live in fear of some volatile god who was poised to smite you, and you'd think of yourself like a worm.

How different, then, when the Hebrew story emerges in response to the Enuma! Many scholars consider Genesis a polemic against the Babylonian creation story, meaning that it is written against it, meant to combat the ideas and narratives presented in it.

Nowadays, if you disagree with someone's position (the gods are out of control, humans are worthless), you would write up an essay which tore down their points and then build up your own argument. Back then, however, they would communicate these truths with stories. Jesus Himself did this with numerous parables, which we also understand to be *true* but not *literal*… we just have an easier time with them than Genesis for some reason.

The surrounding cultures believed that humans were accidents and slaves, but this new story says that we humans have the *ruah* of God inside of us! *Ruah* means breath, wind, or spirit.

God made the world Himself and called it *good*.

Then He specifically forms humans as special among the rest of creation. He walks with them in the garden.

Are you getting the idea here of how different the Genesis creation story is from the Babylonian one?

See how it can be true and meaningful but not literal?

&

Psychologists like Carl Jung and Sigmund Freud had another understanding of these ancient myths, and while I really like certain aspects of their approach, it falls apart eventually upon further examination. Let's look at it.

Jung (pronounced *'Young,'* FYI), known for his psychological archetypes, said that all ancient myths are imprinted on the subconscious of all human minds, and that's why a story written 4,000 years ago still communicates so much truth today. That's why the jealousy between Cain and Abel still reveals so much about sibling, or human rivalry, and how that idea has not changed much in four millennia.

He says that these stories are *true* in the sense that they are still acted out today every day. Every time a brother gets angry at, or jealous of his brother, he is embodying the reality of the story from Genesis 4. In that sense, the stories become more real today than if we read them literally as happening 5k years ago.

In other words, which is more real: two brothers in strife in 2021, or two brothers who may or may not have been literally real back in 3,000 BC? If you think about it like this, the 'realness' of Cain and Abel as historical humans dissolves some in light of us applying the principles to our own lives and living them out. It simply becomes less important. Of greater worth is living without jealousy, anger, violence.

Even one of the first church fathers, Origen, understood much of the Bible to be allegorical rather than historical, and he is still hailed as a church father rather than a heretic. He saw the human as a tripartite self, and read history the same way: that some of the Old Testament happened literally (in the body), but other parts, which are impossible to happen literally, must be spiritual metaphors. In *On First Principles*, he writes,

> The reader must endeavor to grasp the entire meaning, connecting by an intellectual process the account of what is literally impossible with the parts that are not impossible but historically true, these being interpreted allegorically in common with the part which, so far as the letter goes, did not happen at all.

His idea of making the literary into reality melds quite well with Jung's concept. Even regarding Christ's historicity, Origen writes, "What good does it do me if Christ was born in Bethlehem once if he is not born again in my heart through faith?" See how he is similarly calling this ancient text to be more real through how we live, how we interact with God today, and how these are ultimately more important than whether King Solomon *actually* slaughtered 22,000 bulls in the temple? (2 Chronicles 7:5)

Will your faith system fall apart if it turns out that it was just 21,993 bulls? Because *gasp* the Bible was wrong!

Or, is that just how ancient authors—writing for an ancient audience—wrote?

Evangelical Christians talk about reading the Bible as carefully and accurately as possible; a noble endeavor. We obviously should. However, what they often mean by that is simply that we should read it literally, take it at face value, and assume that it's literal history and to believe otherwise would be heresy. It is only a post-Enlightenment, post-Scientific Revolution mind that would read the Bible in this way. That is not, ironically, the most accurate way to read the Bible.

Perhaps it is not ultimately necessary for us to know the exact details of our origins. Maybe we can actually get a good idea of where and why and how we are simply by looking at what's before us today. We have scriptures, which we will try to read as accurately as possible, but at the end of the day, all we presently have are the words on the page. Maybe learning how we think, and why we think the way we do will be more helpful than our collective past.

We have our own minds, our life experiences.

We have history to learn from, and science to study.

We have a lot of theorems, ethics, and philosophy to cover, so we will leave the past there and dive into something new.

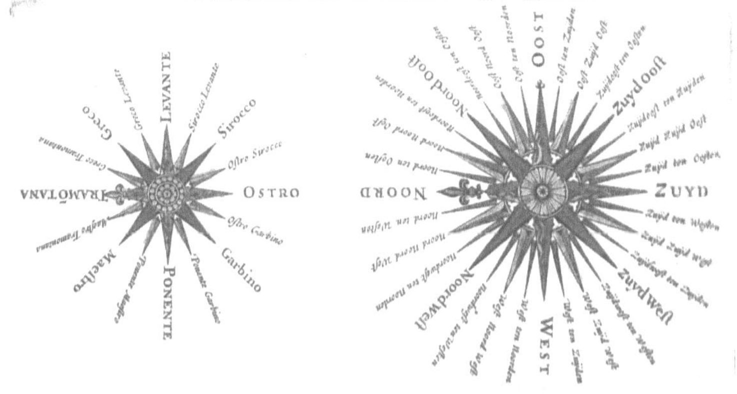

MIND
AJAR
IOANNES BAPTISTA HOMANN
ac. CÆS. REGq. CATH. MAJ.
Geographus, nec non Regiæ Scientiarum
Societatis Berolinensis Membrum.

—William Kingdon Clifford

ow, more than ever, we need a reminder on the benefits of maintaining an open mind. A few weeks ago, I landed on a definition of 'open-minded' which seems accurate:

> A truly open-minded person enters every conversation
> thinking that their belief or opinion might be changed,
> that they may be wrong,
> and that they might learn something new.

Sadly, there are so few people who are truly open-minded by this definition. Most people enter into theological, political, ethical, or scientific conversations with

> Unchangeable beliefs and opinions,
> which are *definitely not wrong*,
> and nothing they hear could convince them otherwise.
> In fact, new information presented
> causes them to double down
> on the side they already take.

You may be reading this and thinking that you are, in fact, in the first category and you are indeed 'open-minded'

...except, of course, if you talk about this category, that one, or these unquestionable beliefs...

In order to be truly open-minded, you need to accept the possibility that you've been wrong about everything and that it was actually your upbringing/experience which causes you to think this way. It takes a ridiculous amount of humility.

So...might you be wrong?

Let me put some skin on it with a recent conversation. I began chatting with one of the billions of people on the internet and it was quickly apparent that she and I had VERY different backgrounds and world views. She was a liberal by every definition of the word: pro-abortion, sex with whomever you want, whenever you want (as long as there's mutual consent), intersectional identity politics, critical theorist (not to be confused with anti-racist!), etc.

Somehow the idea of open-mindedness came up, and naturally, she thought she was the most open-minded person there was. How could she not be?? She was pro-everything! Everything flies! Everything is allowed! She told me that she is the *most* open-minded person there is! I told her that I don't believe abortion is natural or beneficial, but is actually murdering a new human being. Rather than consider my opinion, weigh my beliefs, and hear me out, she immediately shut me down and called me closed-minded, misogynistic, and ignorant.

This seems to be the new definition of open-mindedness: someone who, rather than hearing and weighing all sides, actually is just secular-minded and politically liberal. This is

Neo-Liberalism. Simply because she lets everything fly, she assumed she was open-minded.

True open-mindedness, however, means being able to hear views that vary widely from your own, and rather than shut them down and call them uneducated, listen.
Much easier said than done.

Classical Liberalism, opposed to Neo-Liberalism, is actually pretty cool. I'd consider myself a Classical Liberal. The idea emerged in the early 19th century and the aim was simply to hear all sides of every issue, being open to hearing them all and considering each one.

Neo-Liberalism (what we tend to think of as 'Liberal' today) is moving away from this mindset more and more. Rather than weighing all ideas, they tend to only weigh ones which they already agree with; those that seem the most progressive and least restrictive. Often, the least Christian. Maybe even in extreme cases, those which harm older, wealthier, white men.

As long as something doesn't seem to smell like traditional, conservative Christian values, then it's a-go.

Mark Sayers, in his enlightening podcast *This Cultural Moment*, discusses how the modern Liberal/post-modern movement actually owes much more to Christianity than it wants to admit. The sociological phenomenon of the Pre- and Post-Christian cultures is fascinating. Sayers breaks it down into three stages:

A Pre-Christian culture exists in some sort of tribal, usually animistic society. Think Mayans or African tribes before

Christian missionaries arrived. These cultures typically had less value on human life (especially that of enemy tribes), little to no widespread education, no healthcare, and no democracy.

Then missionaries of some sort arrived and the culture becomes a Christian culture—the second phase. They develop a value on human life, and therefore healthcare, reduced violence, democracy, et al. The values of the image of God (more on this soon) trickle down throughout the entire society.

Eventually, science, reason, and philosophy moved throughout the western world as a result of this peace and education and brought most of these societies to a Post-Christian culture. The important thing to note is, this is not merely a return to the Pre-Christian tribalism. No, the Post-Christian culture attempts to take all it can from the Christian culture, while denying the presence or authority of any god.

Think about it: why does anyone today think people deserve equality, freedom, a voice, healthcare, education, or autonomy? Because they subliminally believe that all people are of some value—a concept which was not present in the Pre-Christian culture. Sayer sums it up succinctly:

We want the kingdom without the king.

We want all the benefits and convenient ethics which the Christian culture provided, without the restrictions and authority of a governing deity. We want Christ's teaching on love and forgiveness without Christ Himself.

Understanding the history of some of today's movements helps inform our decisions when wading through modern issues. Being aware that Neo-Liberalism is essentially an extension of the Christian movement helps us build more bridges with those we disagree with, rather than see them as enemies.

The divide, however, still grows nonetheless. One black professor said that in all his years of teaching in a university, he was never once discriminated against for his skin color, but repeatedly for his conservative values.

Historically, conservative people are the ones painted as the closed-minded sticklers who can't accept things like school dances or having a beer (which is often accurate).

In the past several decades however, a new form of Pharisee has emerged: the closed-minded Liberal. While Catholic nuns at the school dance were once the morality police, there is a new type of ethics monitor: the ones who expect everyone else to speak and act exactly how they see fit.

Their goals are the same as those religious brothers and sisters —they see their way of living as the best practice for all of humanity and expect everyone else to see the same way. The difference is the paradigm on which they built those visions. For the fundamentalist conservatives, it looked like the moral and ethical teachings of the Bible (or their interpretation of it), while for the Neo-Liberals, it emerged from a post-Christian state of secularism, freedom, human autonomy, and, let's be honest, a hedonistic dance atop the grave of God.

Anything that stands in the way of my pleasure is a sin.
And don't get in the way of anyone else's pleasure.
Don't make them feel bad.
Don't restrict *any* autonomy.

I mean, what else do they have to build their ethic upon? Pleasure is a good thing—perhaps not the highest in their view, but one of them—so why stop these people from having sex, or those ones from getting high?

The once open-minded liberals who strove to weigh *all* ideas fairly became locked into a system of humanistic progress, and this one path became the new rulebook for speech and action.

All that is to say this: It doesn't matter if you lean more Conservative or Liberal; religious or atheist; Democrat or Republican. No one is immune to the temptation to close our minds and become locked into a one-way-only understanding of the world.

Like my internet friend proved, simply being licentious and saying *"Everything is okay! If it feels good, do it!"* does not make you open-minded. She wouldn't even hear my reasons for not thinking everything is permissible (like abortion). And that, my friends, is the definition of closed-minded.

Open-minded people aren't just spineless pillows who agree with whomever they're talking with either. I hear plenty of ideas which I disagree with, and after considering their side, my mind leaves the conversation unchanged. The difference between me now and me a few years ago is, now I actually weigh their arguments. Sometimes my mind is changed, sometimes it's not.

In a recent job interview, I was asked what is something I've changed my mind on recently. It was a theologically-related position, so I told them I was raised believing Adam and Eve were literal people who literally spoke with a talking snake. I told them about what I wrote in the previous chapter; that in the past few years, after coming to understand Ancient Near Eastern mythological traditions, and the idea of a polemic response to the *Enuma Elish*—Babylonian creation myths—I changed my mind. I realized that the most accurate reading of the stories is not necessarily literal, but still true. The way poetry is true but far from literal.

Have you changed your mind on anything lately? I want to see a world where opposing ideas are not only heard, but considered.

A social media where rather than hatred being cultivated, ideas can be synthesized and improved upon.

A room where Liberals and Conservatives alike walk in, ready to present their positions, but might have their minds changed, rather than desperate to change the minds of their opponents.

Now, the real test of this chapter is this: Are you reading these words and thinking of all the other people you disagree with? Are you thinking, *Oooh, Mary needs to read this. Then maybe she'd see the light!*? Or are you reading it with humility and applying it to yourself? Are you thinking of conversations where YOU failed to hear/consider the other position?

Let's humble ourselves, learn from others, and hopefully grow in the process.

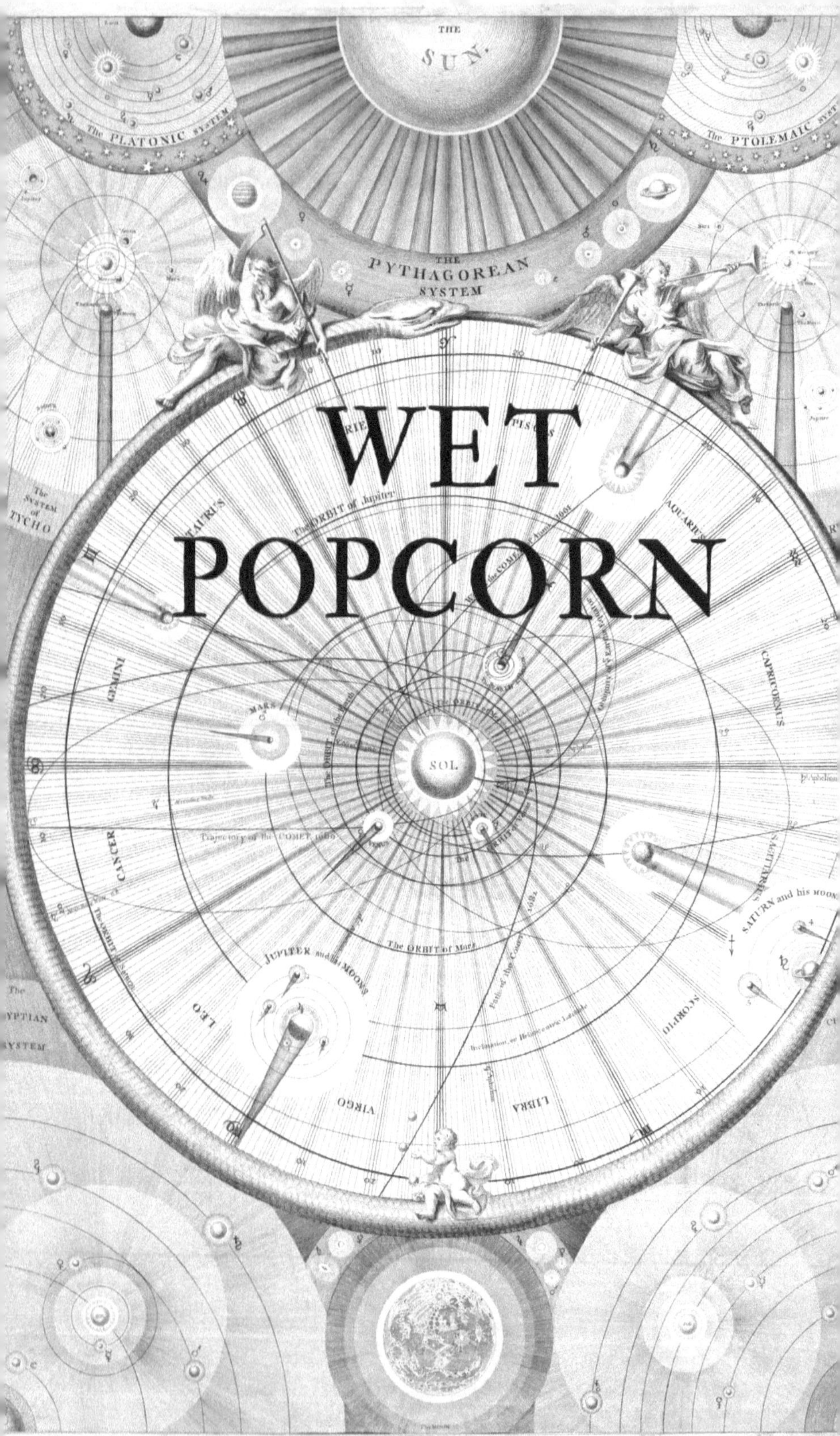

THE SUN.
The PLATONIC SYSTEM
The PTOLEMAIC SYST
THE PYTHAGOREAN SYSTEM
The SYSTEM of TYCHO
The EGYPTIAN SYSTEM
TAURUS
ARIES
PISCES
AQUARIUS
GEMINI
CAPRICORNUS
CANCER
SAGITTARIUS
SATURN and his MOON
LEO
SCORPIO
JUPITER and his MOONS
VIRGO
LIBRA
SOL
MARS
The ORBIT of Jupiter
The ORBIT of Mars
Trajectory of the COMET 1680
WET
POPCORN

—E.M. Forster

uring the Covid-19 pandemic I discovered the YouTube videos of Steven Crowder, a right-wing commentator and comedian. He is famous for his videos where he sits in public places with a sign that says something like, "THERE ARE TWO GENDERS, CHANGE MY MIND."

I watched several of his discussions with people who disagree with him, particularly on sex and gender, and appreciated how he was respectful and cool-headed in his interactions. I also found myself agreeing with everything he was saying, and the way he presented logical, coherent arguments, even when his opponents lost their cool and cussed him out.

Unsurprisingly to us now, as the pandemic rolled into the consciousness of the world, he began posting videos protesting social distancing and mask use, as well as the vaccine. I realized that I partially agreed with some of his points, but several I disagreed with after consulting other sources. All of his loyal followers, however, ate up every word he and other hyper-conservative voices spoke and adopted their stance on Covid just as quickly as their stance on sexuality and gender.

In other words, the values of the tribe mesh together and very few fans challenge Crowder on one point while agreeing with him on another. In fact, you'd be hard pressed to find any conservative people who agree on gender, yet disagreed on Covid mask laws.

This is because belonging to a tribe is easier than thinking for yourself.

It's easier to watch a few Steven Crowder videos, decide that you agree with the way he thinks, and then agree with every video he produces from then on…on any topic.
Let him do all the thinking for you.

In this way, issues conglomerate together and rather than an independent thinker examining a variety of sources and coming to their own conclusions, people tend to think along tribal lines. If two people agree on immigration laws, chances are, they agree on gender pronouns, despite the fact that the two issues are wildly different from one another.

Binaries don't simply exist in a vacuum in which each value gets weighed isolated from its surroundings, but in a family of values which *tend* to go together. To put it simply, most people fall into tribes and end up aligning themselves with the held values of that tribe, rather than examining each value on its own individual merit.

Liberal people, for instance, will tend to agree in their views of sexuality and government, despite the fact that those two arenas have little to do with one another. What does traffic legislation have to do with who you share your bed with? Yet it's hard to find a politically liberal person who has conservative views on sex and vice-versa (Heck, today it's hard to find *anyone* with conservative views of sex!).

Why is this?

It must mean there is something deeper happening than what's on the surface of these arguments. Because a category like Liberalism tends to be rooted in something even bigger than a stance on sexuality or government, but in more profound issues like the nature of existence, the ontology of human beings, and the character of God (or whatever supreme energy they believe in). If we zoom out from individual issues, we should be able to find *why* these tribes agree on so many diverse issues. What is it that causes them to agree?

This is why theology and philosophy are not mere mental exercises, but they trickle down into the real, physical world and shape history. Hitler did not wake up one day merely wanting to kill 11 million people—he was formed by ideas from Nietzsche, Martin Luther, and others.

Mother Teresa did not suddenly feel the urge to move to India and dedicate her life to suffering alongside orphans; her motives were rooted in her beliefs on humanity, justice, and the Image of God.

For this reason, for the deeper spiritual and existential answers they agree upon, Liberal folks will tend to agree with one another on trickle-down issues like sexuality and government. What they believe about authority informs what they believe about everything else.

For Christian folks on one side or the other, this means they will most likely agree on their view of Scripture; whether they see it as high and authoritative, or as simply a helpful collection of ancient suggestions. Others twist certain passages into fringe interpretations, sometimes making the very words on the page mean the opposite of the consensus understanding.

One of the most extreme examples of this was an article I happened upon on Medium's website. They argued that the character Jael from the book of Judges was gender fluid because she did something manly (killing someone with a tent peg). Seems like a stretch, right? Not if you are bent on putting your own worldview anachronistically INTO the pages of the Bible. Let's forget the fact that *no one* back then had even the slightest notion of a human being gender fluid and do what we want with this ancient document…

Understanding God means understanding the Bible.
Understanding the Bible means understanding its context.

In 2015, I taped a ton of colored balloons to myself and wore a tie-dye shirt.

One of my friends dressed as an old, hunched man with glasses, and another became a smiley boy in a Boy Scouts uniform. We were dressing up for our church's Halloween party.

Prior to 2009, no one would have looked at us and known what we were supposed to be. Heck, we wouldn't have known what we were, and wouldn't have dressed up that way.

However, all of our students took one look at the three of us together and instantly knew what we were: The old man, the young boy and the house (balloons) from the film *Up*.

If we were separated from one another, our costumes would not have made much sense and I would have just been a dude covered in balloons. But IN context: a few years after 2009, with the other two leaders, and especially to a group of teenagers who would have grown up with that film, these seemingly random components instantly referenced something they knew.

Yesterday I stumbled upon this meme which communicates the exact same thing, but with far fewer words:

(Please tell me you get that reference too)

The same is true of the Bible. Picking it up, reading it as a 21st century American (or wherever you're from), and assuming that you perfectly *get* it will lead to some disastrous misunderstandings. If you don't do your homework, so to speak, it would be like someone in the year 3,000 looking at me covered in balloons and assuming they knew what was happening. If they didn't know about the film *Up*, didn't know it was Halloween, and didn't see my two accomplices, they'd have a hard time figuring out what on earth I was doing covered in balloons. It's imperative to enter into the thought of the time period we're looking into, not read from your current position.

Context, context, context!

I believe the Bible is written by humans and therefore, it requires a lot of contextual and critical understanding. This is often mishandled by conservative and progressive teachers alike, as we are all guilty of putting what we want *into* the book (or taking the parts we don't like *out*, à la Thomas Jefferson, who took scissors to his Bible and snipped out all the parts he didn't like).

If, on one hand, you believe the Bible fell out of the sky, direct express from God, and is unquestionably, literally true, then you'll likely fall to the conservative side of biblical scholarship.

The other side plants the biblical books deep into the context of world history and emphasizes the *human* elements of scripture. If taken to its extreme, the whole of the Bible is deconstructed away and it is a meaningless heap of Greek,

Hebrew, and Aramaic with no authority whatsoever. Therefore, your ethics and guidelines for life are whatever you want them to be. This delivers one to the modern ethical notion of 'don't hurt other people and live how you want.'

For this reason, let's begin by looking at the nature of God, then humanity, then we will see how that trickles down to inform the beliefs we hold in the areas of government, sexuality, finance, and time.

&

When I was in high school, I went to one Christian winter camp where the speaker explained how he had spent a lot of time thinking about the nature of God.

"I made a list one time," he began. "I sat down and wrote out all the things that describe God. There were dozens of words. Then I began grouping them together until I found that each one can fall into one of two categories."

I was listening intently, eager to see which TWO words could sum up God.

"The two categories that define everything God is and does," he said, "are Loving and Holy."

I thought about it for a while.
Then decided he was probably right.

Holiness.

Love.

These things seemed to be the themes jumping out of the pages of Scripture. One not necessarily more important than the other, but also unable to exist without the other. Let's pause, define our terms, and examine the tension between these two attributes.

HOLY

Several years ago, a photographer named Joey L set out to photograph many of the world's 'holy men' from different religions. He shot them doing their thing, rowing boats across sacred rivers, walking in pilgrimage, and generally living differently than the rest of the world. The portraits are both fascinating and haunting, as the men in the photos—primarily from Ethiopia, Iraq, and India—do not look 'normal' by any definition.

Some have 40-year-long dreadlocks which at first glance look like frayed nautical ropes draped around their shoulders

Others have the ashes of cremated humans smeared across their face while they bathe in the Ganges River. They may flay open their own skin in attempts to appease their gods who are holy but not loving; gods who are only happy when their subjects are not.

Many of the holy people are not so extreme, but the creases which sprawl across their faces sing songs of unique holiness just as loud as the antics of the others. The eyes of each individual in the project draws the viewer in.

Why? Because they are *holy* people.
They are not like the rest of us; they are *other.*

The most simple definition of holy is 'set apart.'
Something holy is unlike the others.
There is something which separates it from the rest.

On my left tricep, I have tattooed a big hollow circle above a small black square. The image is meant to be a meditation on holiness, otherness, and transcendence.

It works on two levels. On one hand, the tattoo represents God and humanity. If He is a big white circle and humans are a small black square, we have as much chance of understanding Him as a small black square would a big white circle. It is different, it is *other*, in every conceivable way.

On the other hand, if the world's population of humans is the big white circle, then Christians are represented by the small black square. God calls us to not look like the rest of the world, but to be holy, set apart.

In other words, if a Christian is living as instructed by God, then she should *not* look like the rest of the world. She should stand out and look dramatically different, the way a small black square would appear to a crowd of big white circles.

This is exactly why the holy men of the world seem so mysterious and intriguing to the rest of us. They have taken the commandment (from Yahweh or their god(s) of choice) seriously, and have set out to be *holy* from everyone else. The prophets of the Bible were not 'normal citizens' by any stretch of the imagination. Imagine stumbling upon Ezekiel, lying on his left side for a year and cooking bread over poop.

Holy people do not blend in.
Holy people do not live or act like the rest of us.
Holy people use their money, bodies, and time differently.

It was said of early Christians that while the rest of Rome was open with their beds (who they slept with) and closed with their wallets (who they gave to), Christians were closed with their beds and open with their wallets.

When God calls His people to be holy, He is not calling them to be cool, relevant, and do the same things as the world.

Very much the opposite.

Several years ago, I was on an outdoor patio enjoying a coffee in a big, busy city. People passed by in a flood of 'normal' humanity and no one paid attention to their fellow citizens. But then, a block up the road, I saw an elderly nun making her way down the sidewalk toward where I was sitting.

A black habit covered her hunched frame as her old feet hobbled her off-white, creased New Balances along. She said nothing as she quietly walked beside the busy street, and I distinctly remember the entire block somehow falling silent as she went by. The rest of the world pressed pause to watch this ancient, holy woman stroll past.

She said nothing, she did nothing, she simply walked. There is something about being in the presence of a *holy* person that shifts the atmosphere. Even the most antagonistic atheists beheld her as someone who had given up money, family, *SEX*, in pursuit of her divine Lover.

You don't need to be religious to acknowledge the dichotomy between the holy and the average. The sexy women pacing the streets in crop tops didn't hold a candle to the aura of this old nun. It wasn't her physical allure or her loud antics that caused the other pedestrians to stop and behold, but the inherent holiness of her presence.

Holiness is a vapid and ethereal concept.

God is holy; He is unlike the rest of us.

He is not a man, but He became one.

He is not an angel, yet He is greater than all other spirits.

He is not a tree, cloud or mountain, yet He created them, then entered into His creation.

In his book *Notes From the Tilt-a-Whirl*, N.D. Wilson writes:

> Why do Christians think of purity, holiness, and even divinity as something with big eyes and soft fur? Why do we so often ignore the beautiful in exchange for the cute? …Holiness is terrible. It comes with the whirlwind. It is a purifying fire…

If you have a god who is only holy, you end up with religions like Islam or Hinduism, where effort and actions purchase your eternal destiny. Make sure not to screw up beneath the careful scrutiny of a holy god or else you'll spend all of eternity—or your next reincarnation—in suffering or insignificance. There is no appeasing a god who is *only* holy. The God of the Bible, Yahweh, repeatedly commands His people to be holy as He is holy (Leviticus 11:44; 1 Peter 1:16)—an impossible task. Jesus and Paul make it clear all throughout the Newer Testament that this is a command which no human can obey.

Holiness is akin to purity.

Something that is 99% pure is not pure at all.

Purity refers only to things which are 100% pure.

So it goes with holiness: there is no point in making efforts to elevate your own holiness from, say, 67% to 68% holy, because in the end, unless you reach 100%, you are doomed.

There is no hope of salvation with a god who is all holy but not loving.

How do we define holiness, much less come to know a holy God who is so *other* than anything we understand? It is impossible without His second attribute.

LOVE

Conversely, the idea of a god who is all loving but not holy is like eating a barrel of wet popcorn. There is no structure, no substance to the essence of the creator. He may be nice—this iteration of God is certainly appealing to our culture, but love without holiness is not only mushy and limp, but ultimately destructive.

Without holiness, there cannot be a form to the universe.

Holiness implies a hierarchy, a system on which the universe is designed. You have God, then everything else. And as creator of said universe, He gets to dictate how things operate. His love does not simply erase all forms of ethics, sin, and truth in favor of some vague idea of grace. Quasi-tolerance. Pseudo-acceptance.

Our eyes interpret the world around us by reading shadows as much as light.

We stare not at the sun, but at everything it illuminates.

When we interpret the history of our own lives, we cannot understand the moments of ecstasy except by knowing the pain of grief, loss, and suffering. They add a sharpened point to the heights of our joy.

To take it a step further into the realm of ethics, let's answer the question of evil. One of the oldest arguments against the existence of a God, much less one who is good, is that evil also exists. In order for something to be deemed evil, you must imply that there is such a thing as good. How do you make a distinction like this, especially with so many diverse cultures coming up with their own slightly-different understandings of right and wrong? If you want to say that something is morally good or bad, you must appeal to a higher authority which defines these characterizations.

Without a definition of good or evil, there is no evil and therefore, no question of evil. You cannot call something 'bad' unless you have a reference point for what is 'good.' If everyone on earth is left to their own understandings of good and evil, there will never be order or agreement.

God, says the theist, is our highest good.
Jesus, states the Christian, is the highest form of humanity.

Relativism is a popular concept today, as it dictates that anyone can decide for themselves what is right and wrong, how they should live, and what ultimate truth is.

It always reminds me of an antique watch I bought at a thrift store once. Around the edges of the watch were the letters N, W, E, and S. It was funny though, because these letters were fixed into the watch body. N was always at the top no matter how you moved it. In other words, the compass letters were purely decorative and not functional whatsoever. North was whichever way you wanted to point it. I always thought it was funny on the part of whoever designed the watch.

This is exactly what relativism is. Each person can define what is right and wrong for themselves. Everyone can orient themselves however they want to the universe, to ethics and morals.

The issue is, the relativist paradigm quickly breaks down when faced with, say, many of the atrocities committed in the 20th century, as many acts were deemed 'universally evil.' After the dissolution of the Nazi regime, Germany was subject to the Nuremberg Trials, which lasted from 1945-49. This was the first time that a punishment was assigned for the category of "crimes against humanity" (although the term itself originated earlier). In other words, these trials established a precedent for certain actions, systems, and policies which are universally immoral. These things will always be wrong.

There is no 'universal evil' without 'universal good,' and the implication here is that there *is* universal good.

Is it 'good' to feed your child?
Is it 'good' to raise him so he doesn't hit other children?

Is it 'good' to raise him to share his bread with others?
Why? What makes this good rather than bad?

There must be a moral Lawgiver handing down these definitions, or else there is no such evil to speak of. Even genocide—generally understood to be universally wrong—falls apart without the notion of the *imago Dei*, which will be discussed soon.

The question of evil instantly falls apart if it is just one human defining evil for themself. Without a larger code of ethics against which to hold the actions of humanity, we lose the question of evil altogether. The argument peters out.

Thus, a god who is loving but not holy begs for no structure on which to rest this call to be and do better; to strive toward growth and progress.

Perhaps this is why, as pointed out by Thomas Cahill in *The Gifts of the Jews*, the Hebrew people were the first to break out of the cyclical mindset of the Sumerian cultures. Outside of the Jewish people, all ancient people on earth believed that life was simply lived in circles: seasons come and go and return; people are born and die but others take their place. There was no concept of forward movement and progress.
Everything happens in a circle.

The Israelites embraced the notion that life, law, and culture can actually progress; that forward motion is not only possible but encouraged by a God who is both gracious (as we stumble and fail forward) and holy (constantly calling us to a higher standard).

A proper view of the Christian God, Yahweh, the *I AM*, requires the believer to hold the proper tension of holiness and love. Neglecting either attribute at the expense of the other is a costly and dangerous mistake.

Finding the balance between the two is the foundation of living out the Christian life; it is our motivation and call forward. It is also the safety net which catches us when we screw up.

That God is loving and holy should come as no surprise to anyone who has been in church for any amount of time. These are the recurring themes of the Bible (if we associate love with similar attributes of mercy, grace, and kindness).

But the Bible does not end by stating that God is these things, The End.

Rather, it implies the continuing work of God through humans in the notion of the *imago Dei*, or the Image of God. Genesis 1 tells us that God made men and women in His image. The word for 'image' is the same one used to describe idols; physical manifestations of the gods which humans can see and touch.

In other words, Amorites and Canaanites whittled little figures that represented their gods and then prayed to them. The Bible gives a different understanding though. If there are any physical representations of Yahweh on earth, it is not a carved wooden statue, but

your mom.

Or your brother.

Or the homeless man you just walked by.

Or the millionaire who just blazed by you in her Tesla.

As you can see in the diagram, many people (in this case, we'll use ancient animistic tribes) would carve an image of their god. Then they would worship the carved image, as it was a representative of their god to them.

In the Biblical paradigm, however, we are told that **we** are the image of God on earth. That means that *we* represent God to the rest of the world, and to one another. When we care for one another, for our planet, and so on, we are being the representatives of God to the world.

Part of the reason God instructs humans not to worship carved images is because it disrupts their proper place in the world. We are not meant to waste our time bowing before things we made with our own hands; we are to fill our time with work, care, love, creativity, and so on, representing God to the world.

Each of us contains this divine spark which is none other than the very breath of God.

Remember that Hebrew word, *ruah*? It has three meanings:

Wind — Breath — Spirit

When God breathes into the nostrils of Adam, He is not just inserting literal air into his lungs, but the actual Spirit of God. God doesn't do this for any of His other creations—He doesn't breathe into the nostrils of deer, guinnea pigs, or alligators, just humans.

All the other animals are animated by the *words* of God; humans come to life with His very breath.

What this means is that humans matter to God because God is inside of humans. It means that when you are rude to another human, you are being rude to the very Spirit of God dwelling inside of them. When you hurt their feelings, you are hurting the very Spirit of God which animates them. And it means that when you feel things deeply in yourself—a sense of justice for oppressed peoples, or when someone wounds you—you are experiencing something deeply profound to the heart of God. Jesus echoes this sentiment in Matthew 25, when He says (in my own translation), 'what you do to one of these people, you do to me.'

It means you are the closest thing to a god walking the earth right now. I don't mean it in some self-empowering, New Age rhetoric, but rather, in the sense that we are God with skin on to one another.

If God created you to be like Him, we need to ask, how then shall we live? How should we treat the others who are made in the image of God? How should we treat the rest of creation?

Well, the short answer is that we should act like God would act.

We need to be loving and forgive others constantly.
But we need to be holy, calling ourselves, creation, and those around us to a higher standard of flourishing and excellence.

When it comes to the nature of humans according to the Bible, there are a few delicate balances which need to be firmly in place before we can discuss the ethics of how to treat our fellow humans, know ourselves, and connect with God. As mentioned above, humans are the only beings on earth who carry within their bones the very Spirit of God.

We are little skin balloons, inflated by Yahweh's almighty breath.

But what is that skin made of? Looking once again to Genesis, we see that we are dust. One of my roommates has a bumper sticker taken from a real church bulletin typo on his laptop:

REMEMBER YOU ARE BUTT DUST

Nothing like a good spelling joke.

Anyway, What does it mean to be made of the crust of the earth but carry the divine spark? It means that we operate within creation but are special. We are not like the rest of creation. We are not the same as moles and tuna fish. We are set apart.

Rob Bell describes it well in his book *Sex God.* I'll summarize:

Animals are bodies without spirit.
Angels are spirits without bodies.
Humans are bodies carved from the dust,
with spirit breathed into us by the mouth of God Himself.

We occupy a special area in all of the universe. This is why, for instance, I can never get AS upset about animal cruelty while there are still child slaves. People boycott dairy farms, and I'm like, "But there are people being sex trafficked right now! Humans!"

Yes, I would LOVE for there to be no more animal cruelty. Of course. I would love for there to be nothing but all-organic, ethical farms.

But in my list of priorities, I'd rather get the injustices against humans sorted out first. As much as I **adore** my pet dogs, Americans tend to elevate their animals to a level the Bible never does. God seems to have no problem accepting thousands of bloody animal carcasses as a sacrifice.

Barbaric? Maybe. But not as barbaric as the nations around Israel which sacrificed children and virgins. From its inception, the Bible has placed infinite value on the lives of humans over animals.

We catch a few scattered verses about angels, but they seem to serve a similar purpose: serving humans in some way or another. The Greek word *angelos* simply means 'messenger,' and most often, that's what they are seen doing in scripture.

Side note: Nowhere in the entire Bible does it say that humans become angels when we die. You may have heard the expression 'heaven just got a new angel' when someone passes away, but…

no it didn't.

It maybe got a new human.

Depending on your understanding of the afterlife, we either are in some sort of spiritual sleep until the resurrection, or spiritually present with God, but in no way do we *become* angels. Humans and angels are ontologically different from one another. Anyway.

Having a proper understanding of humanity within the created order will help us as we move forward in discussing ethics, or *how* to live in the world. You can't know where to go unless you know where (and what) you are right now.

You can't know what right and wrong are unless you know the One who defines them. Part of knowing God means understanding His attributes, which helps us understand why

He leads us the way He does, and therefore, how we should live.

But it's important to remember that God is more real than simple lists of do's and don't's; He does not simply exist in the vacuum of ethical conjecture. So let's look at how we think, followed by how we should think of God's morals.

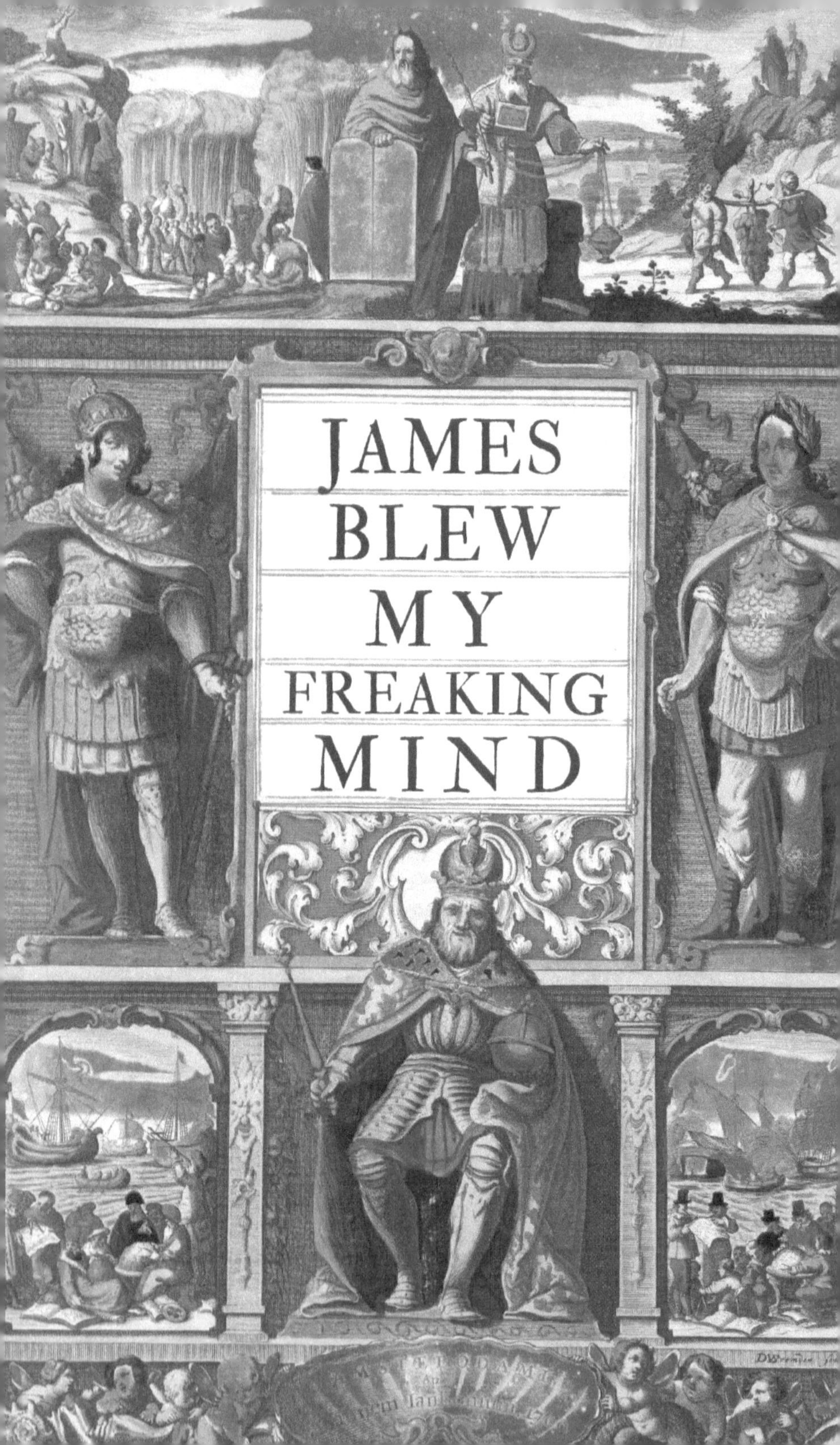
JAMES
BLEW
MY
FREAKING
MIND

very thought you've ever had, every experience you've ever interpreted and every desire you've ever had is, for all intents and purposes, not your own. Perhaps I should say it's 98% not yours, but still. You get the idea. You and I think many thoughts a day, and the majority of the thoughts we have are scaffolded by millennia of people who thought before us, their ideas trickling down into the way we think.

Let me give you an example of just how pliable the human psyche is. Our present culture pushes for individualism at almost every cost.

"Speak your truth" is a phrase we hear constantly.

Well, who exactly discovered that each human is capable of having their own, unique thoughts? When were we given the ability to think for ourselves and present our own interpretations of the reality to the world?

The Sumerian cultures believed that time was cyclical, and that humans were all just essentially spokes on the wheel of time. They had no unique identity. They were not going anywhere.

See how the idea of identity is intricately tied to the idea of time and progress? When you realize that each individual person can bring something unique to the table so that together, you can move forward into something better, you stumble upon both individual value and progress in society. When you think time is just a repeating pattern, and humans are slaves of the gods toiling in circles, then you don't have much room to think or come up with original ideas. If you told an ancient Sumerian to 'speak your own truth,' they would be beyond lost.

This is the culture into which the Hebrew God spoke, radically changing the way humans saw time, themselves, God, and as a consequence, thought.

For instance, in Genesis 16, Abram has raped his slave girl Hagar and sent her away into the wilderness, since he wasn't happy with the heir she gave him. A normal story would focus on the patriarch of the story; the powerful man who overcomes the weak and disposes of them when he's done.

Instead, Genesis pauses to mention a brief interaction between God and Hagar the slave girl. The powerful man had sent her away, but God sees her. She refers to this God as *El-Roi*, or, The Living One Who Sees Me.

Something in her interaction with this divine Being told her that she is seen; that she is not forgotten by the holy mind. That she has a unique identity that is carved out for her.

How different is this story from the surrounding culture which had no concept of progress or individual identity, especially for slave women! And how different are both of these iterations of thought from how we think today!

We are born into the world as a blank slate but from day one, we are having structures of thinking built for us, resting on the foundation of philosophers, writers, stories, and theologians who lie in the ground beneath the feet of our minds.

I just got off the phone with my friend James, who has influenced much of my thinking on the structures of history, philosophy, and the world, and every single conversation with him is like drinking straight from a firehose. There is no 'gentle' switch, and it's fantastic.

Today's conversation was sparked by a relatively simple question from me to him via text: "What's the difference between modernism and postmodernism?" It's the type of thing you can Google and try to decipher for yourself, but talking with an educated friend is so much better.

The firemen arrived and busted the cap off the hydrant.

I put my headphones in while James spoke and I attempted to type up every single thing we discussed as we went.

My mission here is to take the philosophical jargon from our conversation and present it in a digestible and accessible way which doesn't feel like reading the phone book. So in this chapter, I'm attempting to answer four (relatively) simple questions:

What is modernism?
What is postmodernism?
How do these affect our Christian theology and faith?

What can we learn from both sides regarding how we think about the world today?

You'll quickly see that both sides represent very real methods of thought seen today—you'll notice that one category predominantly informs one political party, demographic, etc., and that the other informs another. At the risk of overgeneralizing, I'll try to show why conservative people align more with modernity, while liberal folks will be more postmodern thinkers.

This is why it's so important to understand philosophy—it reveals how we think and why we think that way. Understanding the history of it may help us better understand ourselves as well as those we disagree with.

&

Premodernity

Before we get into the two main camps, I want to paint a bit of a picture of life and thought prior to what we would call 'philosophy.' That word is simply composed of two Greek words:

Philo—"to love"
Sophia—"knowledge"

It is an examination of knowledge, thought, and epistemology (how much we know, how we know what we know, where that knowledge and thinking comes from, what it is possible to know). As long as humans have been on this dusty, humid planet, there has been thinking. For our purposes, however, we will put a historical marker on the criterion Greek philosophers, starting around the 400's BC.

I made my students memorize the order of the heavy hitters with a simple acronym:

SPA. The first day of Greek philosophy was SPA Day.

Socrates: The father of Western thought. Created the Socratic Method, a way of asking questions in order to learn further. At the age of 70, he was forced to choose between drinking poisonous tea or leaving Athens forever. Why? Because he claimed that the Greek gods were not real. More on this soon.

Plato: Some people think Plato invented Socrates as a character and that Plato himself is the originator of the ideas of both of them. Either way, Plato was Socrates' student and is my favorite philosopher because of all of his groundbreaking ideas and metaphors. His brilliant ideas of the Forms and the metaphor of the Cave cause me to refer to him as a "Pre-Christ Christian," if there could be such a thing.

Aristotle: The student of Plato, Aristotle parted ways with his teacher on the nature of existence. In Raphael's painting *The School of Athens*, Plato is seen pointing up at the 'Forms' of the universe, while the more empirical Aristotle is gesturing toward the ground. He tutored Alexander the Great who went on to conquer most of the world and thrust it into a new epoch of global progress. Major proponent of a well-rounded, public education.

And of course, public education creates social mobility. If you don't have a chance to be educated, you'll inevitably end up doing whatever your parents did, in the same social class as them, and so will your kids. For example, if your parents are Honduran tortilla makers, and you have no opportunity for education, how will you learn to be anything else? You won't go on to become an engineer or doctor. You are locked in to the same socioeconomic level as your folks because of a lack of education.

Think about how much we take that for granted in the United States: a poor girl from the South Side of Chicago has the opportunity to attend public school, go on to college, and get a job at NASA.

Social mobility.

Education dramatically changes the face of a society. Interestingly, another major proponent of public education was Martin Luther in the 16th century, the middle of the Renaissance, one of the moments with the most social mobility in human history. (After the Black Death wiped out half the population, opportunities opened up which never would have otherwise.) This mobility is a relatively new addition to the structure of human society—for most of human history, if your ancestors were slaves, so were you. If they were rich rulers, so were you.

Anyway.

As mentioned above, Socrates was killed for denying the existence of the gods. This tells us just how intertwined religious life was with the rest of society prior to these heavy-hitting philosophers.

They were among the first humans ever to imagine a universe in which the gods did not dictate every facet of one's existence. That's how life was done for thousands and thousands of years prior to the Greek philosophers came along and blasted holes in everything.

The gods rule everything and they're chaotic and angry.
No social mobility.
No individual identity, therefore,
no individual ideas or thoughts.
No progress.
Go in circles and then die.

Step into that world for a moment. You take your wagon to the market a few miles away; you don't set out on the road without praying to your god of choice for protection, deliverance from thieves, sickness, and anything else that could befall you.

For longer trips, you'll probably make some sacrifices begging them to keep you safe along the way. There was virtually no area of life untouched by the gods.

Along come the philosophers and suddenly, Socrates is asking questions *of the gods themselves.* Questions like,

What if the gods *don't* actually affect the world that much? What if they don't actually exist?

In a civilization governed entirely by your tribe's deity, this is a big no-no. You don't question the gods because, of course there are gods and now you're in danger of bringing their wrath upon the entire city. No wonder they wanted Socrates to leave Athens.

The chisel of Socrates' questions would eventually tap enough cracks into the minds of the Greeks that years later, they would rule most of the world, first by way of Alexander the Great, then through the Roman Republic which eventually swelled into an Empire which ruled the entire Mediterranean world. Their way of thinking gave us the entire Western world, including our approach to science, medicine, technology, progress, innovation, education, and more.

They blended science with thought and asked questions like, what is the universe made of? What is *this stuff?* How many types of 'stuff' is there? They opened doors which would lead to events like the Scientific and Industrial Revolutions and even the Enlightenment. It is hard to overstate their impact on the face of the world, including how you and I think today.

Pre-philosophical thinking was heavily tribal and lived in fear of their culture's gods. Their religion trickled into every part of their lives. Wars determined not only which nation's military was stronger, but whose gods were stronger.

The Greek philosophers took the first step toward a secular way of thinking, asking questions of reality which no one had asked before in human history. That's not to necessarily say that they were atheists themselves, but the idea that a human could even question *anything* about the gods was novel.

&

Modernism

Philosophy and human thought continued to evolve through many forms for over almost two thousand years, but no shift was as incredibly earth shattering as Modernism. This is the era from which the world's first true atheists emerged and continued the progress toward the Enlightenment and today's secular society. If you were to attach a face to modern philosophy, Descartes is the unchallenged figurehead.

You know his line: *cogito ergo sum.*
Or: *I think, therefore I am.*

That line in itself is earth-shattering, but out of context it's somewhat meaningless. It's not so much where Descartes arrived that matters, as much as how he got there. He began by asking "How do I know what I know? How do I know it's accurate?" (this is all epistemology, remember?) He even wrestled with more preposterous-seeming questions like, "What if a demon is messing with me and making me perceive everything around me wrongly; differently than it really is?"

Now, when we talk about knowledge, it's much broader than you may imagine. How do you know red is red? How do you know what a doughnut tastes like? How do you know another human?

Descartes wanted empirical, unadulterated truth and accuracy in what he knew, and wanted to know that his experience of the world was true and authentic. He tore everything down. All this reasoning led to his realization that he knew that he existed because he was capable of conscious thought.

I think, therefore I am.

By thinking, he empirically proved his own existence. Maybe it doesn't hit you very hard, but this is the nutshell edition.

Descartes wanted a tool with which to do philosophy which he could trust to be accurate. It's as if you had a telescope which was set to 94x magnification, but you thought it was set to 100x. All your measurements would be off because the tool you are using is off. If you can doubt someone's tool or method, you can doubt their knowledge.

Modernists were after solid, universal, concrete truth.

They believed it is possible to arrive at this truth, too. Modernistic thinkers are those who tend to think more in black and whites than in shades of gray, as they are the ones who observe the reality around them and begin to make empirical interpretations of it.

Take a sensitive topic today: the transgender movement. I'll look at it from a postmodern view in a moment, but the modernist would have issue with the trans movement for a simple reason: Men are born as men; women as women. It's simple. It's scientific. It's empirical. It's the way that things are, and it's not open to interpretation.

Modern people have an easier time arriving at concrete conclusions because that is what they are after—empirical, hard proof. Reality. See how this way of thinking could inform a lot of your conservative friends' ways of thought?

&

Postmodernism

In one of my philosophy courses, the professor opened the semester by saying, "Every breakthrough you have this semester will come from you realizing how postmodern you are."

We think this way without even realizing it.

We are the product of those who thought before us.

This modern line of thinking led to two camps: Rationalists, spearheaded by Descartes; and Empiricists, which was led by Locke or Hume. Rationalists asked questions about knowledge, and Empiricists provided what we call modern science, the means of experimentation in order to find answers.

Kant was the first to synthesize the two camps, but the two who sent real shockwaves through modern philosophy were Kierkegaard and Nietzsche. They came along and said 'You guys are fools; it's nice that you want to have sure, certain knowledge, but the fact of the matter is, we're human beings and the ways in which we produce knowledge fundamentally make it so that it's not universal, so it's always couched in human desire and personal experience. No matter how good your method is, your desires are always informing your methods. All your data stems from presuppositions.'

The whole postmodern school is about reorienting away from a search for universal, unimpeachable knowledge and toward local, varied, diverse expression that's constantly changing and being rewritten.

Put simply: Modernists assume and pursue one knowable, universal and concrete truth. Postmodernists realize that, because we are human and are shaped by our culture and desire, knowing this truth in its entirety is foolish. You cannot know 'Truth.' Therefore, truth is somewhat relative.

Take the example of the transgender movement again. If everything in the universe is unknowable, it is not worth trying to grasp it all. Therefore, knowledge is left up to individual experience—you can decide for yourself what is real or not.

Therefore, if a man feels like a woman, who is to stop him from expressing that reality? Who are you to tell him what is real *for him?* His reality as a woman is real inside his mind, and since *you* don't know everything either, trying to stop him would be violence to his humanity, or at least, his reality.

This is where we get phrases like 'live your own truth.' Since there is no universal truth—or at least, no way for one person to comprehend it *all*—all we have left is what we each interpret to be true for ourselves.

It's relativistic and hard to argue against, since you will always seem to simply be expressing 'your own truth,' and enforcing that onto others, rather than attempting to unearth capital-T-Truth.

Both extremes, modernism and postmodernism, have dire consequences, especially in how they relate to Christianity.

&

Another way to see it (with visuals!)

Thousands of years ago, the world seemed simply structured in a foundational hierarchy: At the base you had everything as it existed: the world, birds, dirt, men, women, and so on. This is called metaphysics. Everything simply is what it is, and things are pretty simple.

Resting on top of this was knowledge, or what people were capable of knowing (epistemology). Everything you could know rested upon everything that exists. Then, pulling from what people were capable of knowing came ethics, or the right and wrong way to live.

Millennia later, the bottom two flipped. This started when Descartes questioned the very nature of what people are even

capable of knowing and burped out the phrase "I think therefore I am." Post-modernity saw a reversal of the way things are interpreted and the way things actually are in the universe:

Knowledge became the base of everything, and we wound up with questions like, "If a tree falls in the forest and no one is there to hear it, does it make a sound?" This is a philosophical question because it begs the question of whether anything exists outside of human experience.

Perhaps this is why for the past couple years, voices like Jordan Peterson and Sam Harris—a psychologist and a neuroscientist, respectively—have become some of the most listened-to writers and speakers in the world. Millions of people listen to their takes on history, philosophy, science and other areas, despite the fact that their main training is in how the brain works. Peterson and Harris are popular because modern people are fascinated by how humans think, how humans map out and make sense of the world around them, and why, then, humans act the way they do in response. Because epistemology (knowledge, thought) is now the foundation on which all other sciences rest.

Peterson speaks with incredible knowledge on history, specifically totalitarian regimes, while Harris is better known for his theological stance of atheism. If you're familiar with these two influential figures, have you ever stopped to wonder why our culture at large accepts historical and theological lessons from two neuroscientists?

This is why. It's because the postmodern person believes that how humans see, know, and interpret the world is the beginning of everything else, from history to science to philosophy.

I could go on, but I'd end up chasing a million rabbits down their trails. The important thing here is the hierarchy: The order of the pyramid—especially its foundation—affects how we arrive at our ethical conclusions.

So which is it?

Which way of examining the world is the correct one; how is it made up? If the answer was obvious, we would not be so divided as humans, and we would tend to agree on most, if not all issues.

If your bottom layer, like the modernists and pre-modernists, is metaphysics and you believe that the world *is* the way it presents itself to you and go from there, then you'll have an easier time saying things like, "people born with penises are men and vice versa."

You see the physical, indisputable genitalia (metaphysic), which is the foundation of what we understand to be male and female (epistemology), which supports the idea that men should act/look/function like men (ethics).

However, maybe you believe, like the postmodern folks do, that each person's experience determines the way reality is. You state that complete truth is unknowable and we are all 'blind men touching different parts of the same elephant,' so to speak. Then you'd be more prone to subject reality to the preferences of the individual, saying things like, "if his experience tells him he is a woman, then s/he is."

Their understanding of who they are is not predicated on concrete reality like having a certain reproductive organ, but on who/what they *think* they are (epistemology). Above this is their understanding of reality and they may say things like, 'they just feel like a woman trapped in a male body' (metaphysics), and therefore their ethical solution would be to defy their physical reality and act according to their feelings or knowledge. Because for the postmodern person, experience and knowledge supersede metaphysics.

Modern people look at postmodern people and are baffled by how they can easily deny concrete facts like gender. "It's a dangerous red flag when a society can simply deny the obvious," Jordan Peterson once said. How could someone simply ignore the fact that he was born with a penis? Because his physical body doesn't dictate his gender; his thinking and feeling do. And his experience may tell him that he is actually experiencing life as a female would. Hence, the difference between a modern and postmodern construction of reality.

This is also why it's so hard to listen to conservative and liberal people talk, because from the very foundation of their understanding of the universe, they are starting from very different places. They are merely talking past each other because their structures are fundamentally different.

Ok, you can unfasten your helmet and take a breath.

&

Philosophy in Faith

Most conservative, fundamentalist-type Christians (aka, most Evangelicals) tend to lean toward modernism. After all, don't we believe that there is one universal Truth which is absolute and knowable? Don't we believe you can pick up the Bible and see the words God spoke into human history?

The problems with resolutely modern thinking is that it leads to things like the African missions of the 19th century: White missionaries believed that, because there is one, knowable and absolute truth (and they were the ones who knew it), they not only had to tell native Africans and Americans about Christ, but also conform them to a degree of 'whiteness.' The truth which they knew transcended society, culture and religion, meaning that if an African were to become a Christian, it also meant adopting *every* part of the modern white man's culture as well.

That's a synecdoche of the issue with a completely modern approach to theology. *We* know the full truth, therefore, you must know it exactly like we do.

A postmodern approach would mean that the gospel becomes contextualized to every tribe or individual and they can understand it and interpret it as they please. Taken to its extreme, this postmodern methodology would say that nothing is wrong, and humans can live as Christians *whatever* way they want to read the Scriptures. We could dismiss many of the Bible's instructions, saying that was simply for *that* culture, and doesn't apply to us. Taken to its furthest extreme, postmodern readings of Scripture render it utterly meaningless and its interpretation is left to the whims and desires of the individual.

Don't like Jews? Yank some of the Apostle Paul's writings out of context and use them to exterminate 11 million of them.* Don't like Paul's teachings on homosexuality, premarital sex or gender roles? Just write them off by saying that they were only for his specific culture, not yours.

This is postmodernity.

Modernists fear that a postmodern claim that there is no knowable, universal truth suggests that people will get carried away, modifying the gospel from society to society until no more truth remains. The fear is real and it is valid, but a balance in the middle must be found. The modernist's temptation is to construct an idol of truth and knowledge and bow down to it as the *only* way to know the world.

Postmodernity is not all negative either. It suggests that Christianity can, in fact, be understood by a Native African without conforming to colonial 'whiteness.' It can also be understood and applied as a white capitalistic American, and as an Asian rice farmer alike. It is read with different eyes by each

---

* cf. Martin Luther, Nietzsche, and Hitler

individual, but is no more or less true based on who is reading it.

A seminary professor of mine told us that in order for the gospel to truly take root in a new country, it first must become indigenous and *then* begin to spread throughout the society. Meaning that if I, a white man, were to go to an African tribe and simply try to disciple them into *my* version of Christianity, they would end up not just as Christians, but as *white* Christians.

The beauty of the gospel of Jesus Christ is that it transcends myopic human cultures and can just as comfortably fit into an African tribe as well as an American capitalist culture or an Asian farmland. Whenever we preach the gospel to those outside of our own culture, we must be careful to dissect which elements of our message are merely cultural remnants and which are truly from God, necessary for knowing Him well.

So which camp is right and how do we read the Bible?
And how, then, shall we live?

A professor of James' and mine, Dr. Michael McDuffee, says that the best way for the average Christian to read the Bible is literally. Pick it up and read it. The simplest reading is best. Learn and grow as you go, of course, but if there is no literal reading of the text, then it ultimately is meaningless.

James basically summed up the Christian tension thus:

Modernist theology is largely bunk because it's remarkably arrogant. It's saying that absolute truth exists and *we* have access to it and can describe it beyond the shadow of a doubt. Unchecked, it's a recipe for exploitation and oppression.

However, the ramifications of an unqualified postmodernist theory is equally as dangerous. Because where do you get off the train? How much can we qualify scripture before we're just reading our own desires and interests into what we see in the text?

It's a hard and nearly impossible task, but that doesn't mean we stop trying to grapple with it and understand the Bible we hold in our hands. Understanding these philosophical backgrounds really helps us come to understand how we (how I, Ethan Renoe), read the Bible. How we think. How we comprehend our faith and apply it to our lives.

Yet, until our knowledge is completed and our blinders are removed, we ask, *Maranatha! Come hastily, Lord Jesus! Make our knowledge full and our comprehension accurate.*

&

Modern and Postmodern thought in other areas

Of course this dichotomy is not limited to theology and how we think about the Bible. We see modern and postmodern influences in plenty of issues faced in our day to day lives. I mentioned the trans movement as a perfect example of this, because it posits what is tangibly seen and empirically proven (men have penises; women have vaginas—it's that simple) against the relativistic, individually-determined truth of the person (I *believe* that I'm a woman, therefore I am one). Looking at this issue through the lens of these two camps, we can see why both sides end up where they do.

People on both sides can learn from the other, however, and can always grow into a more holistic balance between two rigid extremes. Modern thinkers need to learn humility which says that no, they don't know *everything* and can learn something new from a different viewpoint. Postmodern thinkers need to be shown that some things *are* universally true and not everything can be left up to individual opinion or preference. Complete relativism is bunk.

We see language like this pop up every time someone says "They can't control MY freedom! They can't tell me how to ________" about whichever hot topic they're discussing. Whether it's sexuality, economics, wearing a mask in public, or any other area of life over which we want autonomy. It's human nature to resist authority, and this is where the kingship of Christ speaks to Democrats and Republicans alike.

To those who think love is love and anyone can marry anyone, Christ asks for authority over our sexuality.

To those who think the government has become too large, no one can take away my freedom, Christ says come and be a slave to me; submit to the governing authorities placed over you (to a degree of course).

Most of us go along with the cultural flow of thought without giving much thought to the history of where this way of thinking came from.

We tend to blindly latch onto any sentiment on love or freedom which sounds good and fits neatly into a soundbite. It's more difficult to build legs for your own way of thinking and ask hard questions about how we arrived where we did.

Think about it—take any hot topic issue and dig down into *why* you think the way you do about it. Many of you will simply say "It's common sense!" This way of thinking stubbornly refuses to hear any other sides and assumes that *your* common sense trumps everyone else's.

Conversely, if you're the 'free love' type who says to just let everyone be themselves, you may need to give some more structure to what you call truth. Perhaps there are some things which are universal and worth standing by.

For instance, I believe men are born to be men, and women to be women, though there is a wide range of what can be defined 'masculine' and 'feminine'. I believe that loving these people—as they are not as they should be (to borrow from Brennan Manning)—is the first priority of the believer. Any sort of moralizing and philosophizing needs to remember that when we talk about trans* people, we are talking about just that— people.

People made in the image of God, people to be loved and embraced and accepted before anything else is done or said.

But I believe that bending the knee to someone's gender dysmorphia will harm them more than help them, the same way giving in to an anorexic person's body dysmorphia would further harm their body.

When I was a personal trainer, one of my first clients was an elderly drag queen. He was the sweetest human being, but he had spent decades pumping his body full of estrogen hormones, and as a result, his body was raging against him. Psychological damage from his past aside, he had *physically* wreaked havoc on his organs and in his late 50's, his body was already shutting down. Remember, you can always trust nature.

Maybe, just maybe, God made male bodies to function a certain way—with more testosterone than estrogen—and vice versa with female frames. Maybe messing around with that intent will always do more harm than good. Rather than looking to heal the psychological damage which causes the gender dysmorphia in the first place, our postmodern culture has decided it's a better idea to embrace the wounded, distorted views of these individuals—because *we* cannot shape *their* truth.

More alarming is how many people—myself included—would be labeled *hateful* for a statement like this. Is it because I hate people who struggle with gender dysmorphia? Because I think they're gross and offensive and I want them to not exist? Quite the opposite: I love them, I'm grateful for every human on earth, and want them to flourish. I do not, however, believe that the way to go about this is to let them go on harming themselves and, like my old client, prematurely destroying their bodies.

Many proponents use the example of hermaphrodites, those born with ambiguous genitalia. "Gender is not so black and white," they argue. These complex cases, however, do not represent the *vast* majority of humans on earth and need to be addressed on a case by case basis.

The exception cannot define the rule.

Many postmodern people like to build an argument based on the 1%, rather than the 99, which is far easier to discern. In fact, according to the Intersex Society of North America, only 1 in 1,500 to 2,000 babies are born with atypical genitalia.

I don't know about you, but I don't want to build my ethics of gender on a 1 in 2,000 case; I'd rather build it on the other 1,999. You don't make nutritional recommendations based on the rare person who's allergic to protein.

Now, to push back against the other side for a moment, there are many stereotypical gender constructs which are more rooted in culture than in actual masculinity or femininity. Like how men:

    drive trucks
    drink beer
    lead (in churches, politics, business, etc)
    have body hair
    are the main income winner of the house
    do construction projects, working with their hands

Some of those items are more serious than others. Obviously anyone can enjoy a beer. When you start asking bigger questions though, like "who should provide for the family?" you get into a lot more grayscale sand traps.

This is an area where there really is no scriptural (and therefore ethical) pushback for why men should be the primary baconwinner in their household. This is where we distinguish between ontological differences and mere cultural differences. What is it that biologically dictates that women can't provide for their families better than men? Nothing. The legs this idea stands on are made of merely cultural fabric.

(I do, however, have one fun thought experiment I once conducted. While living in Guatemala, I noticed that many of the vagabonding, backpacking women were the hippie type who didn't shave their body hair. I wondered why this was a turn-off for me, and feared that I was enslaved by the mere cultural construct of women ridding their bodies of hair.

But then I realized that it may actually be more biological than first glance suggests.

Men produce testosterone, which promotes body hair and muscle, as well as reducing fat. Women produce more estrogen, which inhibits body hair production, inhibits muscle production, and holds onto fat.

So maybe, when a man like myself desires a more hairless woman, he is actually being drawn to *biological* femininity—a woman who produces a healthy amount of estrogen. And when a woman is attracted to a hairy, muscular dude, she is biologically being drawn to his testosterone production. A manly man, biologically speaking. This seems to be slightly more scientific than cultural after all…)

&

So?
Whenever attempting to construct an ethic for *any* category in the world, it's important to determine where you are starting from.

What influences are you taking into account for one stance or another?

Why do you think the way you do?

Are these things based on science, love for others, your experience or the experience of others, or something else?

All of these things are valid bases for constructing an ethical 'good.' Many people, however, do not take the time to examine their sources. We live in an age of memes and soundbytes; where one sentence seems to suffice for an ethical ideal.

THIS sentence will shut them down!

But that is not a holistic approach to living life. It's not a cohesive system of ethics. Until you can identify that "*this camp* is more focused on the experience of various people and wants to serve that while *that camp* is more grounded in science" then you will argue endlessly on Facebook about specific situations and never really arrive anywhere. When you can identify the underlying assumptions of different groups and understand where they are coming from, you can begin to have real conversations that educate both sides.

This is also why what you believe about God must trickle down into the rest of your beliefs. Starting with a slightly faulty paradigm of God, the universe, humanity, et al. will lead you to wildly different conclusions when it comes time to land on one side of an issue or another.

If the universe is open to human interpretation and preference, then yes; let your body become whatever you feel on a given day. If, however, there is some intended order and nature to the universe created by a cause larger than human invention, then perhaps science, reason, and even God may also need to enter into the conversation.

*"Because here's something else that's weird but true: in the day-to day
trenches of adult life, there is actually no such thing as atheism. There
is no such thing as not worshipping. Everybody worships. The only
choice we get is what to worship. And the compelling reason for maybe
choosing some sort of god or spiritual-type thing to worship—be it JC
or Allah, be it YHWH or the Wiccan Mother Goddess, or the Four
Noble Truths, or some inviolable set of ethical principles—is that
pretty much anything else you worship will eat you alive. If you worship
money and things, if they are where you tap real meaning in life, then
you will never have enough, never feel you have enough. It's the truth.
Worship your body and beauty and sexual allure and you will always
feel ugly. And when time and age start showing, you will die a million
deaths before they finally grieve you. On one level, we all know this
stuff already. It's been codified as myths, proverbs, clichés, epigrams,
parables; the skeleton of every great story. The whole trick is keeping
the truth up front in daily consciousness."*

—David Foster Wallace, *This Is Water*

AN ARMY
OF
BADGERS
VS.
JIMINY CRICKET

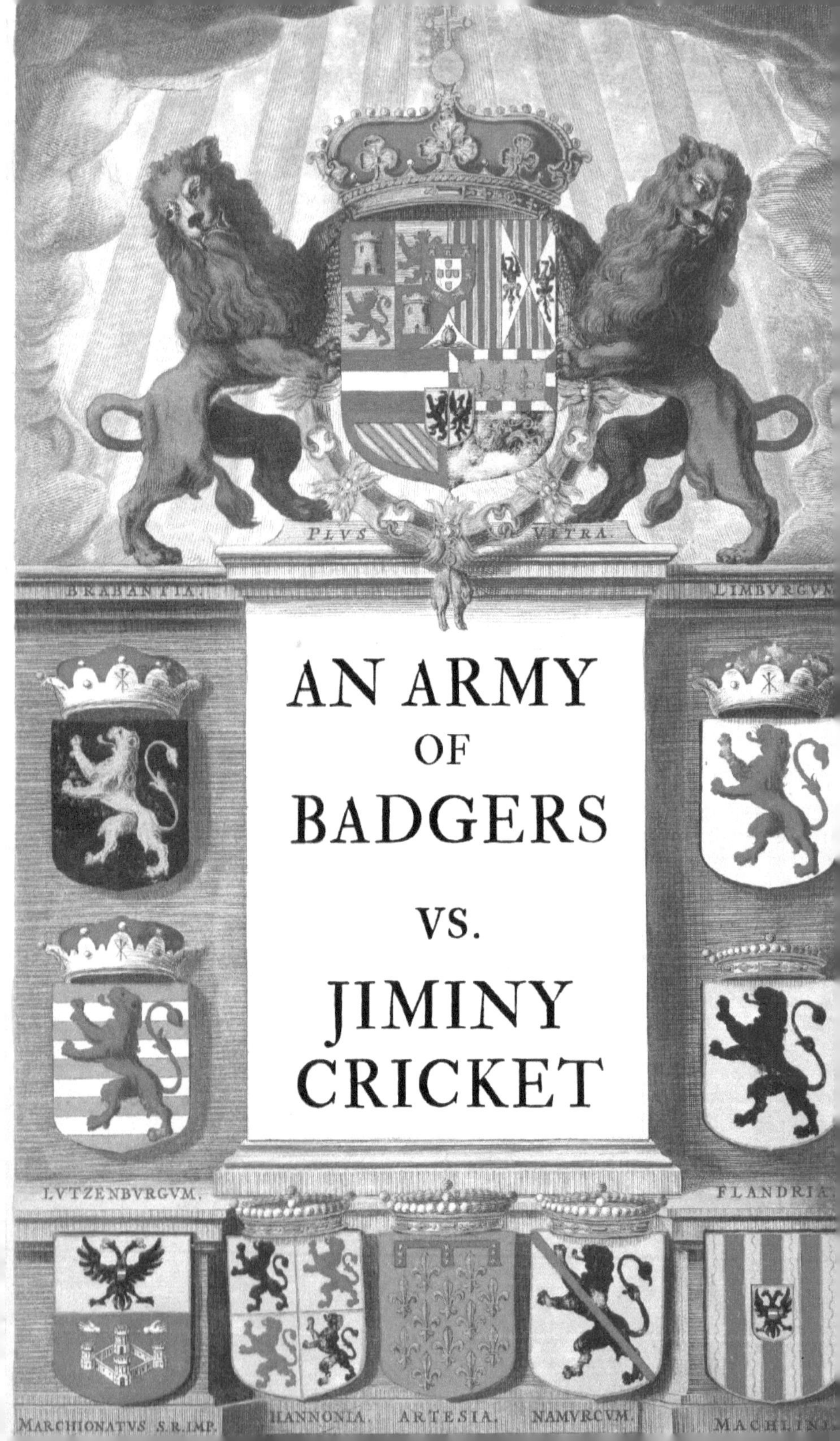

—Silent Planet, "Wasteland"

onight in the shower, for absolutely no reason, I was transported back to 8th grade Bible class when my teacher gave us a creative writing assignment. Everyone else in the class rolled their eyes, but I dove my pen into my notebook and couldn't pull the ideas from my head to the page fast enough, primarily because of the prompt he gave us:

"Write about a day without God."

I should fish through my old papers and find the original story, but mine began with badgers crawling out of their holes and eating people. Then the earth began splitting and peeling apart as the ground on which existence rested, shattered.

A few days later when we shared our creations, I was frankly disappointed/bored with my classmates' stories. I recall pithy sentiments like "I was walking around the mall with my brother and people were stealing things and doing what they wanted," as if God only existed as a Jiminy Cricket character whispering ethical nothings in your ear like a backseat lover. "Don't steal! You'd better be nice to your sister!" Mine was easily the most extreme, but few of the other stories actually conceptualized God as more than a conscience or a moral judge.

Only in hindsight have I caught what this little exercise revealed about the way many of us view God.

For many of us, God exists to monitor the good and bad things we do. When I was a youth pastor, I can't count the number of times a high schooler would accidentally swear in church and then make a guilty face toward me as if they'd just slapped my mother.

"You can't say that in here!" one of their friends would scold them. "You're in CHURCH!"

Why couldn't they swear in a church? Because it's where God lives and because God is a cop who will pull you over if you swear or kiss your boyfriend, but only in places where he can see, like in a church building.

Have you ever felt like this? Like the religion you inherited from your parents or your pastor is nothing more than a moral checklist of do's and don't's, as if God were chiefly concerned with monitoring your behavior? How different this approach to God is than the one the Bible presents! How anemic and weak!

I have been teaching slowly through the book of Mark and am seeing new and glimmering sides of Christ I never saw before. In fact, you'd be surprised how few moralistic instructions come out of His mouth. Whenever there is something like that coming out, He is usually rebuking the Pharisees (religious teachers) for their religious pride and false righteousness. More often, Jesus is demonstrating just how, exactly, God is bigger than their ethical laws on every front.

He calms the storm and the winds and the waves obey Him. (Power over nature)

He heals numerous diseases and disabilities. (Power over human bodies/disease)

He tells demons and other 'unclean spirits' what to do. (Power over spiritual realm)

And yes, He even invades the Jewish religious structures and eradicates them in favor of the outsider. (Power over human religion)

All this is to say that if your god is nothing more than a mere series of ethical codes, you've got Jesus all wrong. You haven't just gotten Him a little wrong; you're answering in a different language. You were asked what 2+2 is and you answered by throwing a baseball at your grandma. You are trying to dig a hole in the ground by climbing a tree and shooting a pistol at the clouds.

That's how wrong you are to fathom God as nothing more than an ethical conscience.

Let me try to explain another way, and you'll have to strap on your philosophy helmets again as we revisit the pyramids from the previous chapter.

At the inception of philosophy, the world seemed pretty simply structured in a foundational hierarchy: At the base you had everything as it existed: the world, birds, dirt, men and women, and so on (metaphysics). It's matter, reality as it is. Upon this was knowledge, or what people were capable of knowing (epistemology). Then, pulling from what people were capable of knowing came ethics, or the right and wrong way to live.

Millennia later, the bottom two flipped. It began when Descartes questioned the very nature of what people are even capable of knowing and burped out the phrase *cogito ergo sum*, or, "I think therefore I am," but we'll come back to him later. Post-modernity saw a flipping of the way things are interpreted and the way things actually are in the universe:

Knowledge became the base of everything, and we wound up with questions like, "If a tree falls in the forest and no one is there to hear it, does it make a sound?"

The important thing here is the top component: No matter what era of philosophy you drop into, you would find ethics at the top of the pyramid. It is the result of how you understand the other two foundations below it. You act according to how you see reality, knowledge, and experience.

Why does this matter? Well, if God only plays in the ethical sphere, then He is not primary, nor is He secondary, but tertiary. He is third-most-important in the construction of the world. The universe exists, I know a bunch of stuff, and oh yah, on top there's God just there to tell me what to do and not do.

"Only God can judge me."

aka,

"God's main duty is judging people's good and bad actions."

It stands to reason, then, that God cannot be merely an ethical entity. He is so much more than that, and so much more foundational.

He informs the metaphysical and the epistemological spheres, yet most of us spend our time relegating Him to the ethical sphere. *"Does God want me to do this? Is this ok?"* This explains a lot of unhealth in our religion in three ways:

1. It makes for far too small of a god. It makes a god who is dependent on other things in the universe, and he will just take care of the ethical sector. Someone/something else made all the stuff and matter and neutrinos and galaxies, but god will be

here to tell us what to do and not do. That sounds more like a demon on your shoulder than the creator of the cosmos.

2. It makes us disproportionally fearful of Him. After all, if He is 100% ethics-based, that has to be His main game. And he's gonna *git* you.

3. Our theology becomes unutterably small. If our God is the God of rules and only rules, then what do we do with beauty? Is God baffled by beauty because it exists outside of his purview? What do we do with secular poets or deep, rich human experiences which seem transcendent in some mystical way? What about what the Irish call Thin Spaces, which are places where the barrier between the natural and the divine seems thinner than others?

Ok, you can unfasten your helmet and take a breath.

Cramming your God into the teeny-tiny box of ethics is clearly unhealthy and a manmade invention, not the way God intended for Himself to be known. This is why, as Eugene Peterson put it, Christ plays in 10,000 places.

Not just in church.
Not just in right and wrong.

It is tragic that so many people see God as nothing more than a small cricket on their shoulder hoping they make the right decisions throughout the day. This is what my classmates' stories betrayed: That they believed in a moral character/ conscience but simply gave it the name of 'God.' How small!

No, God is the God of orangutans, the depths of the ocean, and the depths of our hearts; of blackholes lightyears away, and the distance between former lovers. To pigeonhole Him into a list of rights and wrongs not only pains His heart, but it calls a bottle of brackish water the ocean.

You can often tell if someone has this ethics-only picture of God by the language they use of Him:

Do they speak of Him as if He is the ground of all existence, or as if you're about to break a rule?

Do they speak of Him passionately like a lover speaks of his beloved, or like they're restricted to listening to Christian music and watching Christian movies?

Can you see where I'm going?

How many of us are trapped in this cycle of seeing God through this narrow lens of ethical do's and don't's? It's like trying to take in the sunset while peering through a straw.

I've got plenty more metaphors. If you want them, email me.

God gives us ethical implications, of course, but to assume that this is *all* He is is entirely wrong. It's more akin to the Pharisees' picture of God than the ones Jesus praised: the perspectives of the prostitutes, tax collectors, and outcasts.

Let's be more like those people—the ones who acknowledged how unclean and undeserving they were, and approached God rightly. And when they were around Him, we don't get the impression that he was wagging a finger at them; it seemed more like a party.

Let's find Him everywhere, not just in shameful rulebooks and guilty feelings.

Let's be people who delight in the God who dwells in every single facet of the world.

May He become the ground of your existence, not a mean father unfastening his belt to give you a cosmic whooping.

&

What happens when we attempt to remove God from the ethical equation though?
What if we try to scrub every trace of God (at least, the Judeo-Christian God) from the fabric of our ethical understanding?

People can't escape thinking in terms of good and evil; right and wrong; moral and bad. I became pretty acquainted with the writings of Friedrich Nietzsche this past semester, writing my term paper on his ethics. Nietzsche is less of a philosopher and more of a sledgehammer into the structure of preconceived western principles—principles which rested on those Judeo-Christian assumptions about people and God and life.

The question Nietzsche wrestled with in the late 1800's, and which I have been reflecting on as a result for a few months, is: are these categories real, or are they socially constructed like so many other cultural phenomena?

Let me back up: How do we summarize Nietzsche's ethic in a way that he may approve of?

The more you understand what he wrote, and the context in which it was said, the more you grasp that Sir Friedrich was really less of a philosopher and more of a wrecking ball, and when you fully grasp the scope of his project, you realize that anything less would have failed outright and his name would have blown away in the winds of history like most everyone else.

So what made him rise up above most other notable philosophers? What causes young men to flock to his writings in droves, still today?

I think it's the radical liberation from the chains of social restraint and moral imperatives.

Nietzsche, upon declaring that there is no God and the idea of Him was no longer necessary, but had begun dying in the human psyche, gave with it a warning: He cautioned people that if they disposed of God, then they would also dispose of all morals, ethics, and codes of order as we had always known them historically. If you removed (or attempted to) all traces of Judeo-Christian ethics from the world, you would face chaos and violence unseen heretofore.

In other words, he warned that a storm was brewing and that the death of God could very likely send humanity into a free-for-all tailspin reminiscent of the book of Judges where "Everyone did as he saw fit." Right about the time of his death, the bloodiest century in human history would begin. War would claim more victims at the hands of ideologues than ever before in human history.

The dam had burst. If god was done away with, the leaders of the world needed to come up with fitting, believable, and motivating ideologies to replace him. Naturally, as these were concocted by human minds, they quickly drifted toward simplistic and polarized extremes. How do you describe work, or purpose, or love, or life without a larger meaning than what's right in front of you on earth? That's the problem tyrannical leaders attempted to solve all throughout the 1900's, and their solutions consisted of a lot of propaganda, elevation of the State (or the leader) as a godlike figure, and an attempt at an earthly utopia.

Fun fact: In 1789, at the height of the French Revolution—which defined so much of how we see the world today—a tradition began. Those loyal to the king, who wished for things to stay relatively similar to how they had been, sat on his right. Those who wanted to remove his veto power and therefore upend the present system sat on his left. Therefore the *leftist* ideas became associated with progress and change, while *right* wing ideas were more rooted in present tradition and current order.

Just over 100 years later, the world would see what happens when both of these sides are pushed to their extremes: violence.

Populist (right wing) movements like Hitler's Nazism and Mussolini's fascism resulted in millions upon millions of deaths. In the same vein, leftist regimes led by Stalin, Lenin, and Mao led to, you guessed it, death like the world had never seen before.

And still, people today cling to their 'side,' sure that *this* time, we will get it right and that *this* extremism will finally lead to utopia…

After all, one of the most jarring statements made by one of my grad school history professors was that these dictators on both sides of the aisle were not trying to create a living hell and torture folks indefinitely; they were all trying to make utopia. That's a scary thought, and it only gets scarier the more you chew on it.

It means that the path toward humanistic progress is paved with millions of dead bodies.

Nietzsche outlined this prophetic idea of power usurping right and wrong in a book fittingly titled *Beyond Good and Evil.* He rationed that the ideas of good and evil (as deontological concepts, for you nerds) inherently require a deity to define them, or hand them down to humans.

Put even more simply, if there is such a thing as good and evil, there must be a God who dictates them.

So if there is no god, what are you left with? What Nietzsche constructed to replace morals, as simply as I can understand it, is the idea of strength versus weakness.

The deist (anyone who believes in God) will say that good is better than bad.

In a similar way, Nietzsche would say that strength is better than weakness.

From this developed the idea of the *übermensch*, or overman/superman, and the *üntermensch*, or underman. There are those capable of making their own free decisions, and therefore, their own systems of ethics, and those who follow in the overman's footsteps like sheep.

Nietzsche consistently railed against Christianity because it not only praised weakness and humility, but its founder was someone who voluntarily laid His life down for His enemies. It's a religion for weakness, he would say over and over. And in the mind of Nietzsche, nothing is worse than weakness.

"So if you really believe what Nietzsche taught," someone asked me while I was writing the paper, "why couldn't you just kill everyone you don't like?"

I chewed on it for a while, and realized that the *übermensch* must be smart as well as strong. The prisons of the world are filled with men who think they are supermen simply because they killed someone else (i.e. The Oklahoma City bombers were big Nietzsche fans). But which is more powerful: one murderer, or the ten cops arresting him?

No, in order to enact a new system of ethics, one must be convincing and alluring in some way, as well as strong. Ideas spread like viruses, especially ideas that induce fear or promise of utopia, or both. Hitler promised this to white blondes. He made them scared of those different from them, then promised a perfect land once it was 'purified.'

This is how you get away with murdering 11 million people; not by raising a gun, but the megaphone.

Hitler, heavily influenced by Nietzsche's brave new ethic, would lead much of mid-century Germany on a campaign against everyone Hitler didn't like. Getting thousands of Germans to believe your message and back your ideas all the way to their deaths is real power. Because remember, we are not discussing good versus bad, but power versus weakness. And in Nietzsche's mind, power is ontologically *better* than weakness. It would have been interesting to see what Nietzsche thought of the 20th, bloodiest, century.

After all, his prediction came true.

Now, on a personal level, reading Nietzsche can always be dangerous despite your circumstances, but reading him while your government seems to be fear mongering its citizens into wearing masks and telling you to stay away from other humans, because...they're dangerous...can lead to some ballsy rebellion.

Let's take the 2020 Covid pandemic for example: I revolted against the idea of masks, not only because they made it hard to breathe, I had already had Covid, and then I got vaccinated, but because they also made me into another rule-following sheep.

Is that all I am? I wondered. *Am I just someone who follows rules and does what I'm supposed to because I'm told to?*

Suddenly the thought that I'm just another sheep became more scary than Covid itself. What if, down to my core, I am just an *underman* who does what he's told and is incapable of thinking for himself?

These were the sorts of things I was wrestling with toward the tail end of the pandemic, but fortunately it ended before too long and I could once again live in bare-faced freedom. It wasn't just about the inconvenience of wearing a mask, but the mark of submission to an authority for authority's sake—not always science or safety's sake. After all, the *undermen* outnumber the overmen a thousand to one…Would I rise up?

This small example helps illustrate why so many young men are attracted to Nietzsche's thought. However, we also must remember that taken to its logical extreme, it's deadly.

Anyway, pandemic rant aside, we are still left with Nietzsche's core question: are right and wrong real, or are ethics simply invented by those in power at the moment? You could easily come up with examples of shifting ethical stances which have changed in the last 100 years. A century ago, being gay was outlawed by nearly every US state. It could get you arrested.

Why? because those in power were WASP† and narrow.

Now, the reverse is true. Any hints of discrimination against the LGBT+ community could get you doxxed, disbarred, cancelled, and so on.

The voices in power have spoken.
The people follow.

Did morals themselves change? Is it a matter of right and wrong, or a matter of power vs. weakness? Which is wrong— being homosexual, or discriminating against it? Depends on who you ask...or when you ask.

...or if you can think analytically for yourself.

Remember, I'm not making any argument here for or against homosexuality; I'm looking at how ethics interact with power. We could explore the same idea through the lens of tattoos, women, sexual liberty, nationalism, slavery, race, and a plethora more. Do ethics change, does power change, or does the constantly shifting power dictate what's ethical at the time?

At the end of the day, is power the only thing that matters?

I think Nietzsche might say yes. His idea of The Will to Power, which was left undefined but seems to have implicit meaning in his writing, underscores this entire idea. It has woven its fingers into the fabric of our cultural vernacular, like when we hear now-cliché phrases like "Our greatest fear is not that we are weak, but that we are powerful beyond belief." He thought there was

---

† White, Anglo-Saxon Protestants, or, WASP

an inherent desire inside humanity to rise up and overcome. (Again…it's easy to see why 20-year-old men gravitate toward his ideals.)

But is he correct? Would his narrative seem to (in the words of Wendell Berry)

> Invest in the millennium. Plant sequoias…
> Laugh.
> Laughter is immeasurable. Be joyful
> though you have considered all the facts…
> Ask yourself: Will this satisfy
> a woman satisfied to bear a child?
> Will this disturb the sleep
> of a woman near to giving birth?
> Go with your love to the fields.
> Lie easy in the shade. Rest your head
> in her lap. Swear allegiance
> to what is nighest your thoughts…
> Be like the fox
> who makes more tracks than necessary,
> some in the wrong direction.
> Practice resurrection.

Does his ethic produce more life than death?

One need look no further than the previous century to find the answer to that question. The century of ideologues led to more death and bloodshed than even the ancient warrior-god beliefs before it. It led to more technological advances—advances which Nietzsche may have seen as worthy of the human sacrifices in the name of progress, in the name of strength growing where it can—but to more utter moral failures than ever before.

Are these advances necessary for humanity to progress out of our tribalistic barbarism, or is that barbaric specter an inevitable element of humanity which will haunt us until the end—something we may never fully exorcise until our sanctification is complete? The Christian says yes. We should opt for slower progress in the name of preserving life and humanity.

(**Fun fact:** The term "barbarian" came from Ancient Greece to refer to most non-Greek people. To them, all other tongues sounded like "Bar bar bar bar...")

That, you'll notice, is why it's somewhat easier to paint the USA as the Good Guys when writing historical media. Unlike the extremist regimes of other nations, the USA maintained (most of) the principles of the Declaration of Independence, namely, that all men are created equal. This ancient idea that there is something divine in each person, regardless of color, ability, size, and so on, is utterly revelatory.

Unlike the Third Reich, which determined that Jewish, black, and disabled lives were disposable, the USA tended to hold to our founding principles which, thankfully, come right from the Bible. That divine image is what keeps us afloat, and when we look backward at history (especially in fictionalized tellings of it like war films and books), Americans can celebrate being 'right.' In this case anyway...

Please note that in no way am I endorsing America as the perfect civilization or the pinnacle of human progress. There is so much wrong in our society that needs fixed and we have made so many mistakes in the past that counting them would be as fruitful as counting beach sand.

The root of our American/Judeo-Christian ethic, however, rests on the idea of the *Imago Dei*, the Image of God. You remove that and suddenly, powerful people get to determine whose lives matter and whose don't. Just look what happens when nations dub religion 'the opiate of the masses' and attempt to come up with a replacement code of conduct, or significance to human life.

We may be distracted when certain leaders appeal to strength, offering us freedom and power beyond our wildest dreams, not to mention technological advances which better our lives, but which historically make worse the lives of others we don't know (read: how first world technology consistently leads to more destruction and pollution of developing countries).

Whose lives matter? This question and those like it are where Nietzsche's philosophy begins to fall apart. If strength dictates what is right and wrong, then there is no value to the lives of the weak.

Strength conquers.
Darwin's survival of the fittest wins.
Nature—that thing which selects—decides who lives.

There is more to say to this, but I'll wrap this one up here. Nietzsche is a compelling voice, especially to those who, like him, believe that God is dead, and we can construct our own morals. But beware of embracing this mentality fully—first off, because I believe you can't, and secondly, because you will inevitably discard the humanity of many people. Your ego may swell in an effort to live out your own perceived truth, but the violence done to your fellow humans by this explanation is not excusable.

In lieu of further contending with Nietzsche, how is this for a universal ethical principle:

Pursue that which produces more life than death.

So let's define life and death…

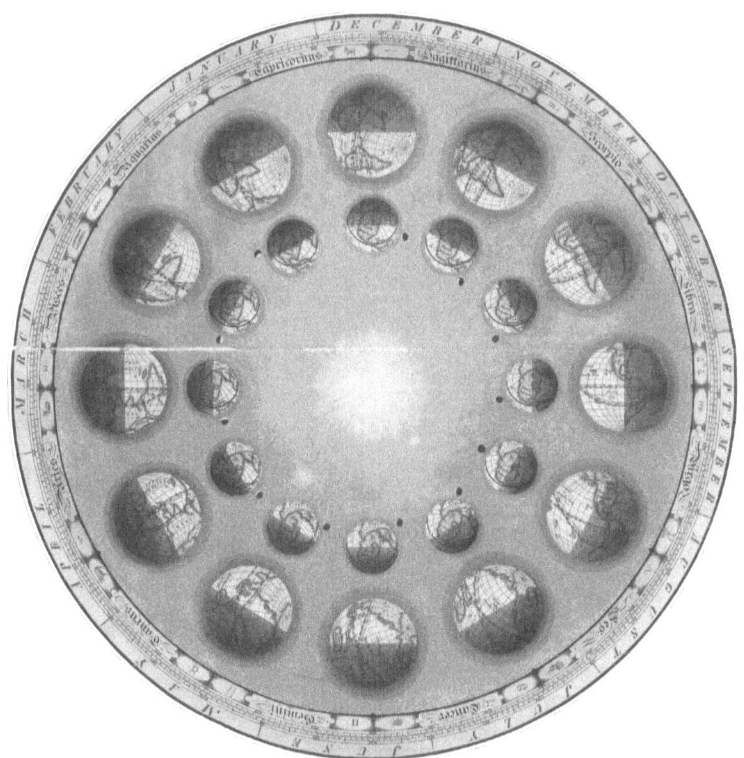

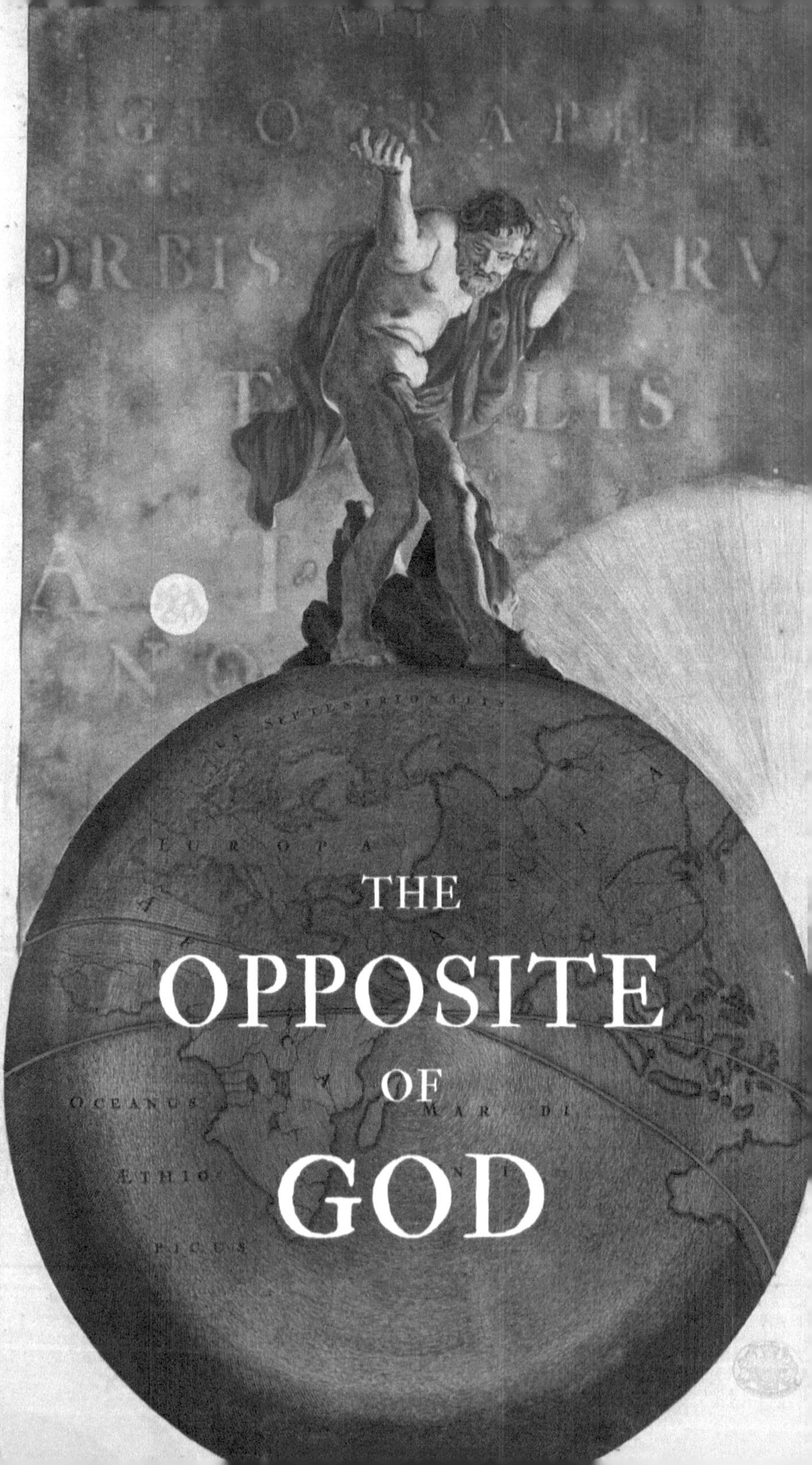

THE
OPPOSITE
OF
GOD

 opened the door and there was Vern, surrounded by a few family members and lawyers. They looked at me as if I were some holy man sent to touch him, or unlock a prophetic word, and nearly apologetically told me, "Sorry…we'll leave you two alone."

I'm just a chaplain at the nursing home and don't know wtf I'm doing.

I sat beside Vern and asked him how he was doing. Then I kicked myself in the head for asking such a stupid question. His wife was in bed in the next room over, "actively dying" as the nursing home employee had put it.

Vern and I exchanged some small talk, our two years of a chaplain/resident relationship straining beneath the weight of the moment. He's blind in one eye and squints with the other, so I don't know if he saw my face or just recognized my voice.

"Anything I can do for you?" I asked.

"What was the sermon on today?" he asked me, genuinely curious. I gave him the two-minute recap of Noah. The dove with a branch. Hope in the darkest season. It seemed fitting in the moment, but at the same time, it felt incredibly hollow.

No, actually, nothing was fitting.

His best friend was dying a room away and I was recounting Bible stories.

Eventually I offered to pray for Vern and his wife and he rose while grasping the handles of his walker. He shuffled his slippers over to the closed door and pushed it open with a frail hand. I barely recognized the body on the bed as Darlene, his beloved since their teen years.

She was fast asleep with her mouth open. It was evident that the tissue paper walls of her organs were fluttering to a halt. Her face was relaxed into a deep slumber—so deep, perhaps, that I wouldn't have known it was her if I didn't see Vern weeping just to look at her frame.

What did he see when beholding the sleeper on the bed? A beautiful maiden? A song? Home? Did her words somehow ring of a sweeter poetry to his ears than everyone else's on earth?

I've never known a love that deep, but I hope to.
Or perhaps I don't.

The deeper the love, the deeper the wound.

And Vern wasn't just being stabbed; he was being sawed apart with a thousand rusty blades.

It wasn't the snoring body in the bed that cut him so deeply, but the soul beneath the skin, the partnership in life and the unbearable pain of divorce by way of death.

I put my hand on Vern's hunched shoulder and began praying for the family. I thanked God for the example of their love and for the life they've shared. I blessed Vern and asked the Holy Spirit to comfort him. I quickly puttered out of things to pray.

What the hell else do you say?

I waited with Vern until the moment felt complete. He sniffled as he had been doing consistently for the past weeks, maybe months. Maybe years, mourning the death before the death.

I'd watched for two years as Darlene's mental state declined slowly for the last season of her life. She'd blurt out cute and irrelevant things during the services and lose track of where she was. And when she was.

Is this where they pictured it ending all those years ago, when they were young and could hold hands instead of walkers? Did they imagine this suburban nursing home in Colorado as the location they'd part ways? Did they expect it'd be in August or were they planning for a winter death?

Here's the thing: There is no poetry in death.

There is no song which conjures its comforts or boasts of its benefits.

You stand there in that August day with your hand on Vern and watch him weep while his wife "actively dies" in front of him.

It's no performance, it's a surrender.
It's an acceptance of the long and dreamless slumber.
It's a scraping of the deepest seabed of human pain.

Darlene didn't stir during the prayer.
She never would again.

She would keep her eyes closed, her mouth open, and sail across the river four days later.

Darlene's departure left a hole in the fabric of her family, as all deaths do. There's not been a death in human history that didn't rattle its community. There are stories of homeless people whose bodies wait in the morgue for 30 days for someone to come and identify it. Then after 30 days, they're cremated.

Even these deaths shredded the fabric of their relationships—
they just died to their friends years ago,
years before their body did.

Death is bad.

I can't help but wonder if death is the opposite of God.

&

Friedrich Nietzsche once used sandcastles as an illustration for life. With all sandcastles, it is inevitable that the sea and the wind will wipe them away within a few hours.

You are given the option, then, to halfheartedly build a few lumps of sand, since after all, it will be gone soon. Or you can throw yourself headlong into crafting a beautiful structure, simply for the sake of doing it, for however long it will last. Will you construct a beautiful castle, regardless of how long or short it will exist? Being a materialist and atheist, Nietzsche applied this to all of life.

All of us are building sandcastles and our wave is coming.

You get to decide how you will throw yourself into your life: Like one possessed and desperate to make something beautiful and original, or hopeless in the face of oblivion?

Until I heard this metaphor, I had never before considered how atheists motivated themselves to live. I know it may sound a bit sophomoric and ignorant, but I had to wonder.

As a lifelong Christian, I grew up knowing that we had purpose as mandated by scripture. The image of God, the salvation of the lost, the inherent value of each and every human soul, and similar ideas motivate the Christian to meaningful action. But what about atheists? From where did they draw their purpose?

Don't think about Nietzsche's inspiration too long: It will soon break down. A zeal for life and for beauty based on little more than, pardon the pun, a sandy foundation will not replace a firm deontological imperative. In other words, humans commanded by God to care for the earth and for one another is more motivating than some vague notion of beauty and "a full life." The Stoic Greeks would call it *eudaimonia*.

Another old saying goes: *you die twice; the day you die and the last time a living person says your name.*

How does it feel to think of fading from the face of the earth entirely? To know that those people 10,000 years in the future will have no idea that you even existed? You may appear in a statistic from time to time, such as the fact that "Over 7 billion people were alive on earth in 2021…" and you were one of them. But that's about it.

In the film *Nomadland*, Frances McDormand's character Fern says, "What is remembered, lives."

While this is poetic, it's not necessarily true.
I may be remembered in 200 years but I'll also be dead.

In the face of death, the Christian becomes both grave and joyous. Too often, in my opinion, we focus on a pithy mode of the deceased "being in a better place," without giving it any further substance. For instance, the evangelist D.L. Moody once said,

> "Some day you will read in the papers that D.L. Moody, of East Northfield, is dead. Don't you believe a word of it! At that moment I shall be more alive than I am now. I shall have gone up higher, that is all; gone out of this old clay tenement into a house that is immortal, a body that death cannot touch, that sin cannot taint, a body like unto His own glorious body. I was born of the flesh in 1837. I was born of the Spirit in 1856. That which is born of the flesh may die. That which is born of the Spirit will live forever."

While he is absolutely correct, is there a line of thinking in this direction that could be considered too far? Could we lean too far into the eschaton that we neglect the life we currently inhabit? The Christian, when balanced properly, can hold the tension between hope in the next life but a focus on this one. We can celebrate the death of a believer but deeply mourn their loss.

Jesus did.

If you've been in church for a while, you likely know the shortest verse in the Bible:

"Jesus wept."

Why was Jesus crying?
Because his friend Lazarus had died.
And Jesus would soon go raise him.
Which begs the question…Why was Jesus crying?

If He knew that Lazarus would rejoin the living in a matter of minutes, why waste time mourning his death?

We also see Jesus, when His friend John the Baptizer dies, retreating by Himself to be alone. He spends the night away from all other people, and I can only assume that He was deeply grieving the loss of the prophet. He could have retorted with another trite quip: "Welp. Don't cry y'all! John is in a better place and we will see him soon! Heck, I could close my eyes and go visit with him now, watch!"

But He doesn't.

Have you ever paused to wonder why Jesus cries in the face of death? Depending on what you believe about the afterlife,

Jesus would likely have been chilling with Lazarus, John, and all the other dead souls in a month or two, after He ascended back to heaven.

My take on it is this: Death is **so** antithetical to the way that God intended the universe to function; it's so repugnant to a God who delights in life, that even a small taste of it causes weeping. Even hearing that Lazarus had temporarily been tucked away in a grave violently disagreed with Jesus' soul.

Humans were not created by God in the hopes that they'd die.

Death is the opposite of life.
Death is the opposite of God.

&

At my college, many of the professors were opposed to singing the song "I'll Fly Away" in chapel.

The old spiritual was written by slaves during the American antebellum and reflects their hope in the next life: they may be slaves now, but one day, this life will end and they will be whisked away to a better place. Swing low, sweet chariot...take me away from here. I wanna leave. The theme shows up often in those spirituals for that very reason. Slaves had reason to hope in the next life: they had very little to hope for in this one.

But us? Those of us who are not enslaved, but are free to do good work, to create, and to care for the world in *this* life? Why should we neglect the concerns and issues facing the world and simply hope for a better one *over there*?

The reason my professors were against singing the song is simple: an almost suicidal desire to move on to the next life removes our focus from the present one. What about the work to be done here and now? What about the people who are suffering today, including but not limited to, modern day slaves? What about Bible translation, creating new art to inspire awe and beauty in the beholders, going for runs in the rain, raising children, teaching the next generation, baking food for hungry people, and everything else?

Are we just supposed to fly away from it all?

Clearly God cares deeply for what we do and how we live in *this* life.

&

When I was living in Guatemala, I was tossing a frisbee with Jake when he asked me a question which shook my theological foundations to the core and caused me to reexamine everything I believed and how I understood scripture. It was a simple question, and he didn't even mean for it to be paradigm-shattering like it was.

He said, "What did the people in the Old Testament—David, Abraham, Moses—what did they believe about the afterlife?"

I scanned the collection of verses locked into my head for easy access.

Then I realized nothing was coming up.

I couldn't think of a single Old Testament reference to the afterlife. I knew that some of the Psalms mentioned *sheol*, or the grave, but I also knew that the Hebrew notion of *sheol* was simply that: the end of life. A cessation of existence. Death. It didn't necessarily refer to the afterlife.

The question haunted me through that afternoon and the following days.

I asked the obscenely educated pastor at our small Episcopal church that Sunday and she didn't hesitate to dive in: "Oh yah! That line of New Testament afterlife thought is a result of the exile to Babylon and their exposure to Zoroastrianism. The Zoroastrians had a huge emphasis on the afterlife, so the Jewish captives there probably picked it up from them..."

It was like that scene in *Fight Club* when the film comes to a screeching halt and Edward Norton voices over, "We have just lost cabin pressure," and he realizes [MAJOR SPOILER OF ONE OF THE GREATEST CINEMATIC TWISTS OF ALL TIME].

I felt like the firm ground I had always stood on of *The Bible Tells Me So And It's All Pretty Simple* suddenly opened up beneath my feet.

You're telling me that everything we as Christians believe about life and purpose and the afterlife and Jesus simply comes from a pagan Babylonian religion?

Nevertheless, she didn't seem too bothered by it. She smiled as she continued to explain.

"Is the trinity described in the Old Testament? We understand that as progressive revelation; God reveals things to humans as history moves forward, and He often uses crazy, unexpected sources to do so. It doesn't mean that all of Zoroastrianism is true, but perhaps the Jews adapted parts of it into their thought and left out the rest. Then Jesus confirms it in the gospels."

My head was still spinning. It didn't sound right.

"Jesus was a Pharisee—" she explained, at which point I slapped her for her heresy. Not really, but I asked her what she meant.

"I mean, of the four major Jewish sects of the day, theirs is the only one that has a firm belief in life after death. So, if Jesus was brought up in a rabbinical tradition, it would have been Pharisaical."

But the Pharisees are the bad guys in the Bible and Jesus couldn't be a bad guy! I thought.

Over the next few weeks and months I began unveiling the Bible as it really was: A book which was collected throughout human history and in real space and time. That means that when Jesus speaks about life after death, He is talking to people who are having arguments and debates in their own time about philosophical and theological issues, just like we do. And His words would be understood a certain way within that historical context. Remember the picture of me covered in balloons?

The thing is, when you don't know the assumptions of the people of the time, you insert your own 21st century assumptions.

The very fact that Sadducees and Pharisees were debating life after death proves that it was not a given in Jewish thought at the time—as it still isn't, with the emergence of Secular Judaism and many Jewish people seeing their traditions as a good way to live without any faith in a coming afterlife.

That means that the majority of the Bible—all of the Old Testament and much of the New Testament—deal with how we should live in *this* life.

It means that people who try to evangelize on the street corners by telling people they're going to hell are dwelling on a small percentage of verses in a very large book. They're missing the point. Perhaps if they spent more time giving to the poor, caring for the sick, and feeding the hungry, they'd win more people into the kingdom of God…

&

There is an old debate among missiology students (those studying missions work): Which is more important—To show up to a hungry African tribe and give them food, or save their souls? The dichotomy typically plays out like this:

Conservative Bible readers think the more urgent need is spiritual. Save their souls first, so that in case they die, they will be in a place where they'll never be hungry again. Isn't it more important to give them eternal salvation than to satisfy their temporary hunger??

More liberal interpreters will say that the Bible clearly talks about feeding the hungry and doling out justice and mercy; that God has a big emphasis on *this* life, arguably more than the next one, in some places.

The struggle is, they're both right. Jesus fed the 5,000 hungry people, but He also taught about saving themselves from *gehenna*, the Greek word from which we get *hell*.

Which matters more, this life or the next one?
Honestly, neither.

You cannot make an argument that one is more important than the other, and this is an area where you see this broader belief trickle down and inform other modes of living. Liberal people will emphasize social justice and healing the world as it is *now,* while conservatives see more weight on where you'll spend eternity, so they focus more on evangelistic efforts to save people's souls…taking care of their bodies is secondary.

Falling into either camp can lead you to live in ways antithetical to the Bible, neglecting either this life or the next one.

&

"I have administrative bones to pick with God, Boo. I'll say God seems to have a kind of laid-back management style I'm not crazy about. I'm pretty much anti-death. God looks by all accounts to be pro-death. I'm not seeing how we can get together on this issue, he and I."

—David Foster Wallace, *Infinite Jest*

If you've read anything I've ever written in the past five years, you know that I'm painfully aware of my own mortality and the imminent death which is coming for each of us. I've ruminated on its finality and the ubiquity of it.

Death dwells in each one of us without exception

Several years ago, the metal band The Ghost Inside were touring across the country when they were in a terrible bus accident. Ten people were injured and one died. A couple years after the crash, they released a song as a reflection on losing of one of their friends in the crash.

The response, according to the band, was not to focus on death and to mourn for the rest of their lives, but to focus on what's left; to live out the rest of their lives with the life that's inside them rather than focusing on the death that awaits them. The song they released the following year cries:

> I don't have it in me to sing of defeat
> Triumph over tragedy
> The beat goes on

They have a sort of resilience many Christians lack. Why are we always talking about death and "What if you get hit by a truck tomorrow? Where will you go?" That's the typical evangelist line. We seem obsessed with death to the point that we miss out on the beauty of life, of inhaling, of flowers and surfing.

This is what prompted Garrett Russel, vocalist of Silent Planet, to write in their song "Dying in Circles,"

> We forgot Your life
> And became a people of death

In an interview, Russell observed that Christians have this obsession with death and convincing people they always need to think about hell and where they spend eternity, almost as if they don't have 80 years here alive to do things and make something beautiful.

Where in the gospels do we see Jesus so concentrated on death? He encounters it a number of times, but what does He do whenever He does? He weeps (John 11), He retreats to a quiet place to be alone (Matt. 14), or He belittles it by saying they're just asleep (John 11, Luke 8).

Jesus seems much more focused on life than death.
Maybe we should be too.

If Jesus has given us life, and life to the fullest (John 10:10), does He seem like a God who is fixated on death?

Another metal song, "Echoes" by August Burns Red screams,

> While mourning the loss,
> I am forced to celebrate
> Celebrate new life,
> celebrate new life

Do you often focus your thoughts, especially your spirituality, on death rather than life? Do you tend toward thinking about what awaits us after the grave and therefore relegate most of your religious reality to then?

This manifests itself in many ways, some of which are incredibly important. For one, if your Christianity is purely relegated to What happens after we die, then you will most likely be incredibly ineffective in this life.

Jesus gives plenty of parables and teachings on how we need to use our time. He talks about the parable of the talents (or *minas*), in which we are responsible to use well what we have been given. In the afterlife? NO! In this life! He teaches that the one who can be trusted with little can be trusted with much. He talks about clothing the naked, feeding the hungry, looking after widows, orphans and prisoners. These are not after-death things. These are things that we can only do while alive.

Too often, our faith floats above us in some vague spiritual cloud at which we will someday arrive, and there is little if any trickle down into our day-to-day lives. It like Hobo Johnson puts it in his song "Mover Awayer":

> Fear the man
> who has heaven in his plans
> so he gets so complacent

Jesus confronted this line of thinking simply by what He did. In theology, it's called the incarnational work of Christ. *Carne*, like meat. He came *into meat* and skin and bones, like us.

He didn't just sit up in heaven and drop down a scroll of instructions on how to join Him up there (cf. every other religion). Jesus seems far less interested in merely telling us what to do, and more focused on joining us, being with us. One of His names, Emmanuel, means *God with us.*

In other words, Jesus wants us to—like Him—use our bodies (while they're alive) to do religious things. What does that mean —doing all your prayers and going to church and Bible study?

I would argue no.
If that is your definition of 'religious things,' you've missed it

The Apostle James clearly tells us that the religion he chose was to look after widows and orphans. Isaiah adds breaking the chains of injustice, setting the oppressed free, sharing our bread, and inviting the homeless into our homes.
Again, none of these things can be done after you die.

You can always tell which Christians are only focused on a religion that begins after death—they're the ones arguing about unprovable theories and doctrines on Facebook. The ones who really know Jesus tend to be the ones hanging with the homeless, giving up their money and possessions, and fighting for justice (usually without posting about it online…).

The Bible tends to put far more emphasis on what we do before we die than on what happens afterward. The entire idea of an afterlife doesn't appear until the prophetic books which are over halfway through the book. In other words, God has an incredible focus on life—on what we do with ours, on how we live, etc.

Have you been like me? Too focused on death to be effective with your life?

Who can praise God from the grave? (Psalm 6:5)

It's important to have a *memento mori* attitude in many things we do, but fixating on our coming death and the life we experience afterward can distract us from the very real life before us now. Death is real, and sadly, we are reminded of that constantly. Mourning and grief are necessary processes.

However, to dwell on them and think of nothing else is not only un-Christlike, but it can distract us from using our lives in the most effective ways possible. Is this not what a demonic enemy would want—for us to waste our lives or whittle them away in fear and philosophy rather than being effective and enjoying our life?

Memento vivire: Remember to live.

Jesus did not come and die simply so we could pontificate about death and the existence which follows. He came so we could have life and life to the fullest, and this tends to begin the very moment people meet Him in the Bible.

You only get to affect this world while you're alive.

Live well now; there is no later.

&

*I hope your parents all told you that you die at the end. Celebrate every moment, celebrate every fucking breath. I'm telling you, life…
it's a birdsong.*

—Johnny Depp, *The Professor*

I was on a date with a girl who grew up in Florida and now lives in California. She had never seen snow in her life.

We got dinner and while we ate, Colorado surprised us with a fluke September blizzard. As we drove from the restaurant, she asked me to pull over so she could throw her first snowball. I obliged and watched as she danced out of the passenger seat and over to the nearest bank of 6-inch powder.

At the ripe old age of 25, she balled it up and flung her first snowball at a stop sign. I enjoyed sitting there watching this moment. It was a dizzying display of wonder and joy.

She climbed back into the car, shivering but ecstatic.

"Look at this!" she nearly screamed in my face, waving her arms all around.

"Look at what?" I asked.

"This! Life! It's in each of us and it's wonderful!"

For some reason, the way she worded that sentence stuck to the inside of my mind and I can't shake it.

Life.
It's inside each of us.

It's in us like a little battery that keeps us going, or the little dash of light that makes the firefly glow.

I began thinking of all humans as bottles filled to the brim with frothy rich milk. The thing is, there is no half-filled. You can't pour out some of your life and keep some for later. You're either filled with life or you're dead.

Maybe a better analogy is a light bulb. It's either singing its loud song of light which fills entire rooms, or it's off.

Some people use the analogy of flickering flames. "His light was flickering out," they may say about an old man.

I don't see it this way.

There are two degrees of life: alive or dead.

There are no two more opposite things in the universe than life and death. Mainly because, there is no in-between. Black and white have shades of grey (more than 50, believe it or not!); hot and cold are simply measures along a big spectrum. But life and death? There is no spectrum. You cannot, in the words of *The Princess Bride*, be "mostly dead all day!" You're dead or you're alive. I think this is why Jesus talks so much about life and death, for there is nothing more extreme than these two.

"Everyone who is among the living has hope!" the writer of Ecclesiastes proclaims. "A sick dog is better than a dead lion."

Why play dead in the land of the living?

Here's an exercise I've been working through the past week: What activities move us toward death and which toward life?

(**Hint**: if you're sweating, you're probably doing something right. Tony Robbins talks about the importance of 'getting into your body.' If you're stuck mentally, or stressed or worried, go for a run. Jump into cold water. Change the state of your body to change your state of mind. Sometimes I think that lifting weights or scuba diving are more philosophical than reading books. They remind you that reality is real; they teach you about the world. Remind your body that reality exists outside of your thoughts. Strain and feel life, entering into a reality unknown to someone who only reads Plato in his room. Likely why Tyler Durden in *Fight Club* tells the narrator to punch him in the face.)

Which activities push us toward isolation and stagnation, and which ones toward community and liveliness? In some ways, is absorbing gratuitous Netflix, video games, and porn practicing for death?

As Wendell Berry said, we should instead "practice resurrection" and that's why I tattooed those two words on my shin.

I witnessed firsthand the effects of *life* the other night when my friends and I went swing dancing. We walked into the dimly lit park as the folksy band rattled off their timeless melodies from the stage. Before the band were two hundred people smiling and moving their bodies. Afterward I wrote this:

> It smells like smoke,
> sweat from every color of skin,
> and alcohol
> at the dance in the park.
> Summer is climaxing and
> I've spent half of it dying.
> I didn't think I understood You.
> Now I know I don't.
> I've seen sorrow blended
> with salvation
> on a dancing black man's face.
> I saw sweat roll down
> like tears
> on the cheek of the old Native.
> I brought a robotic motion
> to the potluck of movement

in the park this evening.
The floor was fast and ferocious
and we dove on in.
After the human rainbow recessed,
we biked the city for a minute.
I'm experimenting with grace.
Tonight I gazed with anger
at the beautiful face of God.
I breathed in His costly perfume.
It smelled like dancing humans.

Here's the thing: No one is ever sad on the dance floor.

You take the life inside of you and turn it into awkward gyrations of your limbs and feet and before you know it, you're living. You're dancing. Sad people don't dance.

You inhale the sweaty air of the dance floor, and can't help but smile.

This is life.

This is what happens to our little bottles of skin when a joyful God breathes life into our bodies and says "go!" Why would God invent music and bodies if He didn't have dancing in mind?

Before my poetry teacher was killed by cancer, we used to sit in poetry club and hiccup out our little poems—life converted into language. Not unlike this book.

What is life?

> Life is a beautiful, magnificent thing…The trouble is you won't fight. You've given in, continually dwelling on sickness and death. But there's something just as inevitable as death, and that's life! Life, Life! Life! Think of all the power that's in the universe, moving the earth, growing the trees. That's the same power within you if you only have courage and the will to use it.
>
> -Charlie Chaplain, *Limelight*

It's what is in you. Sometimes it comes out in dancing, sometimes it's a four stanza poem which shreds your heart. It has also been witnessed in kisses, hugs, rope swings, and a perfectly brewed cup of coffee.

On her walk today, my dog did some phenomenal, tail-wagging sniffing. It was a serious investigation into all the life going on in the world around her.

For others, life comes out of them and into a model train in their basement or a film they direct about time moving backward.

See how the process of creating is an outpouring of life?
See how the restriction of creativity could be an act of death?

Creativity isn't optional.
(neither is dancing)

We have seen people groups throughout history who were squeezed hard, and what came out was works of art/works of life which transcend the molecules which allow for their existence.

We hear the slave spirituals which were lifted up from the chain gangs in a not-too-distant America, and suddenly we too want to go down to their river to pray.

We hear the songs of Zion being sung in a foreign land and like the author of Psalm 137, we weep within the walls of Babylon. "After all," asked Rich Mullins before a car accident took him away from us,
"where have we ever been that was not a foreign land?"

We see communities today squeezed by uneven measures and forced into unjust restrictions (some on their throats, others around their wrists, other restrictions are more invisible), and what do they produce? Artists who elevate the human experience, pushing the limits of the life within us to see how far it can go; how much stretching it can take.

Kendrick Lamar rhythmically pieces together his royal African family before the weight of oppression crushed them, while Nahko Bear sings about his Native American ancestors who opened their own wrists to escape the rule of the white man.

Life and death are not two sides of the same coin.

> *"Part of being alive is wishing you weren't sometimes."*
> —Hobo Johnson, "Sorry, My Dear"

I have known three people this year who heard the sweet song of life and decided it wasn't for them. They decided to lower their light switch; emptying their own bottle.

They got tired of singing the song inside of them.

They believed that the absence of life—or of them—is better than a hard life, or pain, and the darkness won.

Death is not a poem, it's a lie.

It's the opposite of life, which is art, which is beauty, which is all things that grow and are cultivated. Death is not a god to be danced around or joked about, but a termination of all progress, all possibility. All everything.

And if God is in and through everything, death is against Him.

"I am the resurrection and the life," said Jesus in a moment when He was not joking.

What the heck does that mean?

It means He's not kidding when He tells us what to do. He knows how to live and flourish. He knows what is best for us, will make us feel alive.

You want to create a culture of life?

Be creative.
Do beautiful things to one another.
Lift up the bonds of oppression and the yoke of slavery.
Treat others as you would like to be treated.
Fan the flames of life inside one another so each one of you may come roaring to life.

Then pull your life inside out so others can enjoy it too.
Then your life multiplies as your life is shared with others.

Then you dance around when you throw your first snowball at a stop sign.

Why do we go to church? Why do we hug and have book clubs and sing together? Because you're a bottle full of life which is dying to get out of you. Will you let it? Will you let this little flicker of life—the only hope for the world—move your body, sing your songs, and unite mankind?

Or will you continue to dwell prematurely inside your death?

Will your life, the frothy milk bottled inside your bones, rot before TV screens and video game controllers?

Will you tear others down and divide communities with your words and actions? Will you hide the light of all the life in you?

May we be people who pop the lid off the life inside of us.

May we spill it recklessly until at last, when the grave swallows us whole and the lights turn out, we can rest giddy, knowing we didn't let one ounce of our precious, PRECIOUS life go to waste.

WOMEN
WITH
LARGE
FEET

It's 2019 and I'm paddling a canoe across Lago Peten Itza in Guatemala with my best friend Dave. We spent the morning on an ancient dock called Jorge's Rope Swing, and it's already been tagged in my memory as one of the best days of my life.

The turquoise water lapped at the sides of our vessel as we glided through the warm air, heavy with humidity and promising an afternoon thunderstorm. No sooner had we set out from Jorge's than the drizzle began. It never escalated above a pleasant sprinkling as the drops, faint envelopes of goodwill, tapped our arms, shoulders and heads. We slowed our paddling across the jungle-walled lake and just soaked in the moment.

Dave and I drifted past another canoe with some other smiling tourists aboard who also didn't seem to mind the rain. We waved. They smiled, first at us, then up at the clouds blessing them with the refreshing downpour.

It reminded me of other times in my life when I had fortuitously been caught in the rain.

I was on Cape Cod with my good friend Bita in the summer of 2012 when a June storm rolled over the peninsula. We were on the road near Marstons Mills and decided to pull into a forest trailhead so we could run through the muddy trails while the drips dropped around us. Big, fat bulbs of water punched the leaves of the forest around us, creating a natural applause which rose and misted as we sprinted through the puddles and dirt.

We were dressed like Adam as we splashed through the forest, more alive than all the indoor humans of the world combined. Whenever we paused to look around at the clapping world, we saw white mist rising from the forest floor as the rain hit the ground so hard it couldn't help but to jump back into the air.

We smiled and I recalled another moment, two years before *that*, when I was atop a mountain in Thailand and the storm thundered in, trapping us atop the peak with a towering statue of Buddha as he smiled over Chiang Rai. The trees around us this time were wrapped with the orange robes of monks who had left the trunks clothed for some religious ritual.

For me, getting caught outside in a warm rain has always been a timeless moment of great revelation. I can list off dozens more times I rushed outside to catch a rainstorm, or stayed outside enjoying the sprinkle from the clouds which violently tumbled in like a demon tangled in a white dress.

At other times, I witness Beauty in the pages of a good book. The linguistic and poetic utterances communicate holy sentences which seem to transcend time and space, elevating the pages in my hand above a few manmade markings on a white press of wood pulp.

In the words of Rob Bell, *this* is really about *that*. Nothing is inherent in itself as a thing. Nothing is beautiful when abstracted from its surroundings. Pluck a word out of your favorite poem and study the word by itself. It is not nearly as powerful or beautiful without its surrounding bed of flowers, the other words yearning to bloom alongside fellow bulbs of language.

Remember, location and context matter.

Think of your favorite song. The one that moves you to tears because of its raw force or the beauty of its crescendo. Now imagine taking that one note—the one which transforms the entire score and draws the conductor to tears every time—and remove it from the composition. Isolate it.

It's just a C# minor.

It's not that special.
Not that powerful.
Not that beautiful.

Beauty is all about an immersive experience, not an isolated ingredient. You can't dissect beauty, because like humor or a frog, it dies on the operating table. Many of us chase beauty, or rather, these powerful experiences which I cannot tuck into words which fall short of the moving power of a close encounter with beauty.

It's like petting a hungry lion
or making eye contact with a hurricane.

The adrenaline pumps you forward step by step as the dopamine rushes to keep up with all the sensory input being received, whether by rain, language, or a million other mediums through which God reaches out to His people through the beauty of His creation.

Maybe it's another human being who fires you up, sets you on fire. Perhaps your eyes can't seem to capture enough of this person who, though so *other* from you, seems to inhabit a body which was cut out of the earth just for you.

Their green or blue or brown eyes seem composed of fluid depth and like a river, you can never look into the same eyes twice because they are vibrant, alive, fluid. The curves of her hips or his forearms are a mystery you want to spend the rest of your life solving with your fingers. Ten thousand slow dances with her head on your chest wouldn't be enough.

So why can't we capture or describe beauty? Why can't we surrender to this goddess of good fortune who seems to offer us deep and rich experiences which supersoak our souls until we feel like we can't take another drop?

What err is there in enjoying a beautiful life?

There is a logical answer, a holy answer, and of course, a balance to observe.

But first, what is beauty?

&

It seems that everyone is hungry for a beauty that runs deeper than the epidermis.

Many of our definitions of beauty speak of stirrings of eternity, whether it's via a beautiful sunset or being in the presence of a beautiful person. Many say beauty is experiencing life with someone else or seeing in them something rich and far deeper than superficial prettiness, like how Vern saw his dying bride.

Beauty is not subjective.
The first flaw most of us encounter when trying to conceptualize beauty is thinking that it's about us, the beholder. After all, beauty is in *our* eye, right? What this does to us is renders a beauty defined however one sees fit. Just like morals in our culture, beauty comes to be something defined internally by our fleeting wishes and tastes rather than by a much larger, objective source of beauty.

For instance, in some cultures, women with larger feet are more attractive, while in others, women with smaller feet are. Can both be right? Or is defining beauty so narrowly bound to lead to disagreement, and therefore an anemic definition of what is beautiful?

Even within our own culture, notions of beauty shift annually. In the 70's, bell bottom jeans were *in*, but now the skinnier the better. Short bobs were once in, but now longer, natural hair is preferred.

If beauty were subject to the individual, or even to the culture, there would be no absolute beauty to which we may refer. Pedophiles find things beautiful which the larger culture finds repulsive. Pornography programs us to derive the pleasure of beauty from violence, degradation and control.

Describing beauty by means of our own enjoyment of it, then, strips away the grandeur of beauty itself and limits it to the experience of the individual rather than the ontological substance of beauty itself.

For example, standing at the mouth of the Grand Canyon at sunset will invoke feelings of awe and grandeur in the beholder. However, the beauty is not in the person's experience of the canyon, but it is outside of them and they are merely coming into contact with it.

Typically, this person will return home and when they recount the experience to friends, will relay how the experience made them *feel*, rather than relaying the larger beauty which they barely touched. It is through experiences like this, though, that we get to receive a hint of raw, authentic *beauty*, and it is that pure notion of beauty I am attempting to describe here.

The word beauty is something ubiquitous, then. We apply it to supermodels and sunsets alike. Some of us apply it to the gospel: *The beauty of grace.*

That was not meant to disqualify one's experience of coming into contact with beauty, whether it's enjoying a love requited and a bookstore smooch, or standing on top of a mountain as a storm recedes. To be sure, those experiences bring us within inches of beauty itself, but the experience remains outside of ourselves if we limit it to merely subjective definitions.

How, then, do we accurately experience beauty? How do we put it on like a dress and live our lives within it?

Fyodor Dostoevsky predicted that "beauty will save the world,"‡ but how do we come to define this ambiguous word? And how will it go about this incredible feat?

The power of beauty

Lately I've been finding myself reading Scripture and having the choking of sobs well up in my throat and tears edge the corner of my eyes. It has been happening more and more often for some reason.

Just yesterday, as I was in a cafe preparing for a talk on the first two verses of the Bible, I read the verse for the thousandth time, "...and the Spirit of God hovered over the waters." I looked into the verse a bit more, specifically the verb *hovered*. I found that the same Hebrew word is also found in the book of Deuteronomy to describe a mother bird fluttering over the young in her nest, provoking them to flap their wings and take flight. (Deuteronomy 32:11)

I began picturing the Spirit of God fluttering like a mother bird, hovering over the chaos of the pre-diluvian world, whispering *"Come to life! Rise up! Breathe!"* God calls us to rise up and live. He hovers over the chaotic waters which our lives often feel like, calling out to them, telling us not to cower, but to ascend.

---

‡ Fyodor Dostoyevsky, *The Idiot*

Tears lined my eyes and I had to take them away from the words on the page to avoid breaking down in the middle of yet another coffee shop. (And here I am again, swallowing down the sobs in a different cafe…)

Just as when I watched *The Passion of the Christ*, it wasn't the cruelty Jesus endured, or the ripping of flesh from His bones that made me cry; it was a line he delivered to His mother as He lugged the cross up the hill: "Look, mother, I make all things new."

But why?

Why have these non-sad entities been the things that make me cry recently?

I think the beauty wrapped up in these passages from scripture do more than evoke emotions in us because they're pretty poetic phrases. They point to something powerful, something large and real.

Something holy.

And I think that when we encounter something enormous as grace or as powerful as redemption, the only possible response is to weep. Just as my college roommate stated at our friend's wedding: "I cried not because the wedding was sad, but because it was beautiful. There are some things so intensely beautiful that the only possible reaction is to cry." If tears are the body's way of adjusting to reality, then it's not only sad things that would prompt them, but beautiful things, powerful things. Anything that calls for a recalibration to the universe.

It wasn't the bride's dress or the dashing good looks of the groom, but the beauty of the sacrifice to which they were both committing. Because like all things beautiful, marriage points outside itself to a bigger sacrificial work which is at play.

Beauty is a person

I think trying to encapsulate beauty with my own thin words is merely a chasing after a leaf on the wind. My hands may swing lamely after it but continually fall short, because I'm trying to stuff the grandeur of all reality into a 2-dimensional page.

The gospel is something truly beautiful. It is the epitome of sacrifice and giving of the greatest gift ever. However, it is not the action of the gospel which makes it beautiful, but the person who performs the actions. Isaiah 53 tells us that "there was no beauty in Him to draw us to Him." In other words, Jesus was kind of ugly. Yet it is He who defines beauty once and for all.

It was through Him all creation was made, and it is through Him that all creation continues to exist. Not only does He sustain us merely by His being, but He sacrificed Himself so that the cosmos may be made new.

It's not possible to dissect the work of Christ and point to one *part* of it which is the definition of beauty. Yes, sacrifice is beautiful, and so is new life and resurrection. Healing is beautiful, as people are given new health, new limbs, or a sense they had been lacking. But it is not one of these things which encapsulates *beauty*.

It's much bigger.

I think beauty, in essence, is solely defined in the nature and person of God.

He is not beautiful; He is beauty itself.
(Plato wipes a tear from his own eye.)

Therefore, everything God does is beautiful, as is everything He creates. (Sin, therefore, is anything done to skew the perfection of something's or someone's original beauty.) Adam and Eve were beautiful prior to the introduction of sin.

What was their first sin? It was to take their desire for beauty off of *the Creator* and onto *something created*—the fruit. They sacrificed the experience of Beauty Himself for a taste of something merely *beautiful*.

Some sort of conclusion
We catch tastes of beauty and see fleeting glimpses of it throughout our lives. Our notions of beauty sometimes catch the breeze of modern culture and fly away on the winds of whatever is trending at the moment. We are a fickle people chasing whatever we deem to be beautiful that week.

There are real hints of beautiful things in this life: A man being faithful to his wife and loving her well, or, yes, the beauty of a supermodel. God created and perfected sacrifice as well as aesthetics. But as beautiful as these things are, they themselves do not wholly encapsulate *beauty*. They are beauti*ful* because they hold within them some trace of Beauty Himself and reflect an aspect of His person.

Like Plato's concept of the Forms, the idea of Beauty is much larger than any one object or person. We see shadows, or expressions, of the Form of Beauty, but the Form itself is impossible to contain in this imperfect land of Becoming. You can look at a beautiful flower, and it reflects *an* element, or aspect of beauty (until it dies), but it, itself, is not *Beauty.*

It will not be until the next age that our eyes will properly be adjusted to gaze upon Beauty. We will not only catch a glimpse of something beautiful, but we will finally be able to see what we have been longing for in our porn, drug trips, and TV binges.

At last, our descriptions of beauty will not fall short because we will be looking Him in the face. As Paul put it, we will not look through a foggy glass, but we will look upon the face of Beauty with unhindered vision, and He won't disappoint. (1 Corinthians 13:12)

In the end, Beauty will indeed save the world. Not through mere aesthetics or awe, but by nature of *who* Beauty truly is.

TIME

I watched out the window as the city of Philadelphia shrunk beneath us. No matter how many flights I take, there are still a few knots in my stomach which refuse to give up wondering

Will this be the one?
Will this finally be the flight that ends it all?

Some of you may fly a lot, while others rarely or never. I used to love the romantic notion of flying. I used to write a dozen poems per flight, as the idea of flying thousands of miles in a mere few hours was (and is) truly magical.

Nowadays, I plug into my podcasts and try to fall asleep before we touch down.

All human beings find whimsy in novelty.

The first kiss is so much more magical than the 1,528th.

So is the first dance, or the first time in a new city.

I remember the first time I went swing dancing in an ancient castle in Chicago. It was October, 2012 and I will never forget that night as long as I live. The windows were open, allowing a crisp fall breeze to drift in and after a few songs, my friends and I retreated out to the balcony overlooking the city from behind a low stone wall. The entire night could have been straight out of an early two thousands chick flick; it was *that* magical.

But then we went a few weeks later.

And a few weeks after that.

And by the fifth or sixth time, the magic was slipping away. All that beauty of freshness and newness had somehow slipped through our fingers and gotten away from us.

Time marched madly on.

Now I'm flying home from a family vacation to New Jersey. I've been making this trip since I was born, so the traditions and memories from Ocean City run deep in my blood. However, the older I get, the more I see the same thing happening. The magic is slipping away from this tourist trap I once beheld as utopia.

When I was 4, the annual trip to New Jersey contained a sort of magic that has only been captured in pencil-illustrated children's books. But now that I'm older, I see the town as less magical and more money-grabby. Not that I don't enjoy the time with my family and the natural wonder of the ocean, but the trip itself is less...whimsical.

A few weeks ago, I was driving and listening to August Burns Red's song "Echoes." I think it's their masterpiece. There is one part of the song, about a 30-second clip toward the end, which encapsulates all good things about the metalcore genre: power, emotion, brutality, harmony, et al.

I found myself wishing I could just pause the song and somehow dwell in that moment of raw power and emotion. I wanted to stretch the feeling of those 30 seconds out into a shelter and build myself a home.

But of course I can't.

You have your own magical songs. There is a certain line or note that simply speaks to you in some way far richer than words. You wish you could simply put that hook or chorus on repeat and stay there. You just want to soak up the realness in her voice right there, or find a way to encapsulate the crescendo of this one song...but you can't.

And the reason we can't capture the beauty of those musical moments is that time is a necessary component of music.

Without time, you don't have a melody, you just have one note.

Without time, you don't have lyrics, you just have one syllable uttered eternally.

Without time, there is no beauty.

My aging grandfather drove me to the airport an hour ago. I remember when he used to play football with our family, and now he can hardly get in or out of his van—the one with the handicap plates. I think of his weakening body and the various ailments which have seized it and made his hands shake uncontrollably.

My throat swells at 30,000 feet.

My grandfather is aging and will not live on this earth forever. There is great sadness in that, but there is also great beauty. He is a great man and his life, as it rises and falls, will have been utterly spectacular.

Just as a song rises and falls, time wanders its own progression and there is beauty in this progression.

The natural progression of all things is what makes them beautiful.

This is why I still cannot get over the film *Logan*. While most of her superheroes exist in a timeless universe, Marvel chose to show the progression of time and the persistence of age in one of her brightest sons, Wolverine. The beauty of the film comes from the idea that all things age; all things die. And I think the reason this film brought me to tears is because it realizes this truth so graphically.

There is a true, realistic beauty in the progression of time.

That is why the wisest man to ever live, Solomon, wrote that beauty is fleeting. (Proverbs 31:30) As I continue the endless search for my bride, it's easy to be distracted by timely beauty: The look of her face or body as it rests in time *right now*. It's much harder to peer through the exterior and see the things that will truly last; the parts of her which will grow more beautiful with time. The things that I will want holding me when I weep or when my own body begins to break down. The parts of her that I will want by my side even when all of her *present* beauty has faded.

Time kills all things,§
but it also reveals their deepest, most painful beauty.

This is why certain parts of those songs are so freaking powerful. But then the song ends. The experience is over and we move on. And you go to bed and wake up in the slow silence of dawn into another day which has never happened before.

I wonder if a lot of the human struggle is a battle against this time. We try so hard to hold onto things in their present forms that we miss the real beauty of them—the fact that they are in

---

§ Wow! That's a great title for a book…

flux and dying like us. The monstrous crescendo of your favorite song will eventually fade out, just like you will someday.

Maybe this is why we all love photographs so much: They hold the ability to freeze a split second of time in a manageable fashion you can always look back upon.

People in LA pay thousands of dollars to look like they did when they were younger instead of embracing the authentic beauty of age.

They pay a hefty sum to push pause on their body and its appearance.

We want to remember the magic of a concert by preserving it on our phones, but of course these tinny representations do little to convey the transcendence of the night's experience.

So what is the solution? It seems like we are fighting a losing battle as we wage war on the foe of time.

Perhaps the answer is not to battle time, but to find her beauty. Embrace that magical song as it passes by you in your headphones yet again. Enjoy your friends in their present state, instead of wishing they were the way they used to be *back then*.

Time marches madly on.

I wonder if heaven is the summation of all of these passing blips we experience when we hear a great song or hold a baby as it falls asleep. C.S. Lewis notes that these things are simply tastes of what is to come. The difference is, in this world, they come and go. They are not permanent. I can't help but think that heaven is simply an eternity of dwelling in those magical moments. The ones we only wish we could hold onto in this life.

May we be people who age well; a people who suck the life out of every passing second rather than longing for the past or diving into the future. May we learn to recognize the beauty of time as she whizzes past us; the slow-walking seductress leading us to our graves.

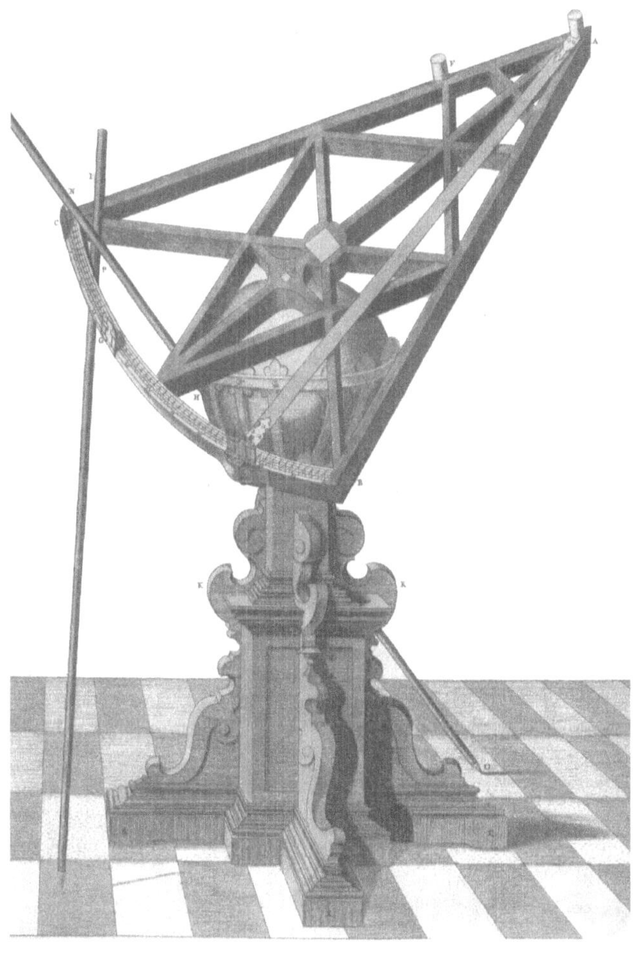

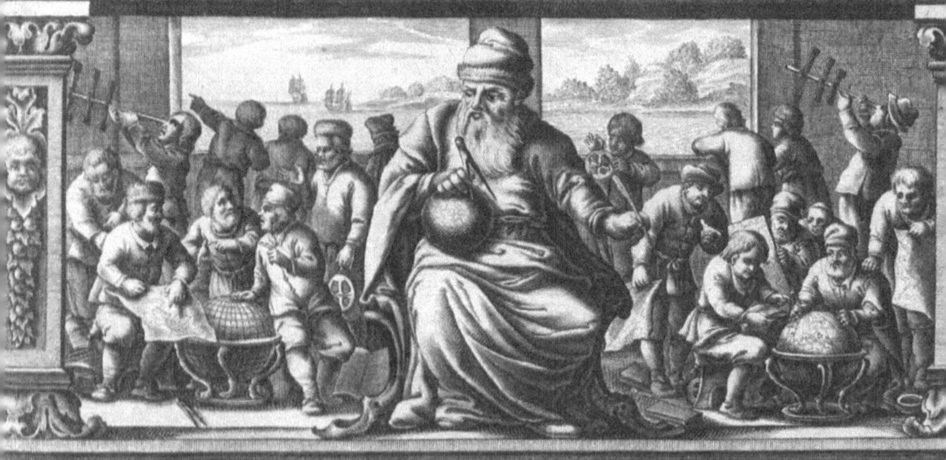

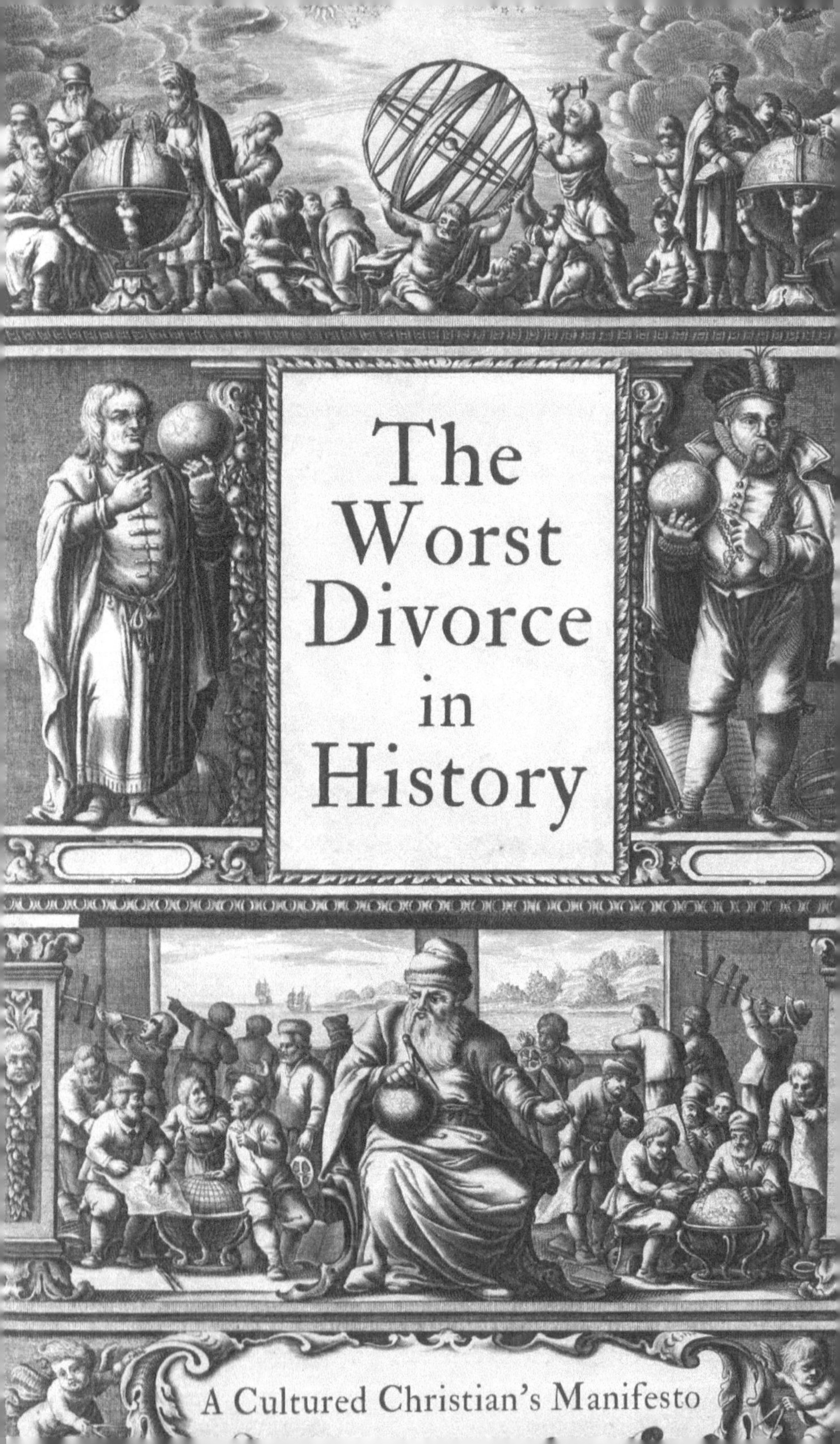
The Worst Divorce in History
A Cultured Christian's Manifesto

everal months ago, my church showed a video to the congregation and by the end of it, not an eye in the auditorium was left dry. A woman in her early 30's was sharing the story of the past 5 years of her life. She was diagnosed with breast cancer, and after a year of struggling with it, was in remission. Some time later, however, it returned and not just to her breasts—but to her bones and blood as well. A year ago, the doctors had told this young woman that she had 5 years to live.

More recently, they reduced that estimation to 5 months.

"There were a lot of things I expected to do," she explained with more strength than I would ever have. "I thought I'd get my doctorate and get married and have kids..." (I'm paraphrasing all this from memory)

She went on to explain how, rather than raging against God, she has adjusted and *expanded* her theology. "People have been asking me, 'how can you love a God who would take your life away from you at such a young age?' But I respond that His goodness and His plan is not predicated on my experience; it doesn't depend on my heath or diagnoses."

She then explained that she herself feels like she is expanding. Initially it sounded a bit woo-woo as she began, but once I caught onto her meaning, it made perfect sense. Rather than hoping in, and being shaped by, earthly things (wealth, job, family, status, friends), she was beginning to tilt toward eternity. She was beginning to eagerly hope more for eternal things than earthly ones.

Inevitably, this is going to make one feel larger.

Philosophers have juggled similar concepts, albeit in the absence of God—the removal of earthly attachments yields freedom. Camus longed for such an experience, and…perhaps he now has it. The Buddha also sought to rid himself of earthly desires, which, according to him, lead to suffering.

While my eyes filled with tears and I watched this brutal five-minute video, an age-old question filled my mind, followed by a newer one. The first was, *What else could possibly matter more than THIS?? What could be more important than knowing Jesus and then connecting others to Him?*

It's not a novel thought. Most Christians, hopefully, ask themselves this on a regular basis. I'm forced to ask myself this every time I hear of something tragic, or weighty, happening.

Two weeks ago, the young woman from the video succumbed to her cancer.

Then my brother's housemate died of Covid-19 during the pandemic. He was 26.

Suddenly I'm forced to ask myself, if I had known him, how much more would every moment have mattered? Would I have benefitted his life in any way? Am I benefitting the lives of those people I *do* know every time I'm with them, the way Jesus benefitted those around *Him?* Did this kid know Jesus in his brief stint on our shared planet?

What else matters during our handful of years on earth more than knowing God and making Him known?

This question implies that there is *nothing* more important than those two sides of the same coin. There is nothing more valuable than knowing Christ and Him crucified (Philippians 3). However, it also implies that many of the things we would otherwise spend our time on (TV, movies, fiction books, art, fashion) would be time wasted, and as John Piper taught us, there is little worse than wasting our lives. And I concur, though I might disagree on some of Piper's application.

This all led to the second question which entered my mind while seated in church, clenching tears back thanks to this woman's testimony. The question was more of a thought than a formulated sentence; after all, like Beckett said, "words are the clothes thoughts wear." So, the question, as well as I can articulate it in language, was something like this:

If nothing else matters but knowing God and introducing others to Him, how do we go about doing this? How do we pursue these two ends?

This led to a myriad of rabbit trail-like thoughts sprawling across my consciousness trying to figure this out. But primarily, it led me to one unavoidable dead-end of reason:

Culture is the language the world speaks. Trying to articulate the gospel of Jesus to a community, while trying to remain removed from its culture, is like trying to share the gospel with a Colombian without first learning Spanish.

Sure, the more sociologically/philosophically inclined among you may point out that language is perhaps the chief element of a culture, but you get the point. Attempting to share the Good News of the victory of Christ to a hurting world while remaining pure of the very culture in which the world partakes is very near impossible and a fruitless effort.

What would be the goal of such an undertaking? To pull others *out* of the culture of the world so they can join you on the sidelines? Sounds like a bummer of a religion to me. Doesn't sound too much like *good* news.

It also requires there to be a singular "Christian culture," and a convert to Christianity must leave their culture and join that one. (Remember the whole modernist idea of "we have the truth and you must become fully like us to understand it"?) In America, we certainly have a Christian culture, and by most appearances, it's the plastic knockoff version of the rest of culture, just with less talent, quality, or honesty.

In my experience, there has been one major exception to this statistic: heavy metal. For at least a decade, the biggest heavy metal bands were Christian bands (August Burns Red, P.O.D., The Devil Wears Prada, The Chariot, etc.), and I've often wondered why these Christian bands could seamlessly skirt the divide between the secular and the sacred. I don't have many explanations of my own, save that many of the themes of the Bible translate well to the metal genre: Just read any of the Older Testament prophets and tell me they *don't* sound like heavy metal lyrics. But I digress.

&

Wait, what are we talking about?
Now before I continue, let's pause and define some of our terms. When I say *culture*, I mean all of it: The images, symbols, language, work, and activities found in every pocket of every civilization. What do we laugh at and recognize at first glance? What references cause connections in our minds and who is leading things like fashion, speech, style, and so on?

And there are hundreds if not thousands of subcultures in the US alone, but there is also a larger, more sweeping idea of *culture*. If we're honest, today it seems to tilt more toward the liberal ideation politically and socially, and has a strong inclination toward freedom, autonomy, peace, and expression. None of these things are bad in and of themselves, but let's pocket that and come back to it.

In past decades, the church has been painted as the Grinch who is opposed to all things fun, expressive, and new. Nothing highlights this better than films like *Footloose*, where the old-school buzzkills are trying to shut down anything that remotely resembles dancing. Why? What was it about the act of dancing that seemed to trigger their fear sensors and prompt them to stomp it out?

I'm no sociologist or historian, but I would guess that it dates back roughly 200 years, give or take, when the cultural power began shifting hands from the church to other rein-holders such as science, reason, politics, and the arts.

For the first 1500 years of her existence, the Church was the dominant source of cultural production. Painters did their best to portray heaven and hell; Handel composed choruses which seemed to elevate the listener far above their fleshly husks as he praised God with deafening *Hallelujahs*; and even the most significant literature was written as means of explaining theology (Luther's 95 Theses, the first publication to 'go viral'), or exploring the human experience of an ethically-rich universe (Dante's *Divine Comedy*).

Rather than poopoo certain forms of art and expression, the church was the main entity in the world *promoting* it! Most, if not all, of the world's most famous artists would not have been known if not for the church. They were rivaled perhaps only by the Medici as patrons of the arts for over a millennium.

Does that sound like the church you know today?

Granted, there are obviously churches with incredible, authentic creative output today who promote art and creativity in all its forms, but that's not the larger perception of the church when critiqued from the outside.

When I say culture, I'm also not referring to simply agreeing with everything the larger population agrees with, and condoning sin or other unnatural activities. Saying that I am, for lack of a better term, "pro-culture" does not mean I simply let myself be carried along by the cultural narrative of the world, wherever it may lead.

Let me give a controversial example.

In 2019, the PreachersNSneakers Instagram account blew up and ignited countless debates on the internet about how pastors should be spending their money. Some (rightly) bemoaned how obnoxious it is for a pastor (or anyone) to wear a $5,000+ outfit.

Others defended them. How? By saying that these expensive duds help them connect better with the culture at large.

"How else is a pastor in LA going to connect with a fashion-heavy culture unless he's wearing Off-White and Gucci??" went the argument.

"I don't know, use your freaking imagination. Shape culture instead of following it," I'd respond.

Most of my outfits, all told, can range from a total of $5 to $75 (shoes, pants, undies, rings, everything), and I have never been accused of being fashion-backward. In fact, quite the opposite. Many people have told this thrift shopper that everything I wear is super cool and they like my style. Perhaps the most empirical proof that I'm certified cool is that on the second day of teaching 7th graders one semester, one of them asked where I got my style from (again, in like a $60 outfit). If a 7th grader thinks you're fashionable, then you have, indeed *made it.*

The reason for that rabbit trail is simple: Being connected to a culture does not require making all the missteps the culture at large does. Relating to a fashion-saturated area like Los Angeles does not necessitate that one become as greedy and materialistic as the rest of the population. All that means is that you've given in to the temptation of avarice; you've caved to the carnal desire of having the same hip material objects your neighbors do.

This is not what I mean by being an active participant in culture.

You don't need to blow outrageous money on your looks in order to connect with your unbelieving neighbors. This applies to our sexual ethics and actions (you don't need to sleep around to relate to people who do), our approach to substances like alcohol (get blasted to relate to alcoholics), et al.

Going back to *Footloose*, it has always puzzled me how Christians could, at any point in Christian history, demonize something which is highly praised and sometimes commanded in Scripture. The same applies to alcohol, as Paul encourages Timothy to have some wine to help his stomach, though I can see why there would be more caution around that one. It's not like you can overdose on dancing.

This, however, seems to be the great perception of Christians to the world. We are not the creative powerhouses we once were; we are the cosmic snobs who drift above the dirty fray which is the rest of the culture. Thank God that Jesus didn't have the same attitude when He looked down from heaven upon this world which, according to astronauts returning into earth's atmosphere, smells like rotting meat.

I recently had two similar conversations with two different people. Their idea of being a good, responsible Christian centered around sharing "the gospel" with all nonbelievers.

It seems pretty cut and dry, right? You tell people the truth; you share with them the four-point structure of salvation coined by Billy Graham so they're saved, and if they reject your method, then the Holy Spirit just hasn't chosen them or enlightened their heart so ¯_(ツ)_/¯

1. God made a good, perfect world

2. We are sinful, separated from God, and can't save ourselves

3. Jesus rebuilt that bridge

4. Believe in Him and you'll be saved!

The problem is, this model is not found verbatim in Scripture. Sure, you could pull up the Romans Road, which are essentially four random verses in the book of Romans which support this model. But what if we did that with other random verses? You could come up with infinite new religions, or paths to God.

This isn't to say that those four points are necessarily *wrong*, just that it's not as cut and dry when you look at the actual pages of your Bible.

Both the guys I chatted with recently seemed to think that this method of salvation, and therefore evangelism, was obvious. They wanted to purge any hint of the world's culture out of them, and saw that the best path toward growing the church was to essentially tell people those four points.

"If your church doesn't preach that message every Sunday— and the reality of hell and the depravity of all humans—then you need to find a new church!" one told me.

I couldn't help but picturing my atheist friends coming to a church where that, and that alone, was the main message. Every week. And I pictured them walking right back out the door.

"No one talked about hell and punishment more than Jesus!" the other protested.

"While that's true," I told him, "look at who He says those things *to*. It's never the sinful outsider, the ashamed prostitutes or the hated tax collectors. It's the pious religious leaders who think they're the most loved by God, and think their good deeds get them god-points."

Jesus' attitude toward outsiders is entirely different.

Think about it: why would prostitutes and 'sinners' flock to Him to hang out all the time if all He ever did was tell them how bad they are? I'm sure there were elements of that in His interactions with them, but how much more grace did He have on them? As discussed before, Jesus was always able to perfectly balance grace and truth, and that also means knowing when to employ slightly more of one or the other.

This is a nuance the men I chatted with seemed to miss. They wanted all truth, all the time. At least, truth as they saw it…

One of them bemoaned the failure of the 'seeker sensitive movement' and I agree—you can't have a church that is completely devoid of truth in favor of the outcast.

But making efforts to speak the language of our culture, to build bridges to them, rather than seeing them as the enemies unless they convert, is a necessity in any effective ministry. That's more of an Islamic principle: convert or kill the infidel. I see those words coming from Muhammed more than Jesus; only, for Christians, God will do the torturing, not us. Doesn't make it less of a weapon.

In Jesus, I see a humble and lowly figure, bending low to meet people where they are and lift them to the higher places. The theology of those two men said, "Meet me here or be rejected. By God. There is no other way."

They weren't building bridges to make it easier to cross over, into the sphere of knowing Jesus; they were building higher fences and telling people to come inside, or else. Their hearts were genuinely to get people inside, but the path to get there was way harder than necessary.

&

How I became a Native American

I once was sitting on a plane beside an elderly Native American man. He said the most *Native American* thing to me I've ever heard.

He asked where I was from and I said I was born in Colorado, "but I'm not a Native American," I quickly clarified.

He protested, "you sound like it to me. You've eaten the food from this land all your life. You are a native."

We kept chatting and he told me that he has spent much of his life working in prisons, helping inmates reform themselves to be more fruitful members of society.

"You know what the difference is between prison programs that are successful versus those that aren't?" he asked me.

How the heck was I supposed to know?

"The successful ones know how to create a *culture* which people enter into. People are formed by a culture, for better or worse. When you have a positive culture, people can point at someone who is violating the values of that culture and say, 'hey bro, you're not benefitting the way we live here right now.' Then that guy has to change to fit in. If the prison doesn't work to create a culture of positivity, of peace, generosity, and love, then people will *act* good before the guards, and go back to the way they were once they're out. But culture actually changes people."

I've thought about that conversation on the plane for years, and applied it in youth ministry and my classroom. People may remember 5% of the words you say, but they will remember 100% of the impression you or your culture made on them. This is why, no matter how many times a church verbally insists, "No, no, God loves you!" someone can still feel rejected for one reason or another. What does the church *feel* like to the outsider? Does it match the words the church uses to describe itself, and its attitude toward outsiders?

Many churches *say* that everyone is welcome in their pews, but when someone with face tattoos enters, they still receive sideways glances and a colder-than-usual reception.

Or, years ago I had a friend who was on the fence about church. She showed up half the time, and even when she did, she was skeptical about being there. Was it because she disagreed with the messages about loving our neighbors as God loved us—the words from the pulpit?

No.

It was because one summer, she showed up to church in a cute summer dress and one of the ladies at the church looked down at the hem and said, "Cute dress…Where's the rest of it?"

From then on, how could my friend avoid going to church without feeling immense judgment, or at least, scrutiny? Who would *want* to be in an environment like that?

Years ago, I realized that **if a lack of love is what drives people out of the church, only a surplus of love will drive**

them back. It is rare that a *purely* logical or scientific motive drives people from church, or draws them to it. It's almost like Jesus told us something similar... (John 13:34)

Creating a culture of love is the only thing that will draw in and then heal a love-starved world.

No one was ever sanctified with measuring sticks, sarcasm, condescending comments, or policing the wardrobes of nervous fence-sitters.

Put a little logic behind that older woman's statement: Her words revealed that she saw the path to salvation was trotted by wearing long enough dresses, and then judging the dresses of others. That's the kingdom she was working toward, and it makes sense that my friend didn't want to go there with her.

Imagine Jesus hanging out with one of the vulnerable prostitutes who seemed to magnetize to Him and rather than encourage her, Jesus says, "Nice toga...where's the rest of it?" How long do you think the crowd of 'sinners' would keep chilling with Him if He had that attitude?

&

Sin is sin, but most are not.

The parts of this culture conversation that seem to be the most volatile are those that are perceived as 'wrong,' but are not really condemned in Scripture. Maybe something is a slippery slope which could slide someone into a life of ruin, but the act being performed at the moment is not actually sinful.

For instance, as mentioned above, alcohol is not only allowed by Scripture, but encouraged at one point. Drunkenness is condemned however, and that is exactly where most people jump to in this conversation, but simply having a drink is not. For humans then, it's far easier to jump to the extreme and simply ban all alcohol, just to ensure no one gets drunk.

The Jewish people reflected this human tendency with how they handled the laws that God gave Moses. They made extra laws, almost as perimeter fences around the laws from God, just to be sure they didn't break those. With the Sabbath law for example, God said not to work on Saturday. The people then, because they were humans and we are all susceptible to fearing the slippery slope, determined that walking more than 2,000 cubits (about 1 kilometer) was 'work.' So just to be sure they didn't work, they measured 2k cubits from where they lived just to be sure they didn't 'work' on Shabbat by crossing that boundary.

It's easier to set tangible lines not to cross than to whole-heartedly engage God's rhythms of work and rest.

Dancing is also a questionable activity despite how highly it is spoken of in Scripture. Ask any good old Baptist and they'll confirm: *Sex leads to dancing.* Why is this?

It likely has roots in the logical fallacy of a slippery slope: Allow dancing and before you know it, your young people will be grinding on each others' bodies and then having sex right there on the dance floor. Or maybe it's because the dancing bodies of women will cause the men watching to think lustful thoughts and stumble into temptation. But here again, dancing itself is not a sin.

There are also a myriad activities, symbols, and words which our culture has appropriated for their own purposes, and to retaliate, the church has simply demonized those *things*.

Symbols must be understood as what they are: something that points to an idea, organization, movement, or so on, but the symbol itself is not evil. Like a road sign with squiggles on it, indicating a dangerous road ahead, the sign refers to danger, but the sign itself is not dangerous.

A current example of this is the rainbow. Our culture has taken it to represent the LGBTQ+ community, and rather than continue an open conversation on how we interact with that community, we've simply begun to bristle whenever we see a rainbow-anything. I'm guilty of it too. I'll see a picture of a rainbow and automatically associate it with the movement, rather than seeing it for the symbol it is. It's become so blatant that some people might see a rainbow-anything, in *any* context and immediately feel some sort of revulsion rise up.

Do they hate colors?
Do they just *loathe* seeing all the different hues at once right next to each other?

Or has the symbol become so associated with an idea with which they disagree that they have come to hate the symbol as well?

See how the meaning beneath the symbol is really what people may disagree with, yet the symbol as a whole is suddenly demonized? Take this rainbow example and you can apply it to nearly everything the church has ever demonized.

It's sad that we are known for having such a fearful mindset.

Even things with darker associations, like pentagrams, Ouja boards, or Tarot cards result in an immediate door closure from Christians. What if we learned to see the people behind these outward symbols or activities rather than writing them off from the start? It doesn't mean Ouja boards aren't dangerous, but I also don't think they are something to fear, and I *definitely* don't think we should avoid those who use them—those fellow people equally made in God's image.

Should someone be turned away from your church's doorstep because her t-shirt has an upside-down star on it? No. The screen printed image will not hurt you. It's just a shirt and some ink.

Should the church hold seances to commune with the dead? Of course not. See how silly it is to make a jump like that?

We could just as easily examine the inverse: Does everyone who wears a cross necklace live a life of repentance, justice, peace, and love? Unfortunately, no. The image of the cross has nearly dissolved into the cultural stream to the point that its original meaning is all but gone. Who sees a cross and thinks of the thousands of people who suffocated to death while nailed to one? (See the chapter on Bleeding Gods)

What if we learned to speak the language of their culture, rather than dismissing it as evil, dangerous, or *bad*?

Isn't that what you would want if you were in their shoes?

Imagine if earlier Christian missionaries had this attitude toward indigenous people they witnessed to:

"Welp, they pray to trees, dance naked, and worship the sun. They're beyond hope. Let's try to get them to be more like us."

Did you notice how one of those things is not inherently antithetical to Scripture, yet it might get lumped in with the others? After all, David was praised for dancing naked.

Are there things that reflect your comfort level among your peers more than the things the Bible actually encourages in us? What are the activities and symbols you see around you which are not inherently evil, yet you shut them down in the holy name of religion nonetheless, maybe just because they make you uncomfortable?

Not everything *associated* with sin is sinful.
Not everything *associated* with evil is evil.

Learning the difference between the two—between associations and actual rebellion—will help us immensely in relating to our culture.

&

Is 'divorce' a bit dramatic?

Now to the title of this chapter. I chose it very carefully for a reason. When two people are married and undergo a divorce, what happens? Practically speaking, they segregate their finances (resources), they change their language, and they sever all other relational ties. I want to focus on the first two for a moment.

Prior to the Reformation, the church was not only a powerhouse of culture, but also of global healing. Who was responsible for feeding the hungry, taking care of the sick, and looking after orphans and widows? Was it the State? Well, sort of. Mainly, it was the church. That's why there are a million hospitals named after saints, and none named after atheists or politicians. And we could debate until we are blue in the face the pros and cons of having a church who holds hands with the king, but it was certainly a care-machine to be reckoned with.

1517 AD. Martin Luther swings his hammer as he pounds the 95 Theses into the All Saints' Church and effectively shatters this mighty entity—the extant catholic church** at the time— into countless denominations and factions with as many

---

** Lower-case c. This simply refers to all Christians everywhere, as opposed to the capital-C Catholic, which refers to the specific Roman Catholic denomination led by the Pope in Italy.

resources to heal the world as an ant has to fix up a house. Unwittingly however, Luther was still an old-school Augustinian, meaning he was holding onto the idea of a theocracy, or a *City of God* where the church is welded to the governing body of society.

The Reformation inevitably led to the Scientific Revolution, the Enlightenment, and ironically, the divorce of the Church from the State. It was a long-lived romance (You could measure it either from the conversion of Constantine, or from the crowning of Charlemagne *by* Pope Leo III. Either one is an equally repugnant representation of Imperial Christianity. Perhaps it began with Constantine and was locked firmly into place by Charlemagne 500 years later. Mix in thousands of other leaders who mixed religion with political power over the last two millennia...), but with the modern day celebration of the separation of Church and State, we can look backward and see that it's probably better when the Church keeps its paws out of royal coffers.

With this divorce, however, the church suffered a loss from the resources of the State, and therefore, can help fewer people per capita, leaving the State to be the great 'Hand That Feeds,' rather than the faithful.

It also seems to have resulted in pulling the Church out of the culture at large, relegating it to the sidelines. No longer are the greatest artists alive creating works to glorify their Maker as encouraged by the Church, but they are patronized by a secular culture which celebrates their creative achievements more than the Church does. And as such, the creations end up more like rap songs focused on wet body parts or how much money one has, rather than the glory of creation or the One who made it.

There was a moment, particularly the Middle Ages through the Renaissance, where the Church championed great artists. The greatest painters, sculptors, writers, and composers created works which still move people to this day. The Sistine Chapel is one of the most famous paintings in the world, featuring Adam reaching out toward the finger of God, and who had that commissioned? The Church! Same with the Pieta, the David statue, Brunelleschi's cathedral dome, and countless others.

Today, the arts are prevailingly secular, with Christians looking more like the copycat who always seems to be three years behind.

In this divorce, the secular State got the creative culture and the financial means of healing the world, and the church is left with…theological debates and the apparent corner on who is in and who's out of heaven? No wonder no one wants to go to church anymore…

And what about the second main effect of a divorce? Well, within a loving relationship, the two members develop a certain language which is spoken only by them. It takes time to build and they know what the other means by their words, even if no one outside the two of them would. It's a sort of secret code known only to the lovers.

When a breakup occurs, reason psychologists, that unique language will never be spoken again.

Their speech to one another becomes cold and alien. It's chiefly legal and robotic now. They communicate *past* one another, rather than *with* one another.

The same has happened in our churches.

The language used seems to alienate outsiders more than draw them in. It may be comforting to those *inside* the church, but does it even make sense to outsiders?

I was recently asked by someone who has been in church for quite some time what the word "grace" means. If you grew up in the church, you take definitions like this for granted, but even something as beautiful and comforting as grace may be alienating to the rest of the world if we can't figure out how to properly translate it to their language.

If you tell someone raised in the church, when they are in an emotional state that "there is so much grace for you," they'll break down and weep. But you say the same words to someone raised in a different context and they'll be unaffected. Maybe they'll say thanks. They'll definitely be confused. Then we wonder why they aren't breaking down and crying and giving their life to Christ *RIGHT NOW!*

After the divorce of Church from Culture, we have lost much of the ability to communicate our intentions or beliefs to those unfamiliar with them.

I can recall many interactions with atheist friends of mine where we may be using similar-sounding words, but saying two completely different things. For instance, I once told a friend I'd be praying for him, and rather than at least acknowledge the kindness of the sentiment, he took offense that I'd condescend to him or try to convert him behind his back. It's almost funny how different the two approaches to that conversation were.

When I, and most Christians I know, offer to pray for someone, it is a sweet, selfless gesture which has only the purest of intentions. Yet when the secular culture hears the same phrase, they take offense.

Why?

Because we have undergone a divorce and no longer speak the same language. To ignore this fact, and to act like nothing has happened and we can just chat with any old atheist and expect to embed the same meaning as they do into our words is just ludicrous.

That's why we need to learn to speak the same language as our culture.

Sure, we may all be speaking English, but we are not speaking the same language. Christians who seek to distance themselves from culture (typically for the purpose of seeking purity or holiness) will never effectively speak into the very world they hope to evangelize. They are Essenes, living outside the bounds of the city, not affected by it, but also not having any significant effect on the population within the city's limits either.

They may seek to obey the commands of James 1, being unpolluted by the world, but in their efforts not to sin via worldly temptation, they make themselves as effective at healing the world as a eunuch is at having babies. Being unpolluted by the world doesn't mean we plug our ears and close our eyes, refusing to participate in any aspect of the world whatsoever; it simply means we don't participate in the sinful acts the world does. And in my opinion, there is a wide berth between familiarizing ourselves with our culture and sinning.

For example, at the risk of sounding too self-righteous, I have never had sex, been drunk, gotten high, or even sworn. Yet I have never felt alienated from our secular culture at large. I can pinpoint cultural references in music, movies, television, and other celebrity phenomena, because it interests me. In that sense, I'm living proof that one can be *in* the world and not *of* it; that you can participate in and contribute to your culture without being polluted by it.

My philosophy of media boiled down to one paragraph is this: Jesus said that it's not what goes *into* a person's body that makes them unclean, but what comes out. If the media you ingest causes you to sin (i.e. if I watched a lot of movies with tons of sex and nudity, it would cause me to spiral down), then avoid it. But just because something is rated R doesn't mean it will automatically make you sin. I can watch people do drugs for days and never be tempted to dabble myself; or hear plenty of foul language and never break my streak of never swearing. Determine what things affect what comes *out* of you and adjust your media *input* accordingly.

Ingesting secular, cultural media does not automatically pollute the sincere believer. I would argue that done well, it can have the opposite effect: building more bridges to our neighbors and secular friends. Familiarizing ourselves with the same things the world talks about can only help our witness, undoing the reeling pain of the divorce we have suffered from it. Just take it in with your brain turned on.

&

Now, bringing this all back to the beginning. I once more ask the question:

What could be more important than knowing Jesus and introducing others to Him?

The answer is still: **Nothing**.

However, to stand on that hill like a glorified martyr earns us no points either. Because someone who touts that phrase and plugs his ears to the cultural songs may very well know Christ, but he will be a failure at introducing others to Him.

If we want to effectively bring others into relationship with The Ground of All Being, then we must first learn to speak their language. We must share their interests and their hobbies. We must listen to (at least some of) the same music and ingest similar media.

Dwelling in our high towers of Christian music and media will **a)** not be enjoyable for us unless we are masochists and **b)** not convince many people that becoming a Christian is worth it.

The stance that Christianity is at odds with culture is outdated. Many people still hold this view, and they are *not* the ones welcoming outsiders into the doors of the church. They are not the ones ministering to those with face tattoos and short dresses.

Many people go too far in the opposite direction too, reducing the spinal column of Christianity to a blubbery pile of mush which can be pushed in whatever direction the culture pleases. This is also not historic Christianity.

True Christians will seek to undo the damage done by this divorce from popular culture. They will seek to participate in it in-depth, to a degree that is not sinful, but is also not keeping the masses at an arm's length.

True Christians will not only absorb the media produced by culture, but contribute to it, subtly being an incarnational witness for Christ in a sea of darkness.

We will not stand back from the world, but will dive in hands-first, ready to get dirty, feed both the mouths hungering for food, and the minds hungering for truth. We will serve and love, even those who hate us.

We will learn the language of the world, using it to communicate truth to an ailing generation.

I like your Christ, I do not like your Christians.
Your Christians are so unlike your Christ.

—Mahatma Ghandi

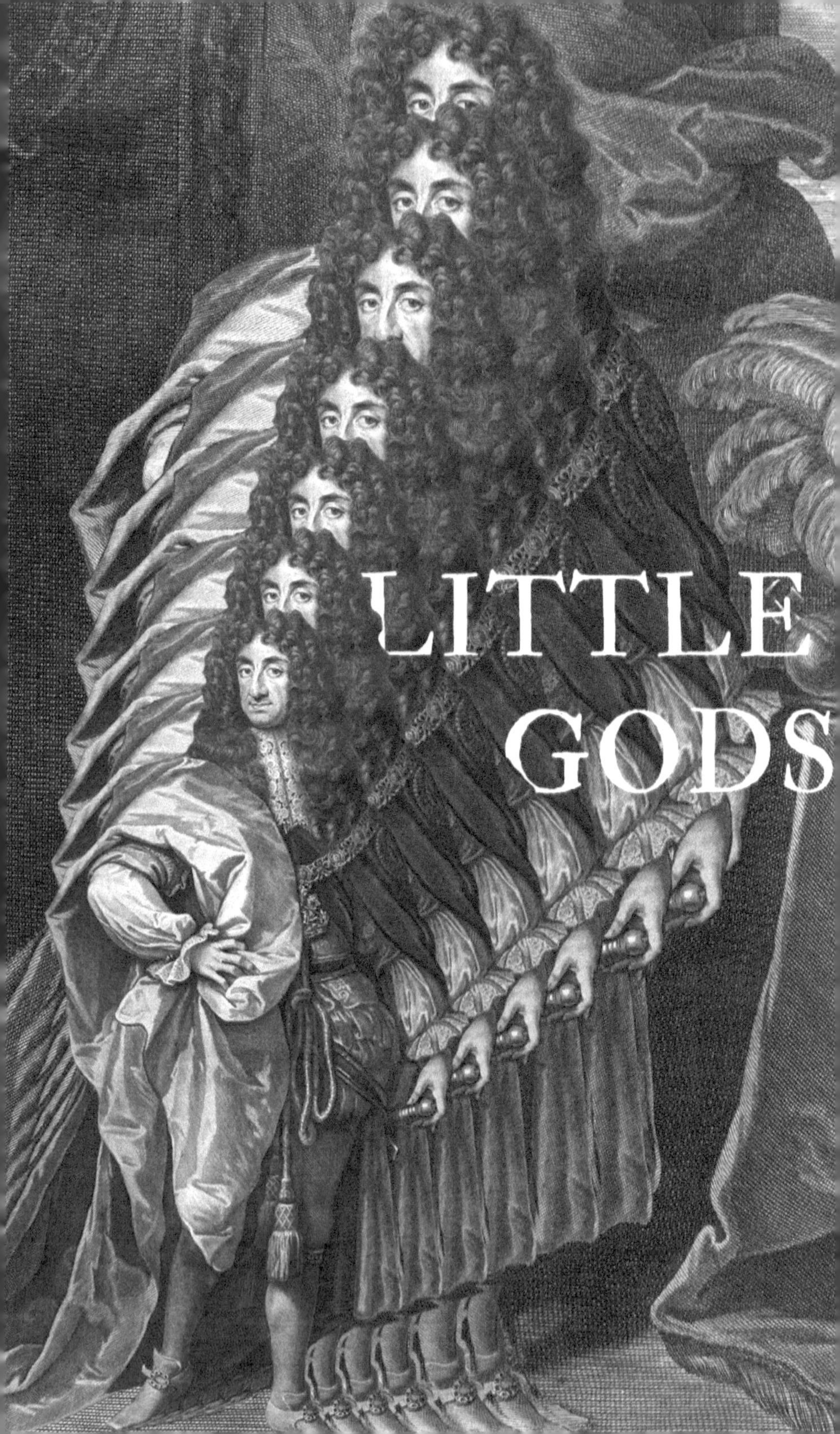

LITTLE
GODS

—Silent Planet, "Northern Fires (Guernica)"

n order for a rocket to make it out of earth's atmosphere, it needs boosters attached to its sides, helping it thrust up off the ground. These boosters are manufactured in a factory in Utah and shipped by train to Florida. Along the route to Florida, the train needs to pass through several tunnels. This means that the dimensions for the rocket boosters need to be able to fit through the tunnel and therefore cannot be wider than 4 feet, 8.5 inches.

Apparently the engineers wanted to make these boosters fatter, but were constrained by these train tunnels. The tunnels are cut to that exact size because the average train gauge (distance between the tracks) is 4'8.5".

Now, why are all train gauges that exact measurement? Because they are based on the distance between wagon wheels which were the predominant means of transportation for centuries (think The Oregon Trail blazing across America).

These wagon dimensions came from across the pond, back in Europe, where everyone built their wagons to fit perfectly into the grooves made in the dirt roads. Many of these roads were part of the Roman road, which spanned the entire Roman Empire for centuries.

Why did Romans decide roads should be four feet, eight and a half inches across? Because their chariots were pulled by two horses, and on average, two horse butts trotting side by side take up that exact amount of space.

In other words, the most technologically advanced form of travel—shooting humans into space—was shaped by the width of two horse bums.

At times, it feels like we have come so far and are totally removed from the past. But then you remember that rocket ships are influenced by Roman horse derrieres and realize that everything is really rooted in the past. We cannot escape history nearly as swiftly as we think.

This does not only apply to engineering fun facts and technology; it applies to everything. We've already examined how the history of philosophy trickles down to influence our daily thoughts still today, and how culture influences our perception of our religious or spiritual beliefs. Now we turn the interrogation light toward something far less divisive and very amiable: Politics.

We may sometimes forget that Democrats and Republicans did not originate alongside Adam and Eve, but are the result of many centuries of experimenting with government, power, equality, and philosophy. Retracing some of these origins may help us better understand the very nature of politics today.

It's just over 1,000 years before Christ would be born and the Israelites start looking around, comparing their nation to the surrounding ones.

They have priests—people who represent Israel before God.

They have prophets—people who are the voice of God to Israel, speaking His words, correcting and rebuking them.

Both of these offices were instituted by anointing the person with oil. They dumped olive oil, a purifying agent, over his head as a symbol, marking him out as special among the people. He talks to God, or he talks to the people from God.

But the Israelites notice that all the nations around them have something that they don't: **kings.**

For generations, the Israelites were led by judges, people who settled internal disputes and make important decisions for Israel. But they didn't have a king. Like the kid who wants the cool new toy his neighbor has, the Israelites thought that filling this position would solve all their issues.

So God gave them Saul—someone they chose because he was tall and handsome, not because he was necessarily a good person (people really have not changed at all in 3,000 years).

A new position which required anointing was introduced. Now there are three types of people who have oil dumped on their heads: prophets, priests, *and* kings. From this idea of anointing, we get the Hebrew term *mashiach*, meaning "anointed one."

We say "Messiah" in English.

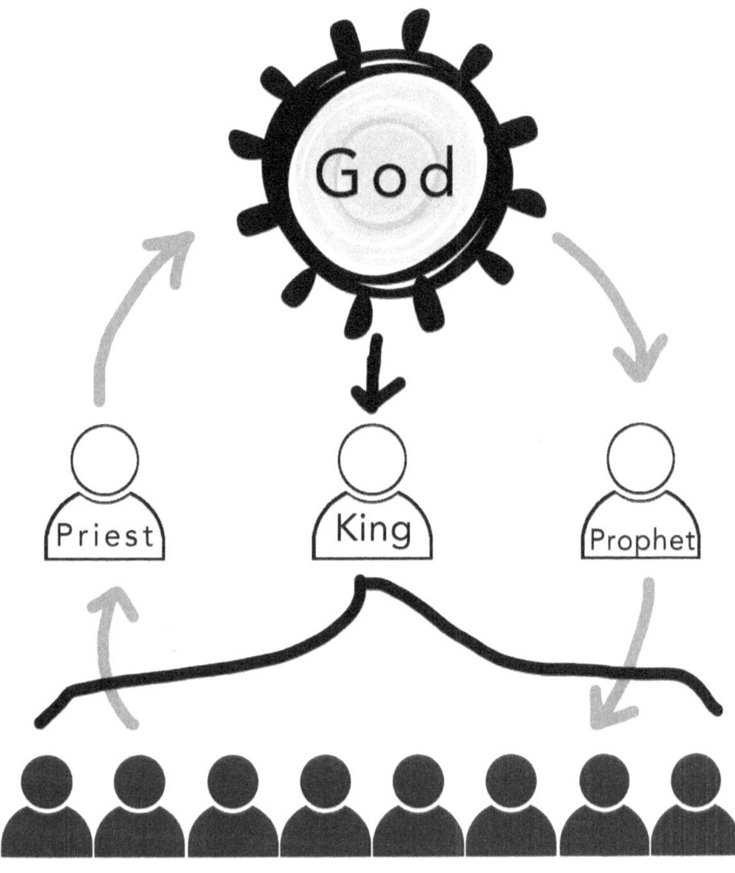

It refers to a person who would fulfill the roles of prophet, priest, AND king, simultaneously. Someone who would speak to people **from** God, take the sins of the people **to** God, and rule over the people **like** God. Israel adopted this hope in a coming Messiah who would fulfill all of these offices.

The kingship continued down through the famed King David, who violently wiped out the surrounding people groups who posed a threat to Israel. God makes a covenant with Dave, and promises that the Messiah will come through his line. This is why, as the Israelites await a Messiah to come and save them, they think that he, too, will be warlike and violently liberate Israel like his ancestor David.

In the oft-overlooked details of the Christmas story, did you ever wonder *why*, exactly, King Herod had all the male babies killed when he heard that the Messiah may have been born? It's because he was familiar with the King David stories and didn't want to end up like one of the surrounding nations he'd wiped out! The possibility of a Messiah meant the possibility of a violent uprising. And warlords are easier to kill when they're infants.

Or later, when Jesus entered into Jerusalem and was greeted by people laying down palm branches (why we celebrate Palm Sunday a week before Easter), they yelled "Hosanna to the *Son of David!*" Hosanna simply means "Save us," so what do you think they expected Him to save them from? Their own sin? Hell?

Of course not! They wanted to be free from Rome, the big, bad human oppressor who ruled over Israel at the time. When they heard that there may be a potential Messiah on the scene, they wanted to cry out to him, hoping he'd save them from Rome.

You can see this thinking embedded in the question asked of Jesus even after His resurrection. In Acts 1:6, Jesus is chilling with His disciples and they ask Him, "At this time, are you now going to restore the kingdom to Israel?" Talk about missing the point. They *still* thought the Messiah's main duty was freeing Israel from Rome.

All this time Jesus has been talking about the kingdom of God as something big and universal, instituted for every person on earth, and they are still focused on the issues of their little tribe. This notion of a warlike Messiah coming to free Israel from Rome is pervasive, and it seems to have taken the New Testament believers many years to fully grasp the mission Jesus had in mind.

Back to the Old Testament: the kingdom passed on to David's son Solomon. This period under these three kings (Saul, David, Solomon) was called the United Monarchy, because after Solomon, the kingdom was ruptured by his sons and there was a massive split between Israel in the north and Judah in the south.

In this period, known as the Divided Monarchy, there were about 2 good kings, and the other dozens of kings were as corrupt and morally bankrupt as possible. They worshipped other gods, persecuted the prophets, and acted cowardly when faced with decisions regarding other nations. Essentially, after hundreds of years, Israel proved that a king would not solve their issues.

If God had not urged them to get a king (which He had not), then it was for good reason, and they should have noticed this.

At the same time, how often do we long for things God doesn't want for us? We have no room to point fingers.

There were already two offices which interacted with God on behalf of the people (prophets and priests), and judges for the tribes who could settle disputes and provide a role of leadership.

In some ways, the desire for a king was a desire for a god they could see. They wanted a person to enthrone; someone they could look up to and point to as representative of their nation. Yahweh wasn't cutting it anymore; they needed a human representative. So God gave them one, and look what happened.

The Old Testament ends with Israel crying out in distress from being carried into exile by Assyria and Babylon. The larger nations had successfully conquered them. Ultimately, these would be replaced by Rome, where Israel is subject when we arrive in the New Testament.

Now, Rome was just a tribe stewing in the background of the Divided Monarchy period, but by the time of Isaiah and Jeremiah (5-600 BC approximately) it would have become a Republic. In 44 BC, a mere handful of years before the birth of Christ, it would transition to the giant Empire we find in the pages of the New Testament, controlling all the land around the Mediterranean. We'll come back to Rome in a moment.

When we read the Bible, we cannot forget that every nation on earth was also morphing and *happening* around its pages. History was being made in China, India, and Central America at the same time that David was killing Goliath, and Jeremiah was thrown into a cistern. It's easy to read the Bible and segregate it from the historical glasses with which we read the rest of the world.

Anyway, God seemed hesitant to give Israel a king, yet gave in to their begging for one. In 1 Samuel 8:7, God says that the people of Israel rejected Him from being their king. We must ask, why this hesitancy?

Well, it seems obvious that God meant to be their leader Himself—after all, they were His chosen people, and He was able to guide them via prophets, ever since Moses and Aaron in the wilderness.

But God was not good enough for them.

They wanted a human they could point to and say, "HERE is our leader! Isn't he strong? Isn't he great? Doesn't he represent us to the surrounding nations?"

To this day, the impulse to hail strong leaders has shown no signs of diminishing. We are still tempted to look at one, single person and proclaim, "THIS person can save our country! They will kick the immigrants out!" or, "They'll open up our borders and welcome the immigrants in!"

Everyone has a different view of how the world should be saved; how the nation will prosper, and we often marry these ideals to the person running for power. He or she is the one who can slap their signature on the bill and save the country.

They can bomb the living daylights out of our enemies and win the war. They can bring peace to our divided nation. And so on.

Israelites in the first century, when Jesus came into the world, found themselves having similar arguments—there were many paths to utopia, and there were monstrous arguments about which one was correct. Within Jewish leadership in particular, we can see how the different sects saw their way as the right one to the prosperity of Israel.

The Sadducees saw that Rome was powerful and huge beyond comprehension, and it would only keep getting bigger. Therefore, they reasoned, the best thing for Israel is to align herself with Rome, so that as Rome grows, Israel—an ally—will also thrive. We are also told throughout the gospels that this group did not believe in the resurrection of the dead ("So they were *sad, you see!*" lol). This lack of belief in the resurrection led them to seek perfection in earthly human society—they believed that if there is no afterlife (a somewhat common Jewish belief), then we should align ourselves with power and flourish in *this* lifetime.

The Zealots were polar opposites, constantly calling for the Jews to rise up and overthrow Rome. This was attempted between the writing of the Old and New Testaments, in an episode called the Maccabean Revolt. In 167 BC, Judas Maccabeus rose up against the then-Roman Republic, fighting for the right for Jews to worship freely, not subject to Rome's practices of emperor worship. They ultimately were successful, and became the only people in the Roman Empire exempt from offering annual incense offerings to Caesar. Zealots wanted to

Sadducees	Zealots
-Liked Rome -Aligning with Rome helps us -No resurrection -Very wealthy	-Hated Rome -Violent rebels -Overthrowing Rome helps us
Essenes	Pharisees
-Hated Rome but didn't do anything about it -Removal from society=purity -Lived outside of society, awaiting Messiah	-Also didn't like Rome, but not violent -Firm belief in afterlife or resurrection

push further, winning complete autonomy from Rome and restoring Israel that way.

The Essenes were the ones who thought the best thing to do was leave. They retreated to the desert and sought to cleanse themselves from society altogether. They waited idly, almost on standby, for the Messiah to come and do all their work for them so they could once again return to a civilized, theocratic Israel. Many people think John the Baptizer was an Essene, as he lived a life of purity out in the wilderness.

The fourth camp, likely the one Jesus was raised in if you recall, were the Pharisees. Theirs is the only one who firmly espouses belief in the afterlife, and does not hope in Rome. Although

Jesus has may disagreements with the Pharisees (they are often painted as the bad guys in modern day messages…sometimes unfairly), He likely came out of this tradition. The Pharisees also resented Rome's rule and sought to return to the Davidic tradition of independence and self-governance, though they were less violent than the Zealots. They were patiently waiting for the Messiah to come and lead them out from under Rome's iron rule.

This is likely why Nicodemus, one of the leaders of the Pharisees, comes to see Jesus at night in John chapter 3. He seems to be prying Jesus, seeing if He just might be the Messiah they have been waiting for.

Throughout the gospels, the various parties try to trick Jesus into answering revealing questions, getting Him to betray which side He was *really* on.

For instance, in Matthew 22, two opposing groups both approach Him and ask whether or not Jews should pay taxes to Caesar. If Jesus says yes, then He's pro-Rome and must align with the Sadducees; if He says no, then He's anti-Rome and therefore on the other side.

Jesus chooses a third (fifth?) option.

He says, "Give to Caesar what is Caesar's, give to God what is God's." He baffles both parties, because on the one hand, He diminishes the importance of both money and Caesar, and on the other hand, He is saying to monetarily obey and pay taxes to those in authority over you.

We are faced with a myriad questions like this today, and how one answers these questions reveals a lot about where we stand politically.

During the Covid-19, crisis, you could tell where someone stood simply by whether or not they wore a mask in public.

You can tell whether someone is a Democrat or Republican today based on their answers to simple questions about immigration, free market, healthcare, and sexual behavior.

What we rarely see, however, is a thoughtful practice of 'zooming out' and deeply examining both sides, landing in a different position, or a diverse assortment of positions, altogether, the way Jesus did. He didn't answer according to their simplistic binary; He reframed the entire question.

Interestingly, we can often lose sight of our positions and our context within a system which often makes us think only in oversimplified dichotomies. We may thing that our red and blue parties are the only possible ways the world can be seen.

In the podcast *This Cultural Moment*, Australian thinker Mark Sayers points out how many attributes of the Right and Left are in flux, and in fact, are nearly opposites in the systems of other countries. Take gun control, for instance. In the United States, it is the Right-leaning conservatives who are in favor of gun ownership and carrying arms; it is the Left who opposes this and wants tighter restrictions on gun ownership. If you have lived in the US for a while, you're accustomed to this line of thinking.

The interesting thing, as pointed out by Sayers, is that in Australia, the issue is flipped. The Conservative party, who prioritizes the traditional family unit and more 'classic' values, is the one fighting *against* guns. If you pause and remove yourself from your American context for a moment, it makes sense: Why would people rooted in Judeo-Christian values, with a high emphasis on family, want more guns around them?

This is why writer and speaker Shane Claiborne, in an interview with Preston Sprinkle, stated that he has a hard time finding a home in any political, or even theological category.

He is anti-gun, but pro-traditional family values. He believes the Bible to be true like theological conservatives, yet daily lives among and fights for the poor, oppressed, and needy minorities like his liberal kinfolk.

If Christians are thinking clearly and elevating our minds above the noise of our immediate context, then we all should feel this way. We should feel like there is no suitable home which perfectly accommodates our kingdom ideals. Jesus said, in one of His most-quoted lines, that His kingdom is not of this world.

To this day, there has nary arisen a single party or regime that fits perfectly with the theocracy described by Jesus. Until the day His kingdom comes rushing in in its fullness, we simply do our best to fit into the authorities placed over us. This means that, in the American democracy for instance, we vote for whichever candidate *best* represents the kingdom values in that specific season.

The error comes when we hold diehard beliefs in one side over the other and are unwilling to acknowledge that our side may have some shifting flaws.

For instance, an elderly mentor of mine has been a lifelong registered Republican. He had never voted Democrat in his life —until 2016. When Donald Trump earned the ticket for the Grand Old Party (GOP), my mentor decided that the party no longer represented the values he hoped for, and at that point had to vote with his left hand for the first time in his life. This is what it looks like when people hold their status as a kingdom-minded individual over their alignment to a political party. It looks like changing when change is necessary, but adhering to your party so long as it *better* represents your Christian values.

Note that I say it *better* represents them, as neither American party has or will ever *fully* embody the values of Christ's kingdom.

This means that there will be some Christians who think through their (two) options when voting, and decide that the Liberal candidate is a better fit for their vision of Christ's kingdom—and they're right. But it also means there will be authentic, scripture-loving Christians who vote for the Republican candidate, and they are also right. It takes a lot of maturity to acknowledge this in others, and to remain cordial when discussing it with those who arrive on the opposite side from us.

The most frustrating point in all of this is when we do our best to strive for a middle balance, but encounter people who centrifugally hurl themselves to an extreme—either one. It's called the Horseshoe Theory, though I think it's less of a theory and more of a law. it's best demonstrated with this simple visual:

center

left   right

far-left far-right

The theory (*cough,* law) states that those on the far right and far left are closer to one another than they are to the actual right or left—their own respective side. We saw this, for instance, in 2017 in Charlottesville, Virginia when a neo-Nazi march kicked off a string of violent riots. Obviously, the racists represented the far right, as they wanted to revive the attitude and dominance of the Third Reich, but then an interesting thing happened. They were met with violent force from the far left as Antifa stormed in to fight them.

The chaos grew until both sides looked essentially the same: smashing windows, destroying property, and fist fighting. The other three categories (center, right and left) criticized the violence as unnecessary and extreme. In some ways, the far right and left are categories unto themselves and are somewhat divorced from their parent party altogether. A reasonable, thoughtful person on the Right may disassociate herself from the Far-Right just as much as she would from the Left. Same with folks on the Left and so on.

We've also seen extremist ideology manifest in other ways recently. Far-Right beliefs often center around blatant racism, such as the German chant of "Blood and Soil!" Their bloodline is pure and their land is theirs. Every other blood is tainted, and anyone who doesn't look like them doesn't belong on their land. This led to Naziism and other, less genocidal displays of racism such as racial segregation, or South African apartheid.

Thoughtful people lately have been asking, however, can the Left also go too far?

It may be more insidious, but ironically, Far-Left ideals look very similar to their counterparts. Recently, with the rise of critical race theory (CRT), many schools have begun adopting 'anti-racist' curriculum. This curriculum teaches students to identify themselves and their classmates by the color of their skin, and think of themselves as either a member of the oppressive class, or the oppressed.

In the February, 2021 faculty meeting of the Dwight-Englewood School, teachers were grouped by their skin color and then addressed. White teachers were discouraged from oppressing their students, and teachers of color were urged to share more of their experiences from their "harsh realities."

CRT urges people to think of themselves by their skin color's identity, rather than as unique individuals. It seems to be a massive step backward, or at least, a step toward the Far-Right ideology of race-defined identity.

This is why, in an interview on Australian television, Jordan Peterson said, "The game of dividing human beings up by their group identity ends in disaster, no matter who plays it and no matter what the reasons are."

It is certainly not a step in the direction of Martin Luther King Jr., who longed for a day when his "four little children will one day live in a nation where they will not be judged by the color of their skin but by the content of their character."

See how the Far-Right and Far-Left, running unchecked, can end up falling into the same traps? In this case, both want to define people by the color of their skin and categorize them accordingly.

You could also examine the twentieth century and see how the Far-Right Nazi Germany does not look too different from the Far-Left Communist China and Russia: both discarded human dignity, killed their own citizens by the millions, and sought for greater control by the State.

This circular approach to politics shows us that we cannot let ourselves get locked into one paradigm of thinking. What if, rather than aligning with one American political 'side,' we filled ourselves with biblical wisdom and applied that to each individual issue? What if we found a way to balance ourselves atop that circle, rather than sliding down onto either toxic side?

In C.S. Lewis' landmark novel *The Screwtape Letters*, one demon, Screwtape, counsels another demon, Wormwood, on how to destroy a person's soul. Keep in mind that this is the perspective of two demons talking about how to destroy a person, and that the "Enemy" is God:

> All extremes, except extreme devotion to the Enemy, are to be encouraged. Not always, of course, but at this period. Some ages are lukewarm and complacent, and then it is our business to soothe them yet faster asleep. Other ages, of which the present is one, are unbalanced and prone to faction, and it is our business to inflame them...

> Whichever he [the human target] adopts, your main task will be the same. Let him begin by treating the Patriotism or the Pacifism as a part of his religion. Then let him, under the influence of partisan spirit, come to regard it as the most important part. Then quietly and gradually nurse him on to the stage at which the religion becomes merely part of the 'cause,' in which Christianity is valued chiefly because of the excellent arguments it can produce in favor of the British war-effort or of Pacifism. The attitude which you want to guard against is that in which temporal affairs are treated primarily as material for obedience. Once you have made the World an end, and faith a means, you have almost won your man, and it makes very little difference what kind of worldly end he is pursuing.

Lewis writes this as WWII was happening, and there were strong sentiments by British Christians for both pacifism and for serving in the military. Lewis' point is NOT which side is better; it's that both sides conducted themselves in a way that ultimately subverted Christ to a mere means of settling political policy. Lewis penned this almost a century ago, and I'm seeing/saying/lamenting this in Christianity in 2021's America.

Don't get locked into one side in an us-versus-them mentality. The more our media and blogs and friends try to polarize us toward an extreme, thus seeing the opposite side as the enemy, the less we embody the kingdom mentality Christ describes.

Although we do not live in a monarchy like the Ancient Israelites, with a king who was anointed by a priest or prophet, our political leaders are still very much stand-ins for God.

They are little gods.

At the end of the day, all power boils down to an attempt to be God. We can demonstrate this in our sexual fantasies, or our desire to have more than our neighbor…don't we all want to be the one who owns the cattle on a thousand hills? (Psalm 50:10)

When we elevate one political leader or another, we are essentially saying, *"Here is the Messiah! Here is the Anointed One! Here is the one who will set things right, the way they are meant to be! To vote against him/her is to vote against GOD"*

All the while, we can forget the fact that Israel also longed for a human leader at the expense of having God be their king. We can forget that we already have a Messiah who has come and, rather than overthrow political regimes and institute new human governments, has overthrown sin and death and instituted a coming kingdom of God, ruled by God.

To get bogged down in the debates about peripheral issues, especially at the cost of burning bridges and hurling stones, is to damage the heart of God. It brings division over unity. It doesn't address issues the way Jesus did: with creativity, imagination, and a perspective that isn't clouded by one side or the other.

Are you able to acknowledge that most Liberal people want what's best for the world, including you?
Can you see that most Conservative folks want the world to prosper and flourish for everyone, including you?

The only difference is, we have different ways of getting there. We have different ideas of what flourishing looks like. But rather than discuss these differences and work together to create a holistic, unified reality of human flourishing, we busy ourselves with simply criticizing the other side rather than working with them. We spend hours on minute issues, becoming so myopic in our approach that we often forget to step back, celebrate our similarities, and work together to make a better society.

In these discussions, remember that we are most often discussing ideas and systems, and a conversation over ideas should never elevate into aggression, much less, violence. Yes, they affect real people in real life, but our debates about the subjects will not solve the problems by themselves, so why become hostile while talking? Why not ask more questions than shout our own answers?

I've learned from even my most extreme Liberal/Conservative friends when I've listened. Even if it's just to understand *why* they believe the way they do, it's helpful in understanding the other.

May we not make little gods of our sides, or their leaders.

May we keep our eyes on The Anointed One, who leads us, speaks to us, and to whom we can always speak.

And may we act with wisdom and peace until He returns to rule His kingdom once and for all.

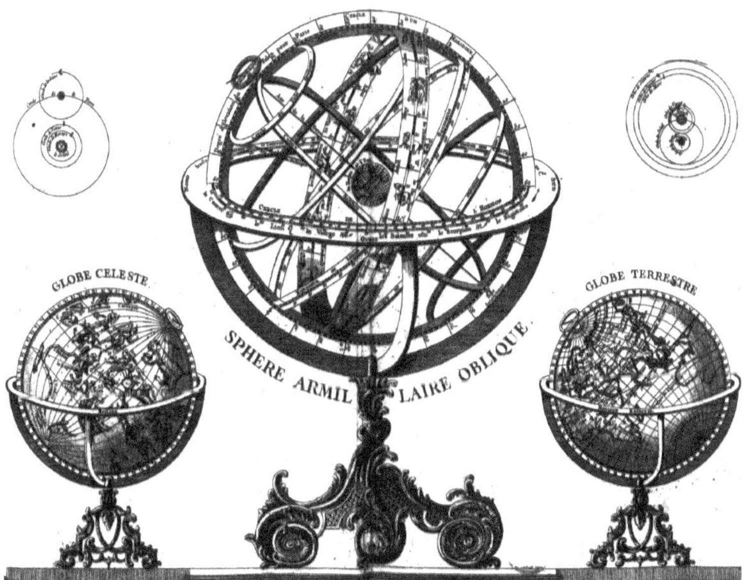

MEXICANA
AFRICA
EVROPA
AS[IA]
PRVANA
MAG
NIC
A SERIES OF
PRECARIOUS
BALANCES
EDITIO   Amstelodami apud Ioannem Ianßonium 1641   VLTIM[A]

very human is daily faced with decisions between two (or more) options. According to Roberts Wesleyan College, adults make around 35,000 decisions *a day* (children make around 3,000). Some are smaller choices like where to eat lunch, or what podcast to play. But others are much larger; they are decisions we will adhere to for months, years, or our entire lives.

Will you be a Democrat or Republican?
Will you marry this woman, that one, or remain single?
Will you be a Christian or Atheist?

These are not small decisions, and where we land on each one will determine a lot about our futures and our lives. The past few years have proven that the human tendency is to gravitate toward one extreme or another, rather than toward a healthy balance in the middle. The slippery hill has many slopes and staying balanced sat the top is harder than sliding down into polarization.

As Christians especially, we must resist the temptation to centrifugally swing toward one end rather than sifting through all the information and making an informed stance somewhere in the gray in-between.

Let's revisit a harmless, peaceful example: American politics.

Christian Democrats will argue that *theirs* is the Christian party, as it aims to treat all people equally and seek justice for all. They have an emphasis on diversity and inclusion which reflects the heart of God. To vote otherwise would simply be un-Christian!

Republicans on the other hand strive toward a traditional view of the family, a value on life in the womb, and on liberty in the work, lives, and actions of citizens. These are equally biblical principles which make a valid case for voting Republican as a believer.

My church reports being split roughly 50/50 between Conservatives and Liberals, and we always tout this as a sign of a healthy church. Why? Because Christians are (or should be) people who are able to recognize the strengths and admit the weaknesses in every side of an issue. Christians are people who can peacefully coexist with people whose views differ from their own.

Swinging to the name-calling extreme of *either* end is the real un-Christian option.

A Christian posture does not opt for a closed-ear stance which sings *"la la la, I can't hear you!"* Rather, a Christian stance is one that can hear all sides of an argument, fairly consider them, and find the balance which rests on the strengths of both extremes.

You may land slightly more toward the Republican side or the Democratic one, and this is perfectly fine. But to assume that the other side has absolutely no merit, and is stupid, insane, and nonsensical is not going to benefit you as you live and think, and it will only vilify fellow humans made in the image of God.

We must always find the balance between extremes.

We must maintain our series of precarious balances, as this is the thought life of all believers.

To lazily topple to one side or the other is not the work of a thinking Christian, but the end result of blindly ingesting the voices of only one biased side or the other.

&

Dogma and Liberty.
Wealth and Poverty.
Expression and Humility.
Discipline and Grace.

Each dichotomy is not only a binary every human must decide between, but one they must construct in the first place. If we say that every path we will walk in life is an attempt to tread out a balance between two extremes, first we must determine which entities are at odds with one another. What *are* the extremes in question here? This may seem easy—and in some cases, it is—but in others, determining said extremes may not prove so simple.

An easy pairing is the balance between wealth and poverty. Clearly an excess of material goods is the opposite of a dearth of them. Absence and presence of resources. Many Christians opt toward a 'poverty mindset,' believing that a good Christian must resist the impulse to accumulate too many material goods and therefore remain poor.

Objects are the enemy.
Money is inherently evil.
Resource control is always sinful.

Many Christians, however, have fallen victim to the opposing theology which is (in my opinion) more destructive. It's a theology which preaches that material possessions are the ultimate good; that your faith will be rewarded in *this* life with riches, a giant house, and perfect children.

See how this is an easy dichotomy to create? Both extremes are detrimental to human flourishing and to a good, robust theology of wealth and possessions.

Other Christians, more wise and faithful, strive to acquire resources in order to use them to further the Kingdom of God, funding missionaries and donating to charities. They do not see material resources as an enemy, but as a good to be put to use for the bettering of the world. They are not greedy and letting their possessions own them, nor are they seeking poverty as a means of proving their devotion.

Attaining this balance is difficult.

Attaining balance in everything is near impossible.

All of life is an examination of extremes and figuring out where to land on the spectrum. It is safe to say that landing on the side of any extreme in any situation is going to be dangerous, even if it is an easier option.

There are other, more abstract spectrums which are not so simple though. For example, compare these verses:

> "Worshippers will worship in spirit and in truth."
> -John 4:24

> "[Jesus was] full of grace and truth."
> -John 1:14

Here we are presented with two pairings which both involve the idea of 'truth.' Which is the more accurate partner of truth: grace or spirit? What do they both mean?

When I was 19 years old, I joined a missions organization which was heavily charismatic. They emphasized the works of the Holy Spirit and were always pursuing mystical experiences, miracles, reading meaning into dreams, and the like. In other words, they were big on the 'spirit,' but often lighter on the 'truth.'

A few years later, I attended Moody Bible Institute, a school known for its academic rigor and its high view of Scripture. After arriving, I soon learned that they were the opposite of the missions organization (on this spectrum, anyway). They perpetually sought truth in God's Word, while sometimes downplaying the mystical elements of God's spiritual nature.

They were focused on 'truth,' sometimes at the cost of the 'spirit.'

Jesus says in John 4, though, that His true worshippers will somehow attain the balance of truth and spirit. They will not neglect one in favor of the other, but will marry the two in a beautiful union that will flourish the believer as an individual, and likely benefit those around them. Spirit without truth spins off into mystical cults and ungrounded experiences; truth without spirit yields dry, religious legalism with rules and dead doctrine.

But as mentioned above, this is not the only dichotomy where truth appears.

What about grace?

We all know people who are so dogmatically obsessed with being accurate in their beliefs that they forgo love and grace. They are perhaps the easier target to stereotype. They are strict and unloving, only rewarding rule-following behavior.

We also know others who are so gracious and loving that anything could be true and nothing really needs correction. Live however you want because all is forgiven. Cheap grace for everybody! Neither is a healthy way to live, nor does it reflect the heart of Jesus and what He wants for His followers. Jesus often rebuked folks who had improper beliefs or unjust actions. His was not the *laissez-faire* type of licentious ethic.

He is after people who can balance truth and grace, people who do not sacrifice one in order to elevate the other. He doesn't want judgmental religious pricks, nor does he want spineless, feel-good hippies. His kingdom is one where truth and grace can coexist in unity and aid the flourishing of humanity. Sinners are repeatedly accepted as humans and encouraged toward behavior that leads to the flourishing of the world—and this involves saying 'no' sometimes.

&

Terrence Malick opens his masterpiece film *Tree of Life* with a woman whispering,

> *There are two ways through life, the way of Nature and the way of Grace. You have to choose which one you'll follow. Grace doesn't try to please itself; accepts being slighted, forgotten, disliked...Nature only wants to please itself. Get others to please it too...It finds reasons to be unhappy when all the world is shining around it.*

While the Apostle John pairs grace with truth in his gospel, Malick contrasts it with nature. So which one is the true antithesis of grace?

Truth,
Grace,
Nature,
Spirit...

Feels like trying to balance atop a greased up bowling ball.

This is part of the struggle of identifying balance between two reference points. The fact that we are comparing them doesn't mean they are necessarily opposites, or that one is the only element which can be compared to this other one. It simply means that they are worth comparing and having both contribute to our lives and thoughts in different ways.

Are Democrats the polar opposite of Republicans? Do they overlap at any point? Of course they do. There are plenty of shared values between the parties, yet these are more often diminished in order to present the parties as mortal enemies without even a hint of agreement. It also means that there are more than two viable parties to consider, but I digress.

Is grace the opposite of truth? Can the two actually beautifully coexist, both simply revealing different necessary parts of Christian life and thought? Like a right and left arm, grace and truth work together to paddle our canoes forward; a missing or weak one would simply send us in circles.

What this means for us is that everything being compared does not need to be opposite in order to be balanced. Just because two things are held up against the other doesn't mean they are enemies, or that only one can exist at a time. Like grace and truth vibrating in harmonic unison, the most beautiful sounds ring out in the *merging* of good things, not the destruction of one or the other.

It also means that multiple things *can* be compared with one another, and of course there is not enough room in a whole library to weigh out every possible balance. So I won't attempt to. Instead, we will look at several of the most significant examples as a means of determining how to balance ideas, thoughts, decisions, and extremes in the rest of life.

The idea of balance, avoiding extremes, and holding tension have been recurring themes in this book; when considering how to understand the entire universe, we can't hastily adhere ourselves to one side or another. Like children voting the same party as their parents, we cannot always assume that the opinion we heard first is the only correct one.

&

Something else we need to always keep at the forefront of our minds when considering the world, how it works, and how it should work, is the difference between people and ideas. It's something which should seem obvious to everyone. People (human beings) are not the same as ideas (abstract belief or thought structures).

Seems like a pretty simple concept, right?
Perhaps it's not quite as clean cut as it first appears.

For instance, a few weeks ago I had a conversation with someone who was raised in a Presbyterian church which leaned more conservative and held to traditional, historical Christian orthodoxy. To me, those all seem like good things and I would likely agree with everything taught at this church.

However, the people who were leaders in his particular church abused their power, hurt congregants, and rather than purely teaching Christ and Him crucified, used the Bible to control, manipulate, and take money.

What was this person's response? He decided that orthodoxy was a repressive system of belief and if that church was its logical end, he wanted nothing to do with it. He developed a view of the Bible which was substantially different than someone who clings to orthodoxy and became much more progressive and postmodern in his thinking.

He did not distinguish the idea from the people.

This makes a lot of sense though. If someone uses a certain idea—or in many cases, a twisting of a good idea—to hurt you, you're likely going to run the opposite direction of that *idea*.

Here, however, is where my friend neglected to differentiate between people and ideas. Rather than recognize the beauty of orthodoxy and the power of Scripture, or even seeking to understand the whole of them, he associated it in his mind with the abusive people from his upbringing and discarded both. This is what happens when emotions blend with epistemology (the way we construct knowledge; what we know and believe to be true) and it blinds us.

Because my friend experienced a good idea via bad people, he ran from both when he got the chance. Sadly, his is not an isolated story. I've heard this time and time again, and it's easy for emotional wounds from people to cloud our beliefs, and I can't hold this against anyone in the least.

This works the opposite way as well. Take, for instance, a bad idea which affects billions of people worldwide. I have no problem declaring that Islam is a *bad idea* no matter how it is taught, and from its foundations, it has no good to give to the world. I can freely discuss Islam as a bad idea without a second thought.

However, this does not mean that I think all Muslims are bad people. The trouble is, in our current eggshell-sensitive American moment, to say anything against a religion (except Christianity...) is considered hateful. Here again we find ourselves at a place where we need to be able to freely deliberate between the two. I am not harboring hatred toward Muslim *people*, but I am aggressively against the destructive, deceptive *ideas* they believe. I have met numerous kind, lovely Muslim people all over the world.

All this can be summed up simply:

Be gentle on people and hard on ideas.

Modern conversation seems to be hypersensitive to the notion of anyone being hard on ideas, for fear that people will be offended. As a Christian, I invite people to be hard on my beliefs. I myself am hard on my own beliefs, hammering them like a blacksmith in order to root out any impurities and make them stronger. I am not one to blindly believe something that sounds or feels good. I don't adopt soundbites as foundational beliefs. I would wager people like that on *any* side are the same ones who become offended when anyone critiques their beliefs.

This is why so many students who are raised in the church leave it upon graduating high school. They were insulated from these refining blows which would have strengthened and reinforced their knowledge of their faith. Then, when arriving at college and facing the arguments of the rest of the world for the first time, they snap like a brittle sword.

Do I want people to come out and attack me as a person? Of course not! But when someone comes with genuine questions or critiques of my beliefs, it's a chance for both of us to learn and grow and, as YHWH says in Isaiah 1, reason together.

In the gospels, I see Jesus being gentle with most people, save the ones who thought they were more righteous than others, and quick to correct crooked beliefs. Just open to nearly any page of the gospels and you'll see people spouting off superstitious or heretical beliefs and Jesus simply responds with truth. It's almost like He's playing Whack-a-Mole with lies. They keep popping up and he keeps slamming them back down.

Finding this balance of grace and truth as displayed by Jesus is much easier said than done. The key is to always be aware of when you are talking about a person or people, and when you are talking about ideas.

Sometimes, this differentiation will be harder than it seems. Learning how to love people who think differently than you is difficult, but not impossible. When disagreements arise, always remember to root out the ideal differentials rather than attack the person (in philosophy, this is called the Ad Hominem Fallacy. It's often easier to just hurl insults at your opponent than to make strong arguments against theirs).

If more people in the world adopted the ability to discern this dichotomy, there would be much more peace, even in our disagreements. We need this in mind when discussing current topics like abortion, race, police, or homosexuality.

For example, I am staunchly Pro-Life, but would never alienate or shame a woman who had an abortion. When discussing any topic, especially deeply personal ones like these, it's important to not forget the humanity and feelings of all people, regardless of how your beliefs or lifestyles differ. Alienating or dehumanizing anyone is absolutely contrary to the heart of God, going all the way back to Genesis 1—we are all made in God's image. Any time we use other humans as pawns in our theoretical arguments, rather than remembering that these issues affect real human beings like you and I, we are doing it wrong. We are not addressing the world and its problems rightly.

One caveat I'll make, though, is this: Christian leaders form a unique category here. I have a hard time accepting people like Creflo Dollar, Joel Osteen, and Stephen Furtick because of their leech-like abuse of Scripture. Because they rob people in the name of Jesus. Their ideas are harmful and toxic, and I don't know if merely critiquing their ideas is strong enough.

We see Jesus and Paul coming down hard on religious leaders who were misleading people in His name. Paul went so far as to wish they would emasculate themselves, and Jesus called them 'whitewashed tombs.' I would have a hard time extending grace to my friend's pastors from the beginning of this chapter because of the damage they did in the name of Christ.

Of course, if they were to repent and acknowledge their missteps, all would be forgiven, but as long as a Christian leader goes on deceiving and stealing from people, they need to be confronted.

Outside of that, and especially with those outside the Body of Christ, we need to be loving, gentle, and seek understanding. The fact that Christians would ever judge those who don't claim to be fellow followers of Christ boggles my mind. Why should you expect an atheist to have the same sexual ethics as you? Why does it surprise us that a nonbeliever has no issue terminating a fetus? They have no category for the image of God.

We must keep in mind that people start from a million different backgrounds and we must meet them where they are, not where we are. The second we cast a judgmental tone over our discourse, we lose all credibility and any chance of sharing our views with the other person.

Let's build bridges to people while seeking to spread truth in what we believe.

May we be hard on ideas and gentle on people.

We all live under the same sky, but we don't all have the same horizon.

—Konrad Adenauer

CAN THE RICH
BE SAVED?

he ancient Mayan people saw their kings and priests as godlike, if not actual gods themselves. If you've seen the cripplingly violent film *Apocalypto*, you know that the Mayans practiced human sacrifice (a highly contested fact among viable historians; the Mayans seem far less violent than many other ancient people groups. Chances are, they did sacrifice humans but not as frequently and gratuitously as we may imagine).

In the film, the ritual is interrupted by the arrival of rain clouds. They stop and look up at the darkening sky. The gods had provided water for their land. Prisoners make a run for it. You have to watch the movie to know what happens next. ;)

The Mayans saw their rulers as divine not solely because they grew up thinking that, or because they were brainwashed—

it was because the leaders secretly controlled the water supply.

How do you convince an agrarian culture which has yearly seasons of drought that you're not only in charge, but are connected to the supernatural powers? Yield the water and dole it out as you see fit. The people will worship you. They would dam it up miles upstream of their town and only let a little bit trickle down at a time. Then, if they wanted to appear gracious and omnipotent, dump some out for their people.

We see the same thing in *Mad Max: Fury Road*, where Immortan Joe holds back the water supply in order to hold onto his power over the people. Because it's a dystopian future where currency has no meaning and only things of practical value can be exchanged, controlling the water means controlling the people.

The ones with the resources are the gods of the age.

It's easy for us to look at Mayans or *Mad Max* and scoff. *How could they be so foolish?* We know who really controls the resources! All these natural things come from God! Or if you're less spiritual, it comes from precipitation and science, etc. etc.

But today it clicked in for me while listening to "Los Angeles" by Ameer Vann. At one point, he raps,

> I remember back when it was simple
> I ain't have to fight with all my n****s
> **Money complicated every issue**
> Man, it's crazy how they deal with you
> Talk about it like they still with you
> Use my name as a meal ticket
> They don't wanna see me standing now
> Bipolar n***a, I'm manic now
> I want more shit in my bank account
> I want my granny a bigger house
> I grow more hungry like every day
> **I feel like God in a scary way**

The key is in the two lines I bolded above. He is telling the story of how he got rich, then his life grew more complicated. I had heard the last line many times before while listening to the song, but today it clicked in *why* he feels like God now that he has money.

His family and friends can now come to him and beg. They can get on their knees and beg. They can petition the one holding the resources and hope that he is gracious in his dealings with them, that he might say yes and dole out some cash.

The rich are gods, and I'd wager they like that feeling.

Just like the classical cultures of old, the people with the resources are the gods.

He controls who in his neighborhood could get an extra $10 for running an errand. He is in charge of...well, most things. People with money call the shots.

Money is the new water.

I feel like God in a scary way.

Now that natural resources like water, gas, heat, electricity, are somewhat regulated and we don't need to fight over them, fiat currency is the new godmaker.

This isn't a political argument for one side or the other, but think about the stimulus checks that went out during the Coronavirus pandemic.

Who controls those?
The poor people?

The middle class?
Or the ultra rich.

They're giving us money, but try to imagine for a moment how tickled you would be if you were the one pulling the lever to rain dollar bills down on millions of hungry folks.

The power would be intoxicating.

The rich control the water;
the rich control the world.

Rich people don't just live in nicer houses, have cooler toys, and driver hotter cars. They control the downward trickle of resources into the rest of the population. It's inevitable. Historically and sociologically, that is a function of a god, or at the very least, a god-king. From the pharaohs of ancient Egypt to the Caesars of Rome to whom every citizen had to offer an annual pinch of incense, human cultures are littered with power wielded in the form of wealth and resource control.

Show your allegiance.
Get some water.

This is the exact reason that Rome began persecuting Christians in 64 AD—they refused to offer their annual pinch of incense to Caesar, claiming they only worship one God. Up until that point in time, only the Jewish people had an understanding with Rome exempting them from worshiping Caesar. It took roughly 30 years after Jesus' death for Rome to realize that this new group calling themselves Christians was not just a Jewish sect, but a new religion altogether—and they needed to show their allegiance to Rome…or suffer.

Suddenly, as a follower of Jesus, it makes sense why He would say that rich people will have a hard time getting into heaven (Matt. 19:24). The powerful think that they, themselves, are godlike. I previously thought this was simply because they were distracted by their nice, shiny things. Now I believe it's because, as Vann rapped, they "feel like God in a scary way."

What use do you have for God if you are God?

Why would you need to ask God for something when you're the one controlling the resources?

I feel like God in a scary way.

The growth of your wealth and power is not merely distracting you from the kingdom of God; it is antithetical to it to the degree that you think you're in charge of running the world. The wealthy, in a very real way, call the shots and operate as a god to the rest of their citizens.

Perhaps this is why the first beatitude listed by Jesus is,

> Blessed are the poor in spirit,
> for theirs is the kingdom of heaven

You can be rich and still be poor in spirit. There have been countless wealthy people who used their wealth to benefit the world. Francis Chan and Rich Mullins earned millions of dollars and gave it all away to help the world. Twitter CEO Jack Dorsey gave away billions of dollars to help educate women in Africa.

Granted, even acts like this could imbue him with the feeling of a god distributing aid to the millions crying out to him. Only they know their own hearts.

The legendary graphic novel *Watchmen* opens with a monologue from the twisted character Rorschach who stands atop a skyscraper overlooking the city and proclaims,

> The accumulated filth of all their sex and murder will foam up about their waists and all the whores and politicians will look up and shout "Save us!"…

> …and I'll look down, and whisper "no."

The question is,

Do you feel like God in a scary way as the result of what you have? As a result of what you can do or provide?

Are you atop the temple, slicing up virgins for an act until you're ready to hand out some water? Is the feeling of playing God intoxicating you?

You can also be relatively poor and still be rich in spirit. I see this in my gym all the time. I talk to 19-year-olds who sell weed and sneakers and think they're the kings of their neighborhood. By most standards, they are not **rich** rich, yet their hearts betray a mindset of those who are 'rich in spirit.' You probably have more money than them, yet they're anything but 'poor in spirit.'

It's not mere distraction that causes this, as I've heard countless pastors preach ("If you're rich, be careful! Your money can distract you from Jesus!"). Rather, it's the elevation of the self above others. It's the feeling godlike among your peers. It's the control and power you accumulate as you grow richer, and then how you use them.

So regardless of how much money we have, let's grow toward being poor in spirit.

Let's, as Paul instructs in Philippians 2, consider others better than ourselves.

Let's adopt the mindset of Jesus who withheld nothing from those below Him, but joined us, His enemies, and suffered for us instead.

"The Son of Man did not come to be served, but to serve..."

&

Almost as alarming as the oppression of wealth is the new concept of "Luxury Beliefs," a term coined by Rob Henderson. Henderson rose up through the foster care system before joining the military, which eventually led him to attend Yale and Cambridge. Needless to say, he was an outlier among his Ivy League peers; most of them came from already-affluent families and expected to maintain their status down through their family line. Coming from an entirely different background, Henderson was able to gain a unique perspective on the mindset and attitudes of the wealthy.

He points out that through the cheapening of material goods in the last few decades (see the next chapter), wealthy people are less attracted to material displays of wealth. In the past, you flaunted your wealth with a fur coat and flashy jewelry. However, now that H&M is difficult to decipher from Nordstrom, and nearly everyone in the global west has a smartphone, looking good is a less telling display of wealth. (Interestingly, it has also led to a decline in burglary)

So what has come to replace physical displays of wealth? Values and opinions that make the upper class look good while costing them nothing.

For instance, states Henderson, educated, affluent, white people are the most likely to state that marriage is outdated and oppressive. Yet they continue to be the most likely to marry and have children inside of wedlock. It is the lower socio-economic strata that has seen a drastic rise of children born outside of wedlock, being raised in a single-parent household. It's also worth noting that most immigrants from Africa, South America, and Asia (aka, those often most praised by the progressive wealthy) tend to staunchly hold to the traditional family system of one mother and one father. The opinions of the affluent *sound* progressive and therefore make them stand out, all the while not affecting their lives, *and* negatively affecting the lower classes.

Henderson identifies many arenas where this plays out: an opinion or view sounds compelling and novel, doesn't affect the wealthier person, and negatively affects poorer people. Wealthy people were the predominant supporters of the

Defund the Police movement, and they are also the demographic least likely to need police assistance in the event of an emergency, wrapped up in their comfortable gated communities where doors can go unlocked and bikes left outside.

In fact, during the racial riots of 2020 following the murder of George Floyd, many wealthy New Yorkers reportedly fled to their second houses in the Hamptons and hired extra security, all the while shouting "Defund the Police!" and "All Cops Are Bastards!" Their status allowed them to maintain opinions which don't affect them at all, yet make them look good, the way fur coats did last century.

Henderson applies this filter to the idea of White Privilege in an article he wrote for the New York Post:

> White privilege is the luxury belief that took me the longest to understand, because I grew up around poor whites. Often members of the upper-class claim that racial disparities stem from inherent advantages held by whites. Yet Asian Americans are more educated, have higher earnings and live longer than whites. Affluent whites are the most enthusiastic about the idea of white privilege, yet they are the least likely to incur any costs for promoting that belief. Rather, they raise their social standing by talking about their privilege.
>
> In other words, upper-class whites gain status by talking about their high status. When laws are enacted to

combat white privilege, it won't be the privileged whites who are harmed. Poor whites will bear the brunt.

He continues to explain that race had almost become a nonissue in America. The predominant view among working class people was that everyone is equal, regardless of skin color, and had in all practical senses become 'colorblind.' It was not until recent years that educated people began resuscitating the ideas of privilege, critical theory, and labeling humans according to skin color. In other words, there is an established pattern of affluent people seeking to stand out by whatever means necessary—historically with material goods, but now with seemingly philanthropic beliefs.

Friedrich Nietzsche made famous his idea of a hermeneutic of suspicion. He wondered if certain doctrines or ideas, particularly in religious spheres, benefitted those in power, or those coming up with the ideas. The most obvious application of this hermeneutic can be seen in the Catholic church's portrayal of heaven, hell, and purgatory in the Late Middle Ages. By telling people that their deceased relatives are suffering in hell or purgatory, the church created an opportunity to collect money in exchange for indulgences which shortened the amount of time they or their family members would spend in purgatory.

See how the doctrine of hell/purgatory monetarily benefitted the Catholic church? There are other examples where this notion plays out in religious circles, but could we not apply the same hermeneutic to the wealthy demographic and see similar themes?

Do they adopt principles or narratives that make them look good without costing them a thing?

Are their ideas based on truth, or on a desire to appear benevolent?

For instance, taking the seed of racism lying dormant beneath the soil of American history and stoking it back to life as a divisive, righteous battle being fought costs the affluent nothing. It also makes anyone who critiques them appear 'racist,' thus elevating them further. Remember that most of the advocates for White Privilege and Defunding the Police were affluent white people who have little-to-nothing to lose by joining either side—so why not join the one that makes you look most virtuous?

Beliefs don't exist in a vacuum. Not only are they contextual, but often motivated by more than just truth.

Wealth allows a freedom of opinion lower classes can't afford.

&

I grew up hearing it.
You did too.

What was the purpose of the great pyramids in Egypt? Well, they were tombs for the pharaohs of course!

As with nearly everything though, there is much more to the story. In Egypt's Old Kingdom, pharaohs were buried in pyramids. Then, for a stretch during the Middle Kingdom, they were buried scattered across the desert in unmarked locations to prevent grave robbing. Finally, in the New Kingdom—the period which most overlaps with the Biblical historical period—they were all buried in the Valley of Kings.

You've seen films like *The Mummy*, and as fantastic of a film as it is, it still leaves me asking the same question: What about the rest of the population? Where were they buried?

The pharaohs and high priests were buried with gross troves of treasures and wealth. They would sail into the heavenly afterlife like clouds on butter. After all—the materials you were buried with were what you were stuck with for eternity.

But what about the peasants? What about the millions of Egyptians who died in their huts while surrounded by their family and couldn't afford a pyramid, or even a tomb? Those lesser-known images of a human curled up in the hole their family dug behind their home are haunting. Don't think too long about them or you'll choke up like I do. What possessions sail them across the river from which there is no return? A few clay pots. Jars. A fetal-positioned body in a hole?

There was a similar photo to this one in my textbook in middle school. You probably saw it too and whirled right past it. Why? Because the majestic tombs of the pharaohs are way cooler to look at. They were covered in hieroglyphics, paintings, and decorated with gold and silver artifacts.

For some reason, while preparing to teach this to my middle schoolers a few weeks ago, I was struck with an image of what this would have been like. Take a moment and follow me there, five thousand years back.

Put yourself in the shadow of Khufu's pyramid, standing beside a grieving widow who can't afford anything more than a hole in the earth for her late husband. Her best clay pots are tossed into the hole next to his curled and decomposing remains—she'll have to save up for more pots now.

Obviously he wouldn't receive the mummification treatment, so his sacred organs would remain inside his body, causing a questionable result when the gods weighed his offerings and delivered his judgment. The widow would be wracked with fear for the soul of her husband. On top of the grief of losing him in *this* life, she's tormented by the notion that their poverty will ruin his chances at a good afterlife as well.

She wishes she could afford more ornate burial paraphernalia, but she prays to Anubis that he will still be allowed entrance across the River.

A few of his fellow slave friends stand around the hole in the sand. There will be no parade for this man like there is when a pharaoh dies. This is it; the undignified end of all things for this man—-it ends in a small hole surrounded by a dozen mourners.

Maybe he had kids; maybe some died as infants and were given equally spartan burials.

Tears continue running down the cheeks of the poor man's wife as the men begin heaving sand on top of the body and the measly jars. Who will provide for her now?

Logic would tell us that this was the experience of millions of Egyptians over thousands of years upon the death of their loved ones. Only the tippy-top one percent of them were afforded ornate burials, pyramids and tombs. A sarcophagus alone would have cost a fortune.

Granted, in such ancient times, the psychology of 'the self' was drastically different, so who knows how a slave would have seen themselves or their loved ones.

I don't know if that makes it more or less sad…

The point is, who gets to decide that some humans deserve pyramids while others deserve holes in the ground alongside their family's treasured clay jars? Why do some humans—equal partakers of the image of God—warrant parades and the wealth of a nation in their tomb, while others (the majority) are tossed into a hole?

Think again about Hagar, the slave girl of Abraham, who was herself an Egyptian. After being raped by her master and tossed aside, she is in the wilderness and has such an experience with God in Genesis 16 that she gives God the name, *El-Roi*, or, The One Who Sees, in Hebrew. The idea is that, when her master treated her as an object—little more than a means of having a son and being thrown into the wilderness —who saw her?

YHWH, God, *The One Who Sees Me.*

This inherently contrasts the Sumerian/Egyptian view of the self as well. Her identity was not predicated on her place in society —a slave woman—but on who saw her and was with her in her suffering. She didn't perceive herself as a necessary cog in the wheel of society, functioning to support the lives of the wealthy and powerful (as would have been the common mentality at the time), but as an individual unto herself. The Bible is remarkably progressive.

Who stands beside the grieving widow while her late husband is slowly buried in a hole?
El-Roi, the God who sees the grief of the slave and the travail of the overlooked.

The same God who saw the exiled slavewoman stands atop every hole in the earth where another peasant lies curled up, weeping.

Or maybe He's throwing a parade.

Who needs to be buried with gold when 'The Lord is your great reward'? (Gen. 15:1)

Romans 4 even tells us that God 'calls the things that are not as though they were'…who's to say that every peasant doesn't rest in a pyramid of their own in the eyes of this hierarchy-destroying *El-Roi*?

The God Who Sees the Unseen.

The God Who puts Peasants in Pyramids.

The thing which is harder to grasp is that, although our society is far more glossy and 'advanced' on the surface, we still put pharaohs in pyramids and peasants in holes in the ground, so to speak.

I was curious, so I made the mistake of Googling what happens to the bodies of homeless people who die on the streets. This article provided some hope of funerary services being held for the homeless, where their shelter friends could come pay their respects, but then it served up these sentences:

> Many are left unclaimed at the city morgue. After 30 days, they are cremated by a private funeral home and often buried outside the city limits. There is no funeral, no head stone, just a name written in the ledger book of a Maryland or Virginia cemetery.

It blows my mind that since the days of pyramids, we have not progressed as far as we'd like to admit. There are still people slipping through the fingers of society like water, their deaths witnessed only by *El-Roi* as their nameless corpses are conveyed into the cremator. This isn't *that* surprising. After all, what else can the State and those funeral homes do; wrangle up some vocational mourners to come and weep for a stranger?

No, the larger tragedy is that this person was forgotten while they were still alive.

My takeaway from this is simple: May we, as image bearers of God, see one another, preferably before death. May we not let others slip down the stream of civilization unseen until they end up in a hole in the ground.

It's hard to fully grasp the vastness of the difference between the rich and the poor, especially throughout history. Not only do we think and feel differently; not only do we have varying degrees of resources and power, but the poor go where the wind blow.

I was in the gym sauna a few months ago and someone asked me, "Do you know why the South and West sides of Chicago became more impoverished than the other parts?"

I knew the West and South sides were the more poor, crime-ridden areas but didn't know the reason why.

"It's because the wind blows off Lake Michigan to the West and South." I waited for him to explain. "They built the factories on those sides of the city so the smoke from them wouldn't blow *into* the city, but away from it. No one wanted to live in the smoke and smog of course, so the housing there became dirt cheap. There are also stories of them redlining black people and other minorities outside of the city."

I absorbed that for a while. Poor people were relegated to areas in town where even the *air* was unclean. Globally, poorer people can't afford clean food, water, or even air!

Last night I was buying pizza at midnight at a downtown shop and a homeless man came up and started chatting with me. His agenda was clear but I was tired and hungry, eager to get home and sleep. To hurry along his spiel, I pulled a $5 bill out of my pocket and handed it to him as I began walking away. He was still mid-sentence.

Looking back on it, I did the wrong thing. I'd still give him the money, but I'd also
talk to him.
Ask his name.
See him.
Treat him like a fellow bearer of the divine spark.

Without these things, we (the world's elite) are no better than the pharaohs of old, setting up our massive pyramids so the world can remember us after we're gone, while the peasants outside the city walls are digging holes.

Food is holy when you eat it,
when it is used to strengthen a body used to strengthen the world.

—N.D. Wilson, *Notes from the Tilt-a-Whirl*

CHOCOLATE

—David Foster Wallace, *Infinite Jest*

 was sitting on a couch in northern Australia with a Swedish boy who was researching various candy companies. He was looking into where they sourced their cocoa, and whether their practices were ethical and sustainable.

"I will buy Cadbury and Mars," he finally exclaimed, "but I can't buy Hershey…yet."

This was the first time I remember seeing someone who actually took the time to look into the source of where their products came from. Up until that point, I had blithely purchased whatever I wanted from wherever I wanted without giving it a second thought.

I accepted the fact that Oscar Meyer bologna simply burst into existence inside its plastic box on the grocery shelf; Starbucks frappucinos came magically out of the spigot at the shop. My clothes came pre-knit in Target and so on.

I never remotely considered the fact that all of these things I bought came *from* somewhere and had to be sourced, compiled, manufactured, labeled, and marketed before I put my grubby hands on them at the grocery store, or wherever.

Capitalism has knit together a system so airtight—with advertising so attractive and squeaky clean—I didn't need to spend one second pondering the background of my purchases; I simply came upon them in the store aisle and made my happy little transaction.

I was 19 when I sat beside the Swede who was a year younger than me while he did his duty of looking up the candy companies. I, like most people in the global West, had simply never considered looking behind the curtain of these massive companies to discover where they got their goods. I wasn't pro-slave labor or animal torture; I had just never thought about it.

Today, as I encounter folks in my former position, I need to remember that not everyone has had this realization yet. Not everyone has been *enlightened* in order to see behind the curtain as my Swedish friend had.

Often, when I hear a friend discussing which diamond he is going to buy for his girlfriend, trace amounts of ire rise up within me and I'm tempted to scream at him, "Don't you know where these come from?? Don't you care about the 3 million people who have died so you can have your precious little diamond??" I need to calmly remind myself that he, too, is not in *favor* of slavery in developing countries, nor is he aware that such things go into the sale of a little diamond. His purchase is an act programmed by the really, really good marketing of a capitalistic society rather than an educated move of oppression.

But let's back up—who are those 3 million people who died due to the diamond trade and why would my friend's purchase affect that at all? Why would the purchase of a chocolate bar in Indiana oppress poor farmers in Guatemala? And will any of our efforts make any difference at all?

you cannot win.

Several years ago, I made a public resolution. I announced online that I would not buy any *new* clothing except underwear and socks; the rest would come from thrift stores. I patted myself on the back as I figured I was making a dent in the global market which utilized sweatshops and paid fabric farmers measly pennies for their arduous labor. I read several articles on the sourcing of clothes and educated myself. I read that, ironically, large brands like Nike, Adidas, and H&M were more likely to ethically source their clothes because not only do they have the financial means to do so, but they are under a much larger magnifying glass. Due to their behemoth resources and publicity, these companies have actually been working toward making all of their clothing just and sustainable, which has been great to see.

Smaller chic boutiques, however, who order small-batch lines from Malaysia are under next to no accountability, nor do they have the means to check *all* of their sourcing, so they are more likely to use unjust production practices. Unexpected, right?

I attempted to bypass all of it, therefore, by shopping exclusively at thrift stores. That way, I figured, all my money would be supporting these nonprofit organizations who employ many people who struggle to find other employment and do a lot of other good for their communities. Plus, I save a lot of money.

After a few months, however, I read another article which pooped on my resolution. Thrift stores, it turned out, can be almost as detrimental to developing countries as the rest of the clothing brands.

The way it works is, when a shirt doesn't sell in a thrift store, they eventually need to get it out of the store. Once they have a shipping container of unwanted clothes, Goodwill or the Arc will ship it over to a country like Nigeria and basically dump the giant crate of clothes into a random town. Sounds like a good thing, right? Poorer folks end up with nice clothes from the USA and don't have to wander around in old, tattered rags.

The downside is that local shirt makers are put out of business because who would buy a local shirt from *him* when they could get free *American* clothes from this crate that showed up? These deliveries disrupt the local economy and put artisans out of work.

Buy new clothes, support slave labor and sweatshops.
Buy thrift stores and harm foreign economies.
Buy no clothes and get arrested.

Are you feeling hopeless yet?

Although our world is constantly evolving and slowly getting better about how we live and do business, there is virtually no perfect way to shop. Unless you are willing to spend collective days compiling data on where everything in your life comes from (or live on a farm and don't even use money), you are going to inevitably purchase things which were once handled by a poorer, oppressed human being.

Hopefully, a few decades from now, this will be a thing of the past and injustice will be eradicated from the world. Right now, however, we are still in a place of improvement and growth and need to find the balance between being ignorant, being educated, and using our money as best as we can to promote justice and sustainability.

Why does my dollar matter?

When my friend was about to propose to his girlfriend, he was talking about which diamond she wanted. She was getting picky about her cut and I couldn't hold back my frustration any longer.

"Why does it matter??" I burst out. "Y'all are being so picky about something that a 6-year-old African boy probably mined out of the earth, and you're just going to dump money into that industry!" (My next book is on how to make and keep friends.)

He looked at me and with a totally straight face said, "Well yah, but whether or not I buy a diamond won't shut down the industry. I won't stop it by boycotting, so I may as well just get it."

This cavalier attitude is what leads entire nations to become populations of accidentally oppressive consumers.

If it won't make a difference, I may as well do the wrong thing is essentially what that attitude says. If you're aware of how your diamond came about, shouldn't you be held responsible for contributing to that process or not?

To make it more relevant, I'm writing this in the heat of presidential campaigning season, 2020: Biden vs. Trump.

Imagine if I went to a democrat and told them to contribute $5 to Trump's campaign.

"Not in a million years would I support that racist misogynist!" would be the response.

But why? It's only five bucks. It won't make or break the election.

What we do with our resources reveals what we support.

Sure, your $5 won't help Trump win the election, yet the act of endorsing the opponent monetarily causes our stomach to churn. We don't just vote with our mouths and our votes, but with our wallets.

You alone are not responsible to shut down the trade of blood diamonds. You are, however, responsible for what you do with *your* money. You are in control of where you allocate it and how it is used. Will you use it to support violent African militias and human slavery, or will you opt to spend your thousands of dollars in a more human direction?

This is what Jesus meant when He said that the person who can be trusted with little can also be trusted with much, and to whom much is given, more will be given. Why? Because you are responsible for what you're given.

I, Ethan Renoe, am not responsible to shut down the diamond trade. God (hopefully) won't judge me because I didn't single-handedly put an end to it. That's a silly line of thinking, right?

So what *am* I responsible for? I'm responsible for what I *have* been given. I'm responsible for the $491 in my bank account and where it goes. So that means that when it's my turn to ponder a nice ring for my beloved, I will have to consider conscientiously throwing more money at the violent diamond trade, or choosing somewhere else to put my money for her ring.

See how you really *are* responsible for what you do with what you have? Even if it won't make a visible difference in the grand scheme of things, you can with a clear conscience say that you didn't contribute to a global system of oppression.

But why is the diamond issue (and many others like it) so bad? Is it even relevant anymore? It's 2021; hasn't the diamond trade been cleaned up by now?

Well, for starters, only 28% of diamonds are even verified to not support violence. That means that 72% of diamonds you see people wearing *may* have come from the hands of African children, enslaved by masters or overrun by terrorist groups. It doesn't mean 72% *did*, but it means they could have. And that's not a risk I'd like to take.

I'm not exaggerating; look into it for yourself.

And no, I will not purchase a lab-created or mine-verified diamond either. The issue with buying from the 28% of verified vendors is that it perpetuates the demand for *all* diamonds to continue to be hustled. Buying ethically sourced diamonds doesn't discriminate in how it creates a demand, and as long as that demand is there, people will also continue the *unethical* sourcing of them. People will still see the nice jewel on my wife's finger and want their own, or want to buy one for their woman.

The sooner we can end the tradition itself—the sooner diamonds become divorced from marriage, so to speak—the sooner demand will die down and the price will deflate, thus funding fewer militias, slaves, and child soldiers.

The tradition of giving a diamond to your beloved isn't even that old. Less than 100 years ago, DeBeers Diamond Co. launched the "Diamonds are forever" marketing campaign, thus marrying the costly stones to romance.

74 years ago, to be specific.
That's it.

I am not trying to upend some ancient, biblical principle of giving a diamond ring to your girl—I'm zooming out enough to see a marketing trend which we have been duped into buying. And we fall for it so hard that we happily overlook the oppression and murder of **millions** of human beings in order to have them. Westerners have bought this schema hook line and sinker to the point that I'm telling them millions of people have died for these stones **and they argue back!**

Because without a diamond…how can your love be forever?

And people think they're not sheep being manipulated by capitalist marketing. This is why I will never buy a diamond, even a fake one, because by keeping that tradition alive, in some small way, we perpetuate this system of slavery, oppression and violence.

anyways.

I'll get off that horse. I don't want to get bogged down in the messiness of this one subject, but rather want to address the bigger question: How can I possibly spend my money ethically, keeping all this in mind?

Does it mean boycotting everything except the tomatoes you grew in your back yard? I've presented my stance and as you can see, I heavily gravitate toward the research-before-purchase line of thought.

But I still have an iPhone which supposedly employs unethical factories in China.

But I'll still eat food I'm served without always verifying its origin.

Where is the axis of this balance? How do we decide where a purchase stops being ethical and starts being oppressive?

As mentioned above, the world is slowly waking up to the corruptness of its economic system, and this is a great thing. We are slowly turning toward supporting farmers in developing countries rather than exploiting them.

I have hope that this shift will continue to move toward sustainability rather than oppression. But in the mean time, maintaining that balance proves quite difficult. After all, for years, growing up in the USA, I never gave a second thought to my purchases or my waste—where it went after I was done with it.

If you're like me, you were born with the 'gift' of blindness. We were born with the option to look at the effect we were having on the world...or to look the other way. I hope that after reading this chapter, you're motivated to slowly educate yourself about the products you invest in. Look where your dollar is going, because for that, we *are* responsible. On the surface, it may feel like an innocent purchase of a diamond ring for your betrothed, but if even five of those dollars ended up funding Al-Qaeda (yes, that's real), then why would you want to support them?

There are some big items on which I've dug in my heels, diamonds being one of them. In other areas, like food and drinks, I do my best to look behind the curtain, but also have grace on products I'm unsure of. In other words, I'm less of a 'sustainability Nazi' for smaller items, despite doing my best to do diligent research on all things.

Clothing is somewhere in the middle, as we have plenty of options to choose from when it comes to where we buy our garments, and it's not too hard to do a quick Google search of your favorite retailers. And even though they're not perfect, I'll always support thrift stores.

One way you can never go wrong, though, is to simply reduce your consumption.

Reduce and reuse.
Buy fewer clothes.
Eat less sugar.

FIRE
HYDRANTS
&
FIGHT
CLUB

aptism:

The welcoming of the unholy into the realm of the holy.

The reclaiming of what God meant for good which man twisted downward into the intentions of the wicked.

The straightening of what was bent.

In the 1960's, firehoses were used on black protesters in the streets of Birmingham, Alabama. According to Diane McWhorter, the hoses were set to a pressure that would "peel the bark off trees," and turned on students who were peacefully protesting in the street. It ripped shirts off their bodies and pushed them over cars. It bruised them and broke their skin.

But what if this weapon could be used on the black community for something else?

The music video for Leon Bridges' song "River" shows the lives of several black people in America at various points in their lives. No context is given and no real storyline is presented, but one theme screams through the quiet lives of the people: we are all waiting for deliverance. In the mundanity of our day to day lives, we are looking for baptism. We are looking for cleansing and the rushing water of God to come and renew us.

It's for this reason that one little girl in the video makes her way down empty city streets, curiously glancing around her neighborhood. At the end, she rounds a corner and finds all the people from her community gathered together, singing and dancing in what looks like rain.

She gets closer and sees that it is not rain, but a firehose tapped into a hydrant which two people are aiming upward, letting the stream rain down on the neighbors.

This tool which was once weaponized against the black community is now being used to baptize them. The water which once punched holes in their flesh now washes away their sin and rejuvenates them.

It's an image of baptism. It's akin to the idea in Micah 4 where,

> They will beat their swords into plowshares
> and their spears into pruning hooks.
> Nation will not take up sword against nation,
> nor will they train for war anymore.

These tools which were once used to hurt other humans, other image bearers of the divine, are now used to harvest food and provide for their communities.

When there is no more war, there will be no more use for weapons. When there is no more racism, fire hydrants are used for baptism (and fighting fires) rather than oppressing protesters.

We don't live in a racism-free world yet, but the "River" music video paints a picture of what it could look like, what form baptism can take.

Baptism doesn't mean turning the hose back on those who used it against you; it means completely reimagining what the hose can be used for in the first place. A lot of human efforts to change systems end up using the same techniques as the former oppressors. Slaves rise up violently against their masters and become new masters to new slaves and repeat the cycle of violence.

They don't lift the yoke of slavery; they just trade places with their masters.

This happened to the nation of Israel in the Bible. They were constantly oppressed by nations surrounding them which were far larger and more powerful, but when given the opportunity, they would rise up and eviscerate their enemies. This doesn't seem to be what God meant in Genesis 12, when He told Abram that his offspring would be a blessing to all nations.

It's a theme repeated all throughout human history. It's the logical outcome of the film *Fight Club*—if a sequel were to be made, it would show the insanity of their plan.

(If you haven't seen *Fight Club*, this will spoil part of it.)

Tyler Durden (played by the devilishly handsome Brad Pitt) reduces all of modern culture to a pile of rubbish. First he blows holes in the lives we *think* we want, created by advertising and

IKEA catalogues, and instead, prompts men to return to their primal instincts of aggression and human connection.

This spreads like a cancer through the world until Durden hatches larger and larger plans, aiming not just to disrupt the commercial status quo, but the entire world economy. He plants bombs in every skyscraper housing the major credit card companies. No one will get hurt, he explains, because "the buildings are empty! Security, maintenance all our people!" The film concludes with the skyscrapers which house the major banks and credit card companies tumbling to the ground as vans filled with nitroglycerin explode in their basements.

Earlier in the film, Tyler explains his vision for a future world, one that may be less comfortable but is far more honest:

> In the world I see, you are stalking elk through the damp canyon forests around the ruins of Rockefeller Center. You'll wear leather clothes that will last you the rest of your life. You'll climb the wrist-thick kudzu vines that wrap the Sears Tower. And when you look down, you'll see tiny figures pounding corn, laying strips of venison on the empty car pool lane of some abandoned superhighway.

This nihilistic view of the world is flawed though. Tyler Durden's image of his ideal future which is a return to a tribal civilization may represent the world immediately after he implodes the American system, but what about a year later? What about a decade later?

People do not stay in their state of distress, but always rebuild and return to their vision of 'normal.' Tyler's destruction of the economy would indeed dislodge the current world elite, but it would also replace them with a new elite.

If Tyler Durden overthrows the old regime, he simply becomes the new one.

This is the problem with all stories in which the weaker, less powerful actors rise up and overthrow a corrupt power system. They employ the same means which once enslaved them, resulting in a new elite which becomes just as corrupt and oppressive.

This is one of the logical flaws in Marx's vision of Communism. One stage on the path to the enlightened state is called the Dictatorship of the Proletariat, or in layman's terms, the Rule of the Poor. After a violent upheaval of a powerful governmental system, there is an intermediate, transitionary stage in which the poor rule over the rich in order to transition into the communistic state, dispersing the wealth, power, and labor equally among the people.

This approach to political power has never worked...Why? Because when humans get a taste of power and wealth, they become the same corrupt, oppressive regime as the one they just unseated. The Dictatorship of the Proletariat doesn't remain in this stage for long, because, well, the proletariat is no longer the proletariat...they have become the new elite.

As satisfying as Quentin Tarantino's "rewritten history" films are to watch, they share this same flaw. The most notable are

Django Unchained and *Inglourious Basterds*, in which black slaves rise up against their white masters, and Jews rise up against Nazis, respectively. The use of violence against their oppressors doesn't do anything to change (baptize) the world and rid it of evil. Instead, it perpetuates the cycle. The only thing that has changed is who holds the whip.

This is why baptism is so needed.

The reverend Martin Luther King Jr. knew this, which is why he implored his followers not to raise arms against the corrupt American system in which they lived, but to peacefully fight for equality. He led one of the world's most significant campaigns for change in history without firing a gun or lifting a blade. And what did it do? It led to lasting change on the face of America which—although far from perfect—has come a long way from the early 1900's thanks to their nonviolent movement.

&

Baptism is a third option.

When faced with a vitriolic, baited question, Jesus rarely picked a side, but presented a surprising new option. We often get so wrapped up inside the dichotomy that is presented to us by the media that we forget that we ourselves have imagination; we have the ability to conceive of new solutions and stances.

Picture a bikini-clad model on the cover of *Sports Illustrated*. Actually, don't picture her. You know what I mean.

The world presents this image to us and we are meant to ingest it and think, *Dang! She's so sexy! Let me soak up every inch of this body and lust over the sexual objet before me.*

The Christian response, or at least the one I grew up with, was to "Bounce Your Eyes." Look away from her immediately. Don't linger on this image, because you will fall into temptation and sin.

What I realized recently is that both of these options treat the woman on the cover more like an object than a human. The publishers treat her as a sexy goddess, elevating her beyond the stature of a normal person. The American church vilifies her, saying 'Look away from that, *it's BAD!*"

Neither one sees that model as God sees her.

Let's think about two monks standing on the sidewalk in New York City.

A hooker walks by them in skimpy shorts and a bra. One monk jerks his vision away from her and looks the other way. A moment later he looks at his friend, who is still staring at the woman, and rebukes him.

"Brother! Why are you looking at something so *unclean*!?"

He sees a tear in his friend's eye as he continues staring at the prostitute. He didn't see some*thing* bad, but a human. And determining which humans are good and which are bad is an impossible and foolish task.

Which monk was more pure? Perhaps both responded appropriately, but the monk with the purer vision was the one who could look at the woman, see through the sexy attire, and see a little, wounded girl instead. He could see someone hurting, looking for love, and in need of grace.

The church typically falls into two camps: Embrace the cultural flow and adapt (Everything is permissible! Go for it! God accepts everything you do!), or plug our ears and avert our eyes. We can bury our heads in the sand and effectively bury our witness to the world. As long as we dwell in either of these camps, we are playing by the rules of the world. We are conceding that they have the arena and we'll play within *their* bounds.

What if we could look at the Sports Illustrated cover and see a woman made in the image of God, rather than a sexy object... or a BAD person? This would be a truly revolutionary approach to the sexual conversation—humanizing people. The world, for all its talk of sexual liberation, still treats that model more like a sexual object than a person. And if we simply bounce our vision away from her, we do too.

The third option here is to baptize our eyes. To see every person we see, not as sexual objects, bad people, banging bodies, or wicked seductresses; but as brothers and sisters beloved by God.

&

The music video for "River" reflects this power because it resists the urge to turn the hose back on the ones who once sprayed them, but to turn it upward, letting the water rain down in a flood of baptism, of new life.

Think about how we can expand this notion of baptism into multiple arenas of our lives—areas where we may still be thinking in terms of *them* versus *us*.

If someone has been oppressing you, your instinct is to spray the hose back at them. And those are the only possible two ways to see the situation.

You merely think of ways to get them back, to hurt them the way they've hurt you. There could not possibly be another use for the firehose. This is a black and white way of thinking. It lacks imagination and seems to be the opposite of the God I believe in—a God who is creative and progressive. A God who gets excited to make things new and find new ways to flourish.

What situations in your life need to be 'baptized'?

What areas need a creative touch in order to flourish into fitful life before being dragged down into a cycle of violent death?

&

We saw this outdated way of thinking unfold recently in the wake of the tragic murder of George Floyd. People were rightly outraged at the situation and our country erupted into violent protest. Buildings were destroyed, property was ruined, and worst of all, more people died as a result. Hundreds more were injured.

The country was quick to polarize into two warring factions: either you were on the side of the violent protesters, or you were a racist who supported the killing of George Floyd.

For weeks it seemed like there was no middle ground. Anyone who opened their mouth trying to find a balanced center was quickly ripped apart on social media by one or both sides. Both sides became the digital police of what language you could and couldn't use.

It was one of the least 'balanced' periods I've ever witnessed.

Were police wrong to use deadly force on George Floyd? Yes. Were the rioters wrong to loot and destroy property? Yes.

But a balanced mindset was scarcely seen online as people were forced toward supporting one side or the other. It also became evident (as it always does) that most people posting about the events were undereducated and overly emotional. Most of us gravitate toward news sources which promote ideas we already believe to be true and agree with, so rather than striving toward balanced understanding of situations, we amplify the opinions of the side we agree with.

Unlike the marches led by Luther King Jr., these protests were violent and angry. They sought to destroy, just as the police had destroyed. They used the same method as the oppressor, and what happened? Only further destruction. If Christians are to be a source of light and healing to the world, we cannot fight the way the world fights; we cannot polarize and angrily yell with our ears plugged the way the world does.

When we are polarized by one extreme or another, not only are we often just being manipulated by larger forces like news, movies, celebrities, et al., but we are playing directly into the hand of the enemy. Whatever you believe about satan or demons, if there is some force working to destroy humans, it starts winning when we pick sides and treat our fellow citizens as hostiles.

This is exactly what Paul was trying to prevent in Ephesians 6 when he wrote that "our struggle is not against flesh and blood, but against the rulers, against the authorities, against the powers of this dark world and against the spiritual forces of evil in the heavenly realms."

If other humans are ultimately the enemy, then yes, choose your side carefully and set out to destroy the other. But if there is something larger at work; if there are unseen forces using our own power against us; if fellow humans are *not* the enemy, then we need to reevaluate how we treat those we disagree with.

&

A few years ago I finally realized how there can be such different beliefs held by those who disagree with one another. One side does not want to hurt people while the other is trying to protect them—that's what one side or the other will what you to think, but it doesn't accurately reflect society's thought.

In American politics for instance, Republicans would have you believe that Democrats are out to destroy humanity by killing babies and shuttering churches. Democrats try their best to paint Republicans as outdated troglodytes who are stupid and uneducated.

I recently talked with someone who would lean heavily to the left. I began to say something about conservatives, and she cut me off with: "The difference is that progressive people want what's best for the world, while conservatives only want what's best for them and their immediate family."

I thought to myself, *what a fitting summation of why the world is so divided.* This embodied the very closed-eared mindset which leads to violence and distrust on either side. If you're starting with the presupposition that your antagonist is selfish, myopic, uneducated, and so on, you will never be able to converse with them; you'll only be able to talk down to them... and think you're winning.

Remember, however, that this goes both ways—conservatives have just as many caricatures of liberals which may or may not be true at an individual level.

What is important to remember is this:

People on both sides of an issue likely want what is best for them, their family, and their community. They are working toward *their vision* of human flourishing.

No, your political rivals are not the reincarnation of Hitler set on annihilating mankind. Nor are they the antichrist. They likely want all humans to flourish (including you). The two of you simply have different ideas of how to get there, and of what 'flourishing' looks like.

Keeping this in mind should help tame the vitriol in your next political conversation. If you can assume that your verbal sparring partner wants what's best for the world—as you do— you should be able to treat them with more dignity and respect, rather than anger and condescension. Pretend like you're working together to solve a problem rather than fighting a rival faction for control of the crown.

(Also remember that Facebook arguments won't change anyone's mind, nor will they overturn rancid power structures.)

Is it possible to baptize the conversations you have on social media?

Rather than turning the verbal firehose on those you disagree with, what would it look like to turn a disagreement into creative energy which unites people and moves us forward?

What would that look like?

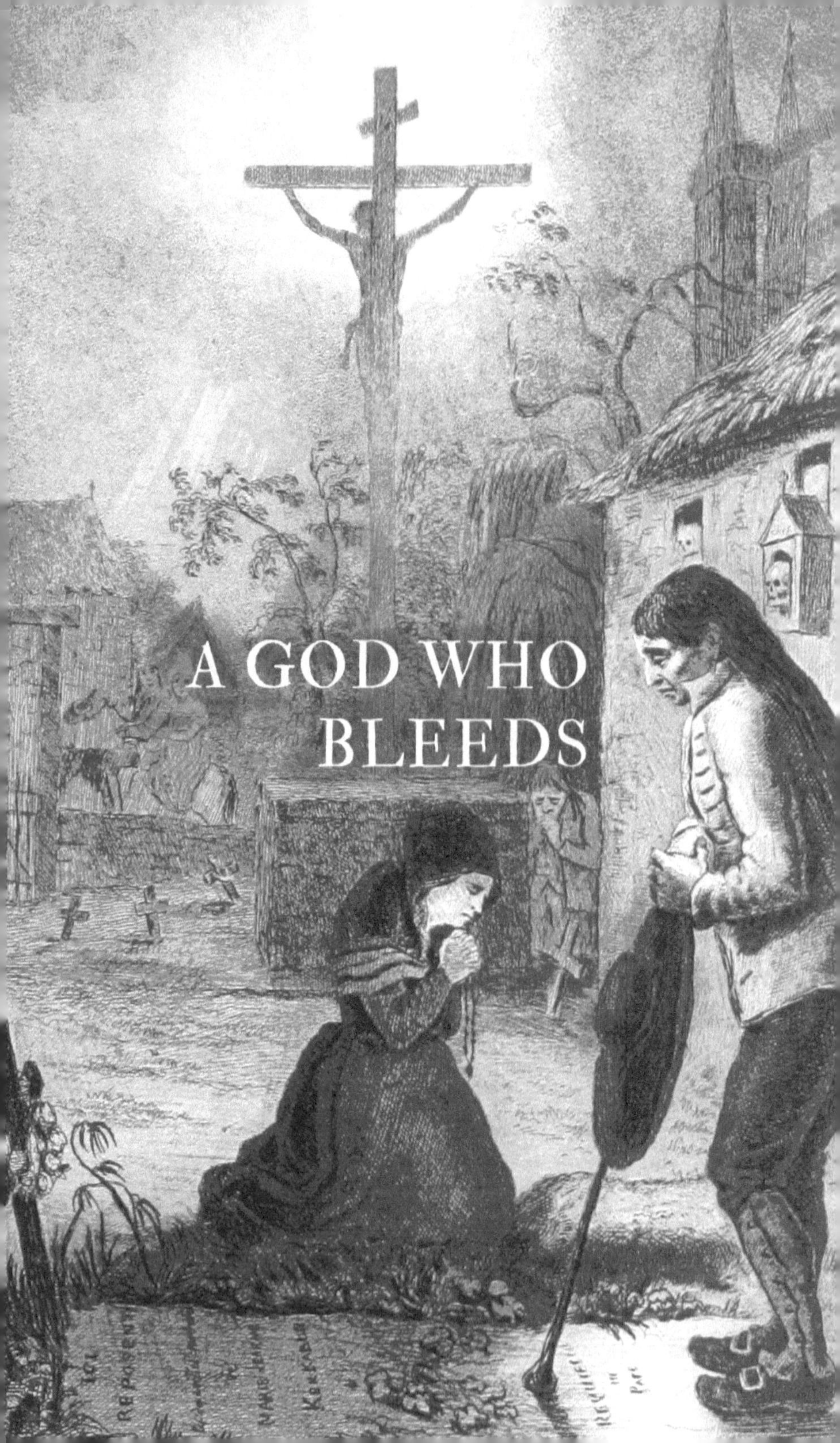

A GOD WHO BLEEDS

—Silent Planet, "XX (City Grave)"

he end of all things will be a Terrence Malick film: A hazy collection of colors, emotions and sweeping shots of nature. At your best, you will be gathered atop a mountain, soaking in the scenery and mesmerized by the breadth of the land, from the horizon down to your toes.

Like the toes which once dripped crimson blood from the midpoint of a Roman crucifix, yours are not that different. All accounted for, you should have ten—five per foot—and they can all bend in one direction, curling like wild french fries beside your happy meal. Happy heel.

There is debate as to how exactly Roman crucifixions were carried out, particularly that of Jesus of Nazareth. Did they use nails or only rope? Did Christ carry both beams of His cross up the hill, or just the horizontal crossbeam? Were His feet pierced with one nail through the top of His feet, or the more ergonomically correct position of one foot on either side of the post with the nail through the side of the heel, under the ankle?

I believe that whatever position the Messiah was in, He was affixed there for hours.

In real time,

in human history.

Not in the abstract myths we often conjure up as we read the Bible—often thinking of it in terms of lofty, theological imagination more than actual history and time and place and Rome and Nazareth and water and poop and blood.

These are real things.

This is the way God interacts with humans.

Jesus is not a theological quandary, but a man who, at one point in history, yet forever, was/is pinned to a tree, accursed.

"Anyone hung on a tree is under God's curse."
  -God, Deuteronomy 21:32, roughly 1350 BC

"Forgive them, for they know not what they're doing."
  -God, being hung on a tree, roughly 36 AD

I daily forget the reality of Jesus, the man, the carpenter from Galilee. I don't spend enough time meditating on the fact that God entered INTO humanity, and the world still hasn't recovered. We have modern-day plagues which wipe us out by the thousands, and we ask God why He sits up in heaven, looking down on our misery.

The same God we ripped the back off of, the way you open up the hood of your car to see what's going on inside.

"How does my car work?" I've asked mechanics working on my vehicle. They point to tubes and switches and levers.

"How does God work?" you may have asked the Roman centurions peeling the skin off his scapulas.

"Well," they reply, "so far He bleeds just like every other crook."

"We've cracked Him open…feel free to take a look inside."

The scholars may piece together their theology of salvation the way a mechanic constructs a combustion engine: lots of moving parts which operate *just so*, and as long as each of the units follows the basic rules of physics, everything will go on swimmingly.

How does God piece together salvation? Look at the life of Jesus, the carpenter from the armpit of Rome: With countless meals in the homes of prostitutes, tax collectors, and 'sinners.'

As if there were people here who are not 'sinners.'

How does Jesus piece together salvation? With buckets of His own blood. And now we're back to the toes of the Divine. The moment God dripped His own blood from almighty toes onto the dirt below, the salvific work was complete.

Yesterday a 14-year-old took his own life here in Colorado. His parents have been friends with mine for decades. What do we do with such pain? I began slamming this post out of my keyboard as an attempt to figure it out, and keep coming back to nothing else but Jesus on the cross: an image to which we have become desensitized. A symbol we sling around our necks as a fashion statement, as if God Himself were not being wrenched apart; each of His molecules shuddering under the weight of His suffering.

Does God know our pain?
The Bible tells me so.

It tells me that I cling to a God who doesn't just *know* it, but has experienced it. The way you can read a hundred books about losing a child but you know nothing until it happens to you.

His skin couldn't hold back its blood, even before the torture began. In the Garden of Gethsemane, His trepidation squeezed the blood from its capillaries before the execution even began.

When someone is crucified, they die of asphyxiation. They can't breathe. Imagine being drowned in air, but not because you're underwater, but because you can't push yourself up—on the nails in your feet—to get a breath. And your skin has mostly been stripped away, and you're nailed to a tree.

If the victim wouldn't die quickly enough, Romans would either break their legs so they could no longer push themselves up, or light a fire at the foot of the cross so they suffocated in the smoke.

800 years before Jesus found Himself on Golgotha, the psalmist predicted that none of His bones would be broken. Sure enough, in 36 AD, Jesus breathed His last before the guards had to come by and shatter His tibias. Perhaps we've become too numb to the language of crucifixion, which is why I'm attempting to breathe some new air into the lungs of our imagination.

Jesus suffocated to death.

He tried to bring oxygen into His lungs, but reached a point where His body couldn't accommodate it.

It's interesting how today we have riots and protests when people are suffocated to death, but we take the suffocation of Christ for granted. I imagine Him pushing Himself up on the ankle-nails and groaning "I can't breathe." Seems like even today, Christ continues to identify more with the weak, oppressed victim than the powerful victor.

Crucifixion was such a painful way to die, in fact, that they had to coin a new term to capture it. *Ex* is Latin for "out of," and *cruc* is Latin for "cross." When something is *excruciating*, it is so painful that it could only come out of the cross.

Your stubbed toe is not excruciating.

Losing your son to suicide might be.

The tradition of carrying your own death machine (as typified in the story of Abram making his son Isaac carry the wood for his own sacrifice up Mount Moriah) was a built-in part of the process. Not only is crucifixion painful beyond comprehension, but it was humiliating. The victim was stripped naked, flogged (skin ripped off of most of the body), and then forced to carry their death machine through public areas—still naked. Then they were splayed to the beams and left to die—still naked.

Jesus was likely *not* exempt from this practice. Jesus was not only tortured, but humiliated. You think you are too shameful to stand in the presence of God? Fortunately for us, Jesus knows shame.

Not only did He absolve us of our sins, suffering in the place we deserved, but He absorbed our shame as well, when He was paraded nude across town and displayed before all of the onlookers. God doesn't only meet us in our pain, but in our deepest of shames—perhaps a place which is harder for us to fathom finding God in. Or being found by Him.

And in the midst of these 'evil days,' that brings a bit of comfort: knowing we're not alone, but surrounded by a God who works in all things, knows all things—from experience, not from reading about it—and has bled for all things.

That's the only type of God who can truly make

all

things

new.

&

The God who bleeds; the God who makes the world new, doesn't do it in a sanitized, G-rated way. He is not worried about such protections.

'Clean' can mean a lot of things. First and foremost, it's a state of being orderly and untainted by unwanted dirt, clutter, dust, mess, and so on.

For the most part, our American Christianity is squeaky-clean. Our understanding of the Bible is squeaky-clean.

C.S. Lewis said of Aslan the lion, who represents God, "Of course he's not safe…but he's good."

The American church, especially Christian media, may or may not be good…but it's safe.

The issue with this is that the Bible is anything but squeaky-clean, and the world in which we live (including our own lives) are far from clean. This seems to be a simple summation of why so many people struggle to rectify being a Christian when they look at the world around them, the lives of Christians around them, and their own lives.

We sanitize our faith to the point that is it ineffective, like bleaching yogurt because it has some bacteria in it (which is the whole point…).

Perhaps a better metaphor is our own gut health. I recently began learning about gut health and how our entire immune system is basically the 'good' bacteria in our stomachs. I grew up thinking that all bacteria were 'bad,' and we should just kill them. I've learned the hard way that, if you kill all the bacteria in your body with an antibiotic grenade, you will have no immune defense and will get sick constantly.

We essentially do the same thing with the world, with the Bible. Welp, this doesn't fit into my worldview as 'good' so it can't be from God. Gotta sanitize this and that…Christians can only make G-rated movies, etc.

Forcing our faith through such a strainer creates a series of impossible dichotomies for us to answer for. Like why are there X-rated parts of the Bible? Well…because there are X-rated parts of the world and they are not hidden from the eyes of God.

You may have grown up under Veggie Tales and thought that the siege of Jericho involved slushies being thrown and Monty Python-esque taunts exchanged, rather than violence and the slaughter of women and children. I'm a big fan of Veggie Tales for the record…for kids. But when it's time to move from milk to meat in our faith, that means cultivating a more nuanced, more sophisticated and complicated understanding of the Bible and how, exactly, it plugs into the world around us.

A G-rated religion has nothing to say to an X-rated world.

I don't think I've ever met a Christian who was terrified of the world who was effective at reaching it. By that, I mean those people who only watch G-rated films, cite selected Bible verses to prove their points, and have never set foot in a bar/club/bad part of town.

I observed a painful image of irony yesterday. I was in a coffee shop and saw a dude in his early 20's, completely decked out in Christian garb. His hat was from a popular Christian TV show, his t-shirt said something witty about Jesus, and he had the bracelets. All of the bracelets.

The irony, I realized, is that he is adamantly trying to tell the world he's a Christian. I have to commend him for his boldness —that deserves some credit for sure. However, I can't help but wonder how effective his message is at bringing people into the fold; how many people does his wardrobe rope into the kingdom of God?

Looking at this kid, I realized that the harder you try to declare your own faith to the world, the less the world is interested. We (myself included...the tacky Christian apparel is a major turn off even to a fellow believer) look at him and think that he's a bit out of pace with the rest of the culture; he's not exactly in touch with the conversations happening around him, on a societal scale.

This sheltered homeschool type of Christian who is scared of tattoos and gay people, which is often how our faith looks to the outsider. It's embarrassing. The most effective Christians are those like Father Greg Boyle (founder of Homeboy Industries, which ministers to hundreds of former gang members. I cannot recommend his book *Tattoos on the Heart* highly enough!) who don't fear the dark bits of the world, but dive on into them, shedding light and hope where there was none.

It makes me chuckle when people ask *how a Christian could watch a horror film*, as if it was the most sinful genre.

As if it were more sinful than a licentious episode of Friends where the harmless protagonists sleep around daily—fun!

As if the Bible wasn't chock-full of horror tales of its own.

Some of the most prominent Christians in Hollywood made *The Conjuring* films, not just to make a quality horror flick, but to be evangelistic in reminding people about the power of the spiritual realm. And they were pretty successful. This is what it looks like for Christians to relay spiritual truths to a violent, not-clean world without sacrificing quality or Christian integrity (the first *Conjuring* film was rated R, not for violence, language, or sex, but purely for terror. The demonstrated that you don't need graphic excess to make a quality, spooky flick).

Addressing this in my own faith also means that I have to admit that 'my house is not in order.' By that, I mean my system of theology still has a hefty amount of clutter and nooks with which I am unfamiliar. I have a lot of questions which will likely remain unanswered until death, and there are two ways to approach this: pretend I know the answers/force some answer upon those questions which would inevitably do them some injustice, or become alright with a little mystery, with a little mess.

American Christianity tends to pretend it has all the answers; that its structures and systems are secure and faultless, that you can *know it all* about God.

As someone who has worked behind the scenes of this church-machine for over a decade, I can tell you that your pastors don't know all the answers. If they never answer 'I don't know' to at least some of your questions, they are either deceiving themselves or you.

There are no airtight pistons in this mechanism.

This scares many people.

It scares me.

The comfort we can take in this is that Jesus Himself doesn't shy away from our questions and doubts, from the areas where our theology seems to disconnect. When Thomas expressed some doubts about Christ's resurrection, Jesus didn't scold him with a line about getting his faith in order; He let Tom touch the nailholes in His hands. He submitted divine omniscience to human investigation, a hungry lack of faith.

We may have to wait a little longer to stick our pinkies into the divine wounds, but I like to think Jesus will still let us if we need to. I think He's less like the strict Catholic nuns scolding us for straying from the path of perfect faith, and more like, well, Jesus letting Thomas touch His hands. (speaking of unclean, think about putting your finger in a 3-day-old nail wound…).

No, the Bible is not clean by any sense of the word. It is not devoid of violence, sex, prostitutes, and a little confusion.

The world is not a clean place.

Your life is not a clean life.

And that's exactly how it should be.

One of my favorite Bible verses is the second one. I mean the second verse in the entire Bible, before God has dug His hands in to the chaos of the prediluvian world and made it into something orderly and functional.

> *Now the earth was formless and empty, darkness was over the surface of the deep, and the Spirit of God was hovering over the waters.*

Two Hebrew words:

Tohu-va-vohu: The most fun to say out loud. Try it. It means 'wild and waste,' or chaos. Or mess.

Rahap: It means hovering. This verse is used in one other place in the Bible to describe a mother bird flapping her wings over her babies in the nest, inviting them to come and take flight; come and rise up.

Imagine this picture: The Spirit of God as a mother bird, calling the mess of the world to rise up and take form; to come to life. She flaps almighty wings over the chaotic waters because she knows exactly what it's capable of, what it can become.

You can almost hear the Spirit calling, *"Rise up, you can do it! Come on! Take flight! Come to life!"*

This is the first image we get of God's Spirit in the Bible—the image of a motherly bird, calling the world to take flight. To rise up. I like to believe this same Spirit is hovering over you and I today, looking at the mess and chaos of our lives and saying, "Come on…you can do it. Rise up."

The Spirit *rahaps* over the *tohu-va-vohu* of our lives still today.
The Spirit calls our world to new life.
This is a message the world needs to hear, the voice of a

mother calling to her young, encouraging us to rise out of the chaos and into vibrant, confident life.

It seems like God likes things that are a little less than perfect, a little chaotic…otherwise, He'd have no work to do.

God still hovers today.
The Spirit isn't scared of the mess of your life.
The Spirit doesn't shy away from the chaos of our world.

&

You've definitely heard it in the songs. Take for instance The Killers, who make Jesus seem like a guy you'd like to bring home to mom & dad:

> *He doesn't look a thing like Jesus*
> *but he talks like a gentleman*
> *like you imagined when you were young*

Think about it for a second…how closely does this line up with the Jesus presented to us in the Bible?

-He's homeless.

-He is relatively ugly.

-He's poor—to the point that women are traveling with & supporting Him. (But He always pays His taxes…sometimes with coins that pop out of fish mouths)

-He sometimes loses His cool and flips over tables in a fit of rage.

-He is constantly, publicly cursing all the pastors in your town whom the rest of the community reveres.

-etc.

Would you really want to bring Him home to ma & pa?

How about another example, this one from Tom Petty regarding the followers of Jesus:

> *She's a good girl, loves her mamma.*
> *Loves Jesus, and America too.*

Same idea. How do we know she's a good girl? Well, because she loves Jesus and 'merica (but we'll ignore that association for now).

It's ironic because the most radical, dedicated Christ followers I know are not necessarily what the world would consider nice, quiet folks like the ones Petty refers to. They're usually the ones who have sold their homes or belongings and live with the poorest of the poor. Or the ones people think are drug addicts because they often spout off prophetic rants or just seem a little crazy in the head.

Rich Mullins went barefoot everywhere, didn't have a home, and gave the vast majority of his money to Native Americans.

Garrett Russell, heavy metal vocalist for Silent Planet, also never wears shoes and, after screaming at the crowd from the stage for an hour, jumps down afterward and tells all his punk rocker, tattooed fans that they're loved and hugs them. He makes time for people—something that's significant to a population that often doesn't receive enough time or love.

Mother Teresa had disgusting feet because she dug through each shoe donation box and pulled out the worst possible pair for herself. "No one is allowed to wear worse shoes than me," she would say.

My friend Josh would always scream at the top of his lungs when he saw me in the streets of Chicago, even from three blocks away, "HEY ETHAN! I LOVE YOU MAN! PRAISE GOD MAN!" Everyone on those three blocks heard, then looked at him and then at me. He's a bit wild and unpredictable, not unlike John the Baptist. Josh and his wife sold all their things and moved to Cambodia a few years ago, where they work with some of the poorest people in the world.

Are these the type of people who come to mind when you hear "Free Falling"? Are these nutjobs the tame Jesus lovers Tom Petty was referring to?

Have we replaced the Jesus of the Bible with some soft, mushy milquetoast? Do we imagine a lamb-hugging dude (which... never happened in the Bible) whose greatest characteristic is that He's really nice?

If that's all Christianity can cough up in regards to its central figure, I'd want nothing to do with it. Nor would most guys I know. Probably most women, for that matter.

What's more, if Jesus is nothing more than nice, that means His followers need to do nothing more than be nice. Is that all the kingdom is about? Is that why I got "your kingdom come" tattooed over my heart, just to remind myself to be more nice?

Niceness alone won't save the world.
Niceness won't overthrow the Third Reich, dole out justice for sex traffickers, or fix systemic racism.

Yet this caricature of Christ has sunk so deeply into our collective subconscious that we blindly accept these references to Nice Guy Jesus without a second thought. Then, when we do get around to cracking our Bibles open, we're surprised that He sometimes says mean things,
that He gets pretty heated and goes nuts,
that He won't let go of this idea that He is actually…God,
that He comes a second time wearing a robe drenched in blood,
that He looks at the religious teachers of His time and basically says f— you. (Matthew 23)

Wait a minute…I thought Jesus was nice!

lol.

Are you reading the Bible through the tainted lens of our culture, or are you reading the Bible as it is? Are you letting Jesus be who He is, as presented in the Bible, or have you also fallen prey to this strange character known as Nice Guy Jesus?

Granted, there are a myriad weird presentations of Jesus in mainstream media. There's Kanye West's Prosperity Jesus ("Man how'd you get so much favor on your side?/ Accept Him as your Lord and Savior, I replied"), or Family Guy's straight-up weird manifestation who sometimes appears in random episodes.

Perhaps some of the more accurate depictions of the Carpenter from Nazareth come from people earnestly seeking answers to the world's most complex questions. Noah Gundersen asked Him through heartrending vibrato,

> Jesus, Jesus, could you tell me what the problem is
> With the world and all the people in it? …
> Jesus, Jesus, there are those that say they love you
> But they have treated me so goddamn mean…
>
> If all the heathens burn in hell,
> do all their children burn as well?
> What about the Muslims and the gays
> and the unwed mothers?
> What about me and all my friends?
> Are we all sinners if we sin?
> Does it even matter in the end if we're unhappy?

More haunting questions are asked by Brand New in their song "Jesus":

> Well, Jesus Christ, I'm not scared to die
> I'm a little bit scared of what comes after
> Do I get the gold chariot?
> Do I float through the ceiling?
> Do I divide and fall apart?
> And at the gates does Thomas ask to see my hands?

The bottom line here is that, if you get your theology (or your Christology) from pop songs, TV shows, or basically anything but the Bible itself, you'll end up with an inaccurate picture of who Jesus is and what He came to do. You'll also get a wide spread of different Jesuses—Weird, nice, nerdy, judgy, goofy... If it's been a while since you've opened the gospels for yourself, you may be surprised at the Jesus you find.

He will not be just nice, nor will He be a tormenting monster trying to throw all the gay people into hell. You'll find a Jesus who snaps when people are thinking too small of God and His kingdom, but one who is also the friend of prostitutes and other outcasts.

He's not just any one of those things either; He is a lot of things.

He is complex, and perhaps this is why every culture, especially ours, has such a hard time categorizing Him. Sadly, evangelicalism seems to have pigeon-holed Him as just a **super nice guy**, most likely because this is a safe bet, and if there's anything we know about evangelical culture, it's that it's safe. (Maybe because people get banned when they're edgy or just use the word 'penis.' Seriously. Google it.)

The Jesus of the Bible is far more interesting (and...true) than any of these mainstream iterations of Him. May we familiarize ourselves with Him so much that we can identify fallacies in misrepresentations, but also see truth wherever it may exist.

As Calvin said,
may we seek Christ purely for the joy of seeking Christ.

My soul is restless till it rests in thee.

—Augustine

WHO THE
LITERAL
F
IS
JESUS

t felt like there was a lump in my lung today on my run. It was most assuredly the normal out-of-breath-ness that comes when you're not exercising the way you should, you feel half-sick, and you start running again. And that's exactly what I was doing—getting back into the habit of my summer runs.

However, with the terror of an invisible and imminent virus floating around,

mixed with my doctor telling me I had cancer a few months ago,

mixed with the fact that I am still sick after 19 months,

tossed in with grief over a local boy who took his own life last week,

it felt like a lot more than a mere burning in my lungs.

Most 28-year-olds believe they're not even close to the halfway point of their lives. I, however, need to continually remind myself that I probably have over half of my own life left.

Jesus says to Lazarus, "this sickness will not end in death," and what does Lazarus go and do?

Die.

Will my sickness end in death? I can't help but wonder if the answer is always going to be no, even after I die.

Because no one born of the Spirit ever really dies...do they?

I don't know what it all means, and I'm not yet convinced it's not all ancient Sanskrit gibberish, but I really want to believe that the man Jesus Christ was as wonderful as I see Him being: A man who critiques toxic power structures, partly those of the political world, but more the religious ones.

A man who gives the finger to the *holier than thou* judges and breaks bread with the sinners.

A man who kills death.

What do you do with a man like that?

Reading through the gospels slowly has been a huge boon in disguise to me in this season. A season filled with doubt — and don't go ooing and ahhing, because doubt, when truly experienced, feels like the thin shelf on which you perched (we will name it 'paradigm' or 'metaphysic') is being shattered and you have no idea what form of existence lies beneath this shelf.

The world might not be the same after this moment, and you definitely will not.

Is it a river running wild as Semuc Champey in Guatemala, waiting to suck you into an underground vortex? Or is it something more sinister—perhaps the one thing more chaotic than water: fire?

That, after all, is what Christians have taught since Dante's Inferno in the 1200's. Abandon, or even question your faith and you might go to that place where you get poked by little devils while dangling from your ankles for eternity.

Is this your image of hell?

Or is it the Dutch painters' from the Late Middle Ages?

I often tell people (Christians, specifically) that 60% of what you believe about the afterlife comes from Dante, 20% from modern cultural staples like *Bruce Almighty*, or *The Good Place*, and maybe 20% is from the Bible. We subconsciously absorb these images and unwittingly adopt them as truth, without really returning to the Bible—something we claim is true and authoritative—and holding them up to it.

The whole idea of the seven circles of hell: Bible or Dante?

If you're a real nerd like me, you may say, "Well, the seven circles are based on the seven deadly sins, so…"

Fun fact: The seven deadly sins aren't in the Bible either.

Mainstream media has a way of seeping into our minds in such a subtle way that we forget what we read where—was that in the Bible or did we see it in an ad on the wall of the subway? Are the seven deadly sins mentioned in Proverbs, or did the film *Se7en* just want us to think that so we attach some spooky religious notions to the premise?

Where do you get your information?

That is perhaps the best question to ask yourself on a regular basis, about anything. Examine why you think the things you do; look at where your thoughts and mental images came from. You may be surprised.

Does God want to tie you up and poke you for eternity, or would he rather pull you apart limb by limb, like in the Renaissance paintings?

Or is it neither, as we will neither drown nor burn, because God doesn't want those things for us?

Because this sickness will not end in death.

This death will not end in death.

My lungs burned as the silky, sexy sunlight slid downward, shooting off pink and blue confetti cannons into the Colorado sky, but all I could think about was what to do with my remaining minutes of life on this side of the casket.

Moreover, how would I ensure that the skirt-wearing Egyptian guard dog gods would grant me safe passage to a pleasant afterlife? How do we know the Hebrews got it right, not the Egyptians? Or maybe the Hittites were the ones with the correct answer to the Great Mystery, but King David wiped them out and here we are, trusting a mentally ill Carpenter from Galilee who says His forefather did the right thing…

See what I'm saying?

History and scriptures are written by winners and passed down by a lot of scared people who are hoping that the straw they grasped was the right one.

The thing I can't escape, however, is Jesus.
The man.
The human.
The one who used the bathroom and slept in the desert and probably got sand in His cheeks.

Hear me out—it's not just Christianese mumbo-jumbo, I promise. Joseph Smith and Muhammad invented the same religion (if you don't believe me, look into it: they both promoted polygamy in a monogamous culture; added to the Bible, began wars with surrounding religions, claimed to meet an angel in private who gave them sacred scriptures which no one else ever saw...the list goes on), and it's garbage. Their messages; the 'truths' they preached were utter manmade nonsense.

Actual feces.
On the level of Harry Potter, but less entertaining.

Joseph and Mo were men.
They died and stayed that way.

The Buddha and Dalai Lama and Ghandi were legit—

(more legit than any American pastor today who wears thousand dollar clothes and preaches new garbage messages. I've heard more accurate truths creep out of my bum after too many chalupas. "I hate, I despise your religious festivals," says

God in Amos 5, "your assemblies are a stench to me…You have lifted up the shrine of your king, the pedestal of your idols, the star of your god—which you made for yourselves.")

—but Buddha, Dalai Lama and Ghandi were not gods. They were also men who died.

Also thrown into the mix is the cultural environment in which these manmade religions took root: They reflect the culture and ethics of the people groups they represent. Mormonism is undeniably a white, American religion, no question about it.

Islam reflects the Medina of Muhammad's youth and doesn't easily bend its message for those outside the Middle Eastern (or Arabic-speaking) world. I mean, one of the five pillars is to go on a pilgrimage to Mecca. Sucks to be handicapped or unable to travel internationally if you're a Muslim. You also must read and recite it only in Arabic. So. lol.

Jesus, however, deconstructs the human, lawful elements of His own religion of Judaism and frees people from the burden of lifting themselves into heaven by following the Code. He embodies, rather than man striving to get to God, God striving to get to man. Since the first sin in Genesis 3, God's response to screwed-up humans has not been to cut them off, but to move toward them. God goes into the garden after the fruit is eaten, *looking for* Adam and Eve. This idea of God moving toward us is perhaps the central theme of the Bible, and its crescendo is in the person of Christ.

God pursued men by becoming one.

Our limited, finite brains can only comprehend so much about the thoughts of the divine, but maybe by looking backward, using history's hindsight, we can actually see the brilliance of how Jesus worked things out in the timeline, and maybe even get a better sense of what the heck God is doing in the world today.

Historically, there is no point in time to which His coming could have been better-suited. The gospel took advantage of the Roman road system which spanned Africa, Europe AND Asia, and used the common, global languages—Latin and Greek—to communicate it. The timing in the belt of history is just too perfect.

Ask yourself—as I am while writing this—

"If I were God (crazy thought, I know, but follow me, as this line of logic has helped me out). If I were some almighty, omnipotent, omniscient Being, and I wanted to interact with humans, how would I do it? When would I do it?" Purely strategically speaking, of course.

And what would I be for/against? Or, what would my message be?

Here's my thought process:

Well, I would first need to show people that no power structures—political, religious, economic, or otherwise—can affect Me, God.

I would humiliate people who thought they were gods and lift up people who felt sub-human.

Because of people's fickle, unbelieving hearts, I would need to show them a few tricks just to wow them with my powers.
Show them I'm really God after all.

Then I would show them two things: Their standard and mine. How much they should sacrifice for one another...Why? Because God Himself is willing to sacrifice for them, to maintain relationship.

It wouldn't be pretty.

Jesus somehow meets my expectations and defies them simultaneously. When I really think about it, it is nearly impossible for me to talk myself away from Him because of the love He shows and the truth He speaks.

Not because I want to—because there are a lot of Christians in the world I'd rather not associate myself with. See above, re: rich, famous pastors.

Not because it's popular.

Not because I believe it easily all the time.

Not because it makes scientific sense.

Not because it's just the way I was raised.

Not because I'm scared of going to hell.

But because *It is what it is.*
God is who God is.
And this Jesus person may not get me all the way to the ground, but He gets me a heck of a lot closer than any other joker who has claimed to carry the truth in his jaw.

Because when I embrace the Bible as true, not just ancient writings or a feel-good manual, Jesus simply *must* be the cause of creation.

The ground of all existence.
The source of knowledge and the foundation of my metaphysic.
That thing that is greater than all things.
That thing that is before all things,
breathing meaning into matter.

Not just the real and metapysical, but
the emotion of an honest song
or the force of a heavy metal one;
the Wind that hovers over creation and
breathes new life into the lungs of the world;
the magnetism of that painting you can't stop staring at
and the terrible length and breadth of the land that makes you
feel like you're sinking when you survey it from atop a cliff.

That God.
Those things.
This reality, here and now.

So on my run, while I was having an existential meltdown over the burning in my lungs, I felt a small voice whisper one of the

names of Yeshua (Jesus' name in Hebrew) into my ear:
The Prince of Peace.

Because no other title will serve to set my fickle, fearful heart at ease. No other person will arrive and put a healing finger on my wounds, like the alien from E.T.

Try as I may to rage against Him indefinitely, I can't bring myself to escape Him.

Perhaps that's the point.

Perhaps it's why marriage is such a strong tool for communicating what life with God is like: Someone you want to escape from and caress at the same time.
A slow way to be crucified.

Perhaps even my anger at God has led me back to Him again, and here I sit, like a little kid who's still pouting about not getting their way while they're wrapped up in the arms of their mother.

So despite my best efforts, I haven't escaped being a Christian quite yet.

Maybe next time I'll get away.

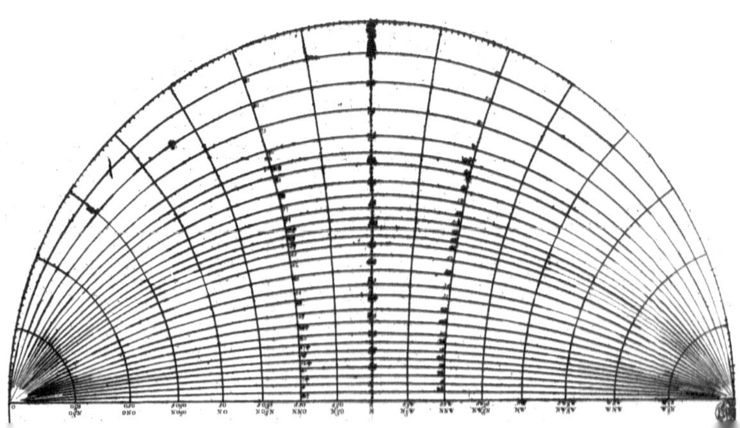

maybe
next time
I'll get
away.

Maybe next time I'll get away.

DISORIENTATION

an apology &
an approach

 ell.

ell.

ell.

Do you understand the entire universe now?

If not, that's only because the subsequent books in this series haven't come out yet.

I have been sitting at my laptop in this coffee shop, alternating between watching Thalassophobic videos on Reddit and pondering how to start this disorientation/conclusion.

The one I have in mind sounds like a forced mashup of Ecclesiastes, Nietzsche, and Annie Dillard. Something poetic, philosophical, and telling you to enjoy life.

But there's even more than that, right? You can backpack Southeast Asia for a decade and still have an unscratched itch for adventure. Knowledge and experience may be the building blocks of life, but they're not the destination. You'll never arrive.

I've written this book, mostly stream of consciousness (sorry if You spent actual money on it and didn't get it on a free Amazon Kindle giveaway thing), and learned a few things myself along the way.

For instance, I've learned that men only want one thing and women only want everything.

I've learned that forgiveness is easy to talk about but hard to say out loud when you really need to.

And that Western people read everything left to right except the order of highway exit signs.

The art of understanding the entire universe begins with the art of, well, understanding, so that's where this book had to begin. It's not a description of the cosmos, but a method, or a lens through which we see. Like I said in the early chapters, this book is a sort of introduction to my 'lens.' My prescription may change over time, with more experience and education, but I'm 30 years old now, so I think I know darn near as much as possible.

I don't know everything about everything, but I know how I approach knowing. Learning. Growing. There's a Zen idea called Beginner's Mind, where no matter how much you know about a subject, you enter a state of mind that tells yourself that you know nothing about it. It's humble. It's the best way to learn.

Enter every book or conversation thinking you know it all and you'll learn nothing.

Maybe I should have put that in the beginning of the book. Forgetter's Mind. ¯_(ツ)_/¯ Oh well.

                                    &

So? May we rebel against the State in discreet and silly ways.
The world, the government, and especially advertisers who
profit off of your emotions want to control how you think, how
you feel, and your desires. So get back at them.

Wipe the snot.

Be childlike and discreet.
Subtly rage against the all-controlling State.

Not until we have wiped our boogers on a thousand statues of
leaders, good and bad alike, and until these have dissolved
back into the carbon cycle that we will really see what matters
in life, that we will feel less like sheep and more like humans.

Statues are for the dead, but these things are for the living:
defacing state-owned things in non-permanent ways;
holding hands,
being friends over being right,
the slowing breath of a woman as she sighs gently into sleep,
and creating things we think are cool.

Loving those who made it difficult for you.

Also, the first breath of air when exiting the airport in a new
country. It's not just oxygen and nitrogen, but discovery.

Add to the list:
watching the angry dance of fire
and the happy-sad lives of dogs;
salt water drying crumbly into all your cracks,

and a recovering alcoholic calling his sponsor when tempted; and first through millionth kisses.

You'll forget leaders and statues and ultimately facts and all the people you never came into contact with (not the least of all bestatued leaders) but you won't forget these things.

So wipe the snot.

Don't conform.

&

I hope this book was helpful.

Maybe it caused some disorientation of sorts and drew up some new maps for you. Perhaps you learned a new fun fact or two.

I'd consider it a success, if nothing else, if you opened your mind just a crack more. If you challenged yourself to stretch your horizons and tried to see things from the other side.

One pastor of mine once preached a sermon that always stuck with me. From my memory, he said:

> People often come to me and tell me they're having a crisis of faith. They sit in my office and lament the fact that their faith seems to be slipping away and they're terrified. Usually in these conversations, I discover that

what they call a 'crisis of faith' is really God taking a sledgehammer and smashing the tiny box in which they used to hold Him. Then their perception of God can grow and expand. If it's done in healthy ways, they'll have one of these crises of faith every few years as God continues to expand in their mind.

So will you grow? Even if you're not a Christian and you've made it this far in this book, I'm grateful for you, and I ask, *Will you let your perception of the world, of God, of people expand?*

Will you ask new questions and pursue honest answers?
Will you dip your toe into the waters of disorientation from time to time, rather than fighting for constant intellectual control?

I hope you do, and I hope a tsunami rises up and sucks you in.

e

A Photo and Description of Ethan

If you're like me, you keep flipping back to this page, especially when the author says something especially jarring or provocative and thinking, *THIS joker said THAT??* Maybe you're not like me and you'll look at the author page once and move on. Like a normal human.

That is indeed a photo of me taken this year, albeit minus a few tattoos I now have as I finish up this book, and my hair's a little longer. Dave took this picture in Mexico City as we began our 30th Birthday Backpacking Bonanza. Gotta look adventurous for the author photo or else no one will think you know anything about the world. But as you now know, or as you soon will if you're pre-stalking the author page, I know a crap ton.

That's because I went to Denver Seminary and Moody Bible Institute (not in that order) and travel a lot and read at least three times a week. I'm a youth pastor and live in Denver with no wife or dogs or cats or fish or anything. I write a lot and post it on ethanrenoe.com or @ethanrenoe on social media.

Other Books by Ethan

Open Hands (#1 best-seller!)
Ethan's shortest, yet most impactful book. It has inspired tears and tattoos (yes, plural). Just read it.

The New Lonely (#1 best-seller!)
Today, everyone seems to be lonely, despite being more connected than ever before! What happened?

All the Immortal Things That Live Inside of Us - Indescribable.

Now Let Me Find A Stopping Place
Every night for ten years, Ethan wrote at least one poem. This collection compiles the best of these poems from around the world, written between 2008-2018.

Time Kills All Things
After blogging consistently for over five years, Ethan collected the best 272 of these posts, converted them into essays, and published this cohesive, 600-page collection on…everything.

Bad Timing (#1 best-seller!)
The dating book the world needed. This book spans over a decade of dating debacles. It's a series of romantic petty crimes and misdemeanors by a very PG-13 Christian.

If you could haunt your house forever (#24 best-seller!)
This is a collection of 29 spooky, weird, eerie, and just plain original short stories. You never know where the next twist will take you! Not for children or the faint of stomach.

Leaving Weather
This first book began as a college senior project and ended up being a unique collection of essays exploring intimacy, faith, and humanity, with aesthetic design and photography.